AF564442

MEMOIRS OF GIANI ZAIL SINGH

MEMOIRS OF
GIANI ZAIL SINGH

THE SEVENTH PRESIDENT OF INIDA

HAR-ANAND
PUBLICATIONS PVT LTD

Reprint, 2001

Published by Ashok Gosain and Ashish Gosain for:
HAR-ANAND PUBLICATIONS PVT LTD
E-49/3, Okhla Industrial Area, Phase-II, New Delhi-110020
Tel: 41603490
E-mail: info@haranandbooks.com/haranand@rediffmail.com
Shop online at: www.haranandbooks.com

@haranand_publications
Har Anand Publications

Printed in India at Megha Printographics

PROLOGUE

Giani Zail Singh, the seventh President of India, took about four years to narrate his memoirs to me. The process started a few months before his tenure in Rashtrapati Bhawan ended and it continued well into 1990, three years after he demited his office. It was not a hurried and regular affair, but a slow and halting process dependent on the leisure and convenience of Gianiji. It was only after my induction as Officer on Special Duty to the President in 1986, subsequent to my superannuation from All India Radio, that I was told by the President that this would be one of my assignments.

What I noted with some discomfort was that Gianiji had not maintained any diary or notes throughout his public career and that he was depending entirely on his memory, recollecting events from his early childhood till the last day of his Presidency. Though I recognized his mental capacity and sometimes marvelled at his long memory and tremendous power of recall, yet some mixing up of sequences and repetition of facts was inevitable. It came in the way of preparing a slick and lucid text. Quite a few drafts were, therefore, prepared and presented to him, when he asked for deletion or addition of certain portions and expressions.

It also became clear that Gianiji did not dwell in great detail on all the significant facts which had become a subject of wide debate in the press and private conversations across the country. That, according to him, was on purpose and he knew exactly what was to be recorded and what was to be left out. He had a knack of separating the chaff from the grain, he benignly averred. In spite of this he was discreetly requested to make his memoirs more detailed and comprehensive, but he preferred to remain content with what is contained in the following pages.

Gianiji personally read the penultimate and final drafts and approved them entirely. But when he started giving hints to his friends and certain visitors that his memoirs were ready for publication and some publishers actually started approaching him, he changed his mind and felt that these should be printed when he is no more. He gave some advice to his son, Joginder Singh, and his daughters, Ms. Joginderpal Kaur, Dr. Gurdip Kaur and Dr. Manjit Kaur, to this effect.

On 24 November 1994, when we met for the last time, he told me that he had something very important to discuss after his return from Punjab, where he was going for a few days. He had been keeping indifferent health for a couple of months. 1 instinctively thought that he wanted to finalize the publication of his memoirs. He left Delhi on 26 November 1994, never to return alive. After three days he met with a serious accident while travelling to Chandigarh from Anandpur Sahib, where he had gone to pay his obeisance at Gurdwara Kesgarh connected with the Tenth Guru, to which he was deeply attached emotionally.

I came to know that when he was wheeled into the Intensive Care Unit of the Post-Graduate Institute of Medical Science and Research at Chandigarh, he asked for me twice, but due to some misunderstanding, I could not be informed. When I went to Chandigarh to ask about his health on 6 December 1994, it was too late, as he had gone into a coma and the visitors were not allowed to see him. He passed away on 25 December 1994.

Whatever appears in the following pages, it records faithfully what Gianiji had narrated and then read and finally approved.

Manohar Singh Batra

CONTENTS

1.	Childhood and Early Youth	9
2.	Rumblings of a Rebellion Against the Ruler	22
3.	A Sham Trial and Jail Sentence	25
4.	Working an Oil Mill like an OX	36
5.	Emancipation From Incarceration	44
6.	From Faridkot to a Wider Arena	46
7.	India Gains Independence	59
8.	The Last Ditch Battle with the Raja	62
9.	Parallel Government	65
10.	A New Dawn	72
11.	Proprietary Rights to Tenants	79
12.	A New Turning	85
13.	Linguistic States	89
14.	Election Woes	97
15.	Exit from the Cabinet	100
16.	Punjabi-Speaking State	104
17.	Rift in the Congress	113
18.	Time for Action	116
19.	Guru Gobind Singh Marg	125
20.	Amity and Goodwill	128
21.	The Emergency and the Opposition	131
22.	Persecution	137
23.	Union Cabinet	144
24.	Congress (I) and the Non-Congress (I) States	150

25.	Public Issues	152
26.	To Rashtrapati Bhavan	158
27.	Sikhs—A Separate Nation?	166
28.	The Methods of the Akalis	171
29.	The Asiad and the Travails	174
30.	Operation Blue Star	177
31.	The Aftermath	186
32.	Last Meeting with Mrs. Indira Gandhi & The Appointment of a New Prime Minister	202
33.	The Holocaust	207
34.	The Massacre of Independent Opinion	211
35.	Differences with Rajiv Gandhi	217
36.	Denial of Information to the President	223
37.	Statehood to Union Territories	228
38.	A Foreign Visit	241
39.	The Constitutional Relationship	244
40.	A Visit After All	249
41.	Evasion of Responsibility	255
42.	Fairfax and Bofors	258
43.	No Desire for a Second Term	268
44.	Conscientious Objectors	272
45.	The Indian Post Office (Amendment) Bill 1986	276
46.	Politicisation of Sikh Faith	280
47.	Sant Jarnail Singh Bhindranwale	289
48.	Some Memorable Meetings	293
49.	Censorship of President's Broadcasts to the Nation	301
50.	My Successor and I	307
	Index	311

Chapter 1

CHILDHOOD AND EARLY YOUTH

I was born on 5 May 1916 in Sandhwan village of the erstwhile princely state of Faridkot. It is now a district in Punjab, in the northern part of the country. My mother was Indi Kaur and father Kishan Singh. He originally came from an artisan family, but also started tilling the land for his livelihood.

1 was hardly nine months when my mother expired. It was a great tragedy, but immediately her elder sister, Daya Kaur, took me under her tender care, and oblivious of everything, 1 started regarding my aunt as my real mother. She herself was childless and brought me up as her own progeny, with all the love and affection she could bestow. I was put on cow's milk for nourishment and started growing up in the typical surroundings of a village with agriculture as its most predominant feature. My father was a deeply religious man, who read and interpreted the Sikh and Hindu holy scriptures. He extensively studied the Sikh traditional history and daily offered prayers in a room, where the Holy Book, *Guru Granth Sahib,* was kept. He came to be regarded as a saintly and pious person in the village and the surrounding areas. I was the fourth and the youngest child in the family and was sent to the school at the age of five. Being the youngest, I received the maximum affection and care all around me. But, at the same time, my foster-mother had a vigilant eye and tried to keep me under strict discipline. Apart from the instruction in the Urdu language that I received at school at Kotkapura, a market town three kilometres from Sandhwan, I

was taught Punjabi at home by my father, who also initiated me into the study of the scriptures from a very early age. My foster-mother was a picture of compassion and love and she encouraged me to learn as much as I could from my father.

I can recall my serious sickness due to small-pox and my mother's prayers for my recovery. It was popularly believed by the rural folk that this dreadful disease was caused by the ire of Goddess Sitala, who had to be propitiated. My mother placed an earthen jar full of water along with some dried dates, coconut, some other dry fruits and a length of spun yam near my pillow. One day, in a semiconscious state, I heard someone's voice from outside and my mother rushed to see who the caller was. She had given strict instructions against anybody entering my room without washing his face, hands and feet, lest the goddess of the small-box got displeased. Luckily, I pulled through the disease without a scar having been left on my body.

At the age of twelve, I fell seriously ill and my pulse rate became very low. No doctor could help me, as my condition was critical. In that state of dismay, the only ray of hope my father could see was in prayer. He carried me in his arms to the room where the holy scripture was, and prayed for my recovery taking a vow that if my life was spared by the Almighty, I would be dedicated to the service of God and His people. The prayer of my father, it is said, was answered and my pulse rate picked up within an hour, though I did not regain consciousness. The village doctor, Hakeemji, as he was called, was sent for. He expressed his delight at the mercy of God. It took me three days to regain consciousness, when the doctor started administering a local medicine to me. I received no nutrition for three days, at the end of which I was allowed a lean diet. Gradually, I started recovering from the illness. Some family elders advised that I should go to pay my obeisance at a Gurdwara, for thanksgiving, which I did alongwith my family.

Among some other recollections of my childhood is the one about the sale of a harvest of about 16 quintals by my father and his bringing home 85 one-rupee silver coins, which he put in a jar handing it over to me. I went on turning the jar upside down and counting the coins over and over again. Father told me that all this money was mine and I could keep it. I retained five coins and returned the rest, but, later, I gave him those five coins too. The next day, my father again gave me all the 85 coins, as if it was a toy, but I did not even cast a glance at them.

This illness had left me too weak and listless. I tried to stand up and take a few steps with the support of the mud-wall of my house. The doctor who had tremendous affection for me; advised that I should always try to stand on my own feet. and never to depend on anyone. In my later life, these words very often echoed in my mind. In different situations, I have interpreted these as an exhortation to take courage in both hands in any adversity and to grapple with problems with fortitude.

It took me about three months to recover from my ailment, when I regained some strength and started running around in the courtyard of my mud-house. After a few days, my father brought from Lahore all the four volumes of the epic *Suraj Prakash* written by a great scholar, Bhai Santokh Singh. The first volume dealt with the life of the first Guru of the Sikhs, Guru Nanak. The second and the third volumes were on the work and achievements of the next eight Gurus and the last volume related to the life story of the tenth Guru, Guru Gobind Singh. This great book was in Hindi language written in Gurmukhi script and represented a marvel of outstanding poetry.

Father was determined to fulfil his vow and did not want me to adopt any other career except the service of the Lord and His creation. He wanted me to devote all my time to the study of religious books. A retired police official, Chanan Singh, who was a close family friend, felt concerned at my father's plans, and paid several visits to dissuade him from pursuing these. He told my father that his decision would be detrimental to my interests in the long run.

There was an ascetic, who was popularly known as Parmahansa. He undertook to teach me Hindi. He made me write Devnagri alphabet with my index finger on the earth. When my finger bled, he asked me to use an iron nail instead of my finger for writing. He argued that for learning letters of the alphabet, one did not need to use a pen and paper. He was a Vedantist by faith. He taught me *Vichara Sagara, Bhavarasamrita, Vichara Mala, Hanuman Natak, Saruktavali* and some other religious works and took pains to explain their meanings to me. He placed less emphasis on writing and more on learning and comprehending. He developed such an involvement in teaching that if I missed going to him for lessons, he would himself come and coax me to accompany him to his class of three or four students. He did not charge any fee from any of us. Teaching was the biggest charity and the best act, he would say, and it did not brook any stinginess. Originally, this ascetic was a Sikh, but had turned a *Sadhu* (mendicant). Clad in ochre robes, with silver-white flowing hair and beard, he lived in close proximity with nature. He insisted on bathing in cold water even at the peak of winter and enjoyed a sparkling health with limpid eyes and a pink spread over his mellowed countenance. He really had an imposing figure. He never allowed me to drop out of my studies. Well-versed in the life-stories of Lord Rama, Lord Krishna, Swami Ramakrishna Parmahansa, Swami Vivekanand and the Sikh Gurus, he was keen to impart his knowledge to others.

Friends and well-wishers of the family started observing that surely the aim of my life was not to become an ascetic. I had been lovingly tutored by my father in the recitation of the Sikh holy scripture, *Guru Granth Sahib,* at a very young age. I had to use a thick cushion to sit comfortably to level up to read the scripture placed on a palanquin. By the age of seven, I could recite the holy book with considerable ease and accuracy. I was already being sought after by the devout, who organized recitations of the holy book in their abodes or gurdwaras.

Wrestling was a popular sport during those days. I was fond of witnessing the wrestling bouts and playing Kabaddi. Listening to *Kirtan,* i.e., recitation of holy hymns set to music by renowned *Ragis* (singers), brought the best out of me as a musician and I took to playing on the harmonium brought by my father from Amritsar. I felt deep joy in singing devotional songs. Ragi Sarwan Singh, who lived about two kilometres from our village, was my harmonium tutor. He was willing to teach me classical singing; but I was not too fond of it, as I preferred to sing in light tunes, which I found more interesting and easy to grasp. Karam Singh Jogi, a singer and preacher, was the most appealing out of the several devotional singers I had occasion to listen to. I started singing *Asa Di Var* every morning, the text of which I knew by heart. My father was of deep conviction that no one should accept monetary compensation or offerings for performing sacred music. According to the Sikh Gurus, anyone accepting remuneration for such tasks would not find favour with the Lord. Such earnings should always be avoided. I never accepted any compensation for performing at a religious function. My services were in heavy demand at congregations, marriages and other community events.

In this process I became involved with an Akali Jatha of Faridkot, as I saw a procession of the Akalis, who were set free from the State ruler's prison, being taken out by the people. During those days the Singh Sabha organization and the Arya Samaj movement were also active. Once the Arya Samaj of Faridkot convened an all-religions' conference, but they could not find a suitable speaker on Sikh religion. The theme was: "Why I love my religion." The Jains, Muslims and the followers of the Sanatan Dharma were well represented, but there was no Sikh exponent. I was asked to speak. I felt very hesitant, as I was not accustomed to making public speeches, and I was not prepared too. But when I went on the dais and spoke, I remember having received warm applause, which gave me great confidence for the future.

Because of my rising reputation as a good religious singer, I was invited by a well-to-do Sikh gentleman, who was deeply involved in the national struggle for freedom. After the religious ceremonies at his residence, I came across three persons, who were described as "saints". The eldest, Baba Ishar Singh, was about 50 years old. The second appeared to be about 40 and the youngest seemed to be in the vicinity of 25 years. The name of my host was Janga Singh, who asked me to stay on for three or four more days to perform *Kirtan* daily. He also asked me to start recitation of the Holy Book. Baba Ishar Singh and his companion named Amar Singh Tegh were good reciters. One early morning, while I was busy singing *Asa Di Var* and giving oral interpretation of the holy hymns, a man from the household came and whispered in my ears to hasten and conclude the session. He refused to tell me the reason. So I did his bidding. I was surprised to notice the absence of the three "saints" from the *Kirtan* that morning.

When I climbed the stairs to the first floor of the house, where I was putting up along with the three "saints" and two other persons, I was asked by the host, Janga Singh to run to Kotkapura and bring Doctor Chanda Singh with me. I noticed the youngest "saint" Jaswant Singh lying on a cot, with his companions and Janga Singh sitting by his side with anxious looks. As I was leaving, I noticed that Jaswant Singh was being coaxed to drink hot milk mixed with clarified butter. He was also being helped to liberal doses of liquor. I was cryptically told that he was not feeling well. It came as more of a little surprise to me to find Janga Singh's wife, Punjab Kaur herself cleansing and mopping the floor. As I stepped out of the house, I saw Janga Singh coming upon my heels. He suddenly tried to take me into confidence and said in a low tone that there was nothing to conceal from me any more. These three were no saints, he said, but revolutionaries engaged in the struggle for national freedom. They had contacts with freedom-fighters like Sardar Bhagat Singh, Sukhdev and Rajguru, who had been sentenced to death for hurling bombs in the central Assembly and the assassination of the British police official, Saunders. Jaswant Singh had received a bullet in his thigh, and if the incident was detected by the police, he would surely be taken into custody and all of them would get into trouble. It was necessary, therefore, that Dr. Chanda Singh should be brought post haste. He should only be told that a man was wounded and needed his immediate help.

I instantly left for Kotkapura on a bicycle and made straight for Dr. Chanda Singh's residence-cum-clinic. But, before I could enter through his door, a man came panting and asked me not to call the doctor, as Jaswant Singh's condition had started improving. He conveyed to me Janga Singh's message that I should return to his house at the earliest possible. Without a moment's delay, I started for the village. On reaching the residence, I was told that the bullet, which had pierced Jaswant Singh's thigh, had been found by Mrs. Janga Singh, while mopping the floor. Now there was no reason to fear. Had the doctor come, it could have created a problem, as he was a retired surgeon of the State, and if anybody else had got the wind of the incident, it could have landed them all in a soup. The young revolutionary had imbibed a generous quota of drinks and liquor was being applied to his wound as well. He was strong and courageous and was bearing the pain without much fuss.

Janga Singh's narrative sharpened my curiosity. These revolutionaries were preparing to put away a traitor, he said, and in the process were planning to confiscate his wealth for the national cause, but a pistol had gone off accidentally resulting in a serious injury to Jaswant Singh. He advised that I should loudly sing devotional songs to the accompaniment of a *dholak* (a percussion instrument) and *cymbals.* In the meantime, they would think of the next step.

Janga Singh was of the view that the injured revolutionary should be taken to the town of Muktsar. After a long discussion, we decided to start on our journey at night under the cover of darkness. We tightly dressed the wound of Jaswant Singh, as there were quite a few hours left for the approach of the night. There was apprehension in the house about any neighbour getting the scent of the trouble. The injured was to be carried on a cot, but in spite of the excruciating pain, he volunteered to walk upto the bullock cart. Summoning all courage, he flung himself into the cart being drawn by two oxen and on a bed of grain. A lot of fodder was heaped over the man to create an impression that we were all going to town to sell the foodgrains. Janga Singh, Sarwan singh and I seated ourselves in the cart and started tor Muktsar, about 25 kilometres away. We left at 8 P.M. and hardly had we trundled some 10 kilometres, when one of the oxen collapsed. We had crossed one village and were quite afar from another. Janga Singh said that he would watch over the sprawling ox and we should take its place and pull the cart upto the village and ask the people to help with some medicine for. the ailing animal. I yoked myself to the cart alongside one ox, and leaving behind the sick ox with Janga Singh as the watchman, we started heaving forward. I was hardly seventeen years old, but drawing upon all my strength, I pulled the cart for about 10 kilometres before reaching the Jhabelwali village, where a sister of Janga Singh resided. We borrowed an ox from the family and yoking it to the cart, reached Muktsar before the crack of the dawn. We made straight for the clinic of Dr Kehar Singh, but since it was too early in the morning, he was still at his residence. We hastened to his place with the confidence that he would help. He was a silent sympathizer of the freedom-fighters. Though he did not overtly participate in the national movement and confront the colonial regime, he secretly helped the freedom-fighters and extended his wholehearted support. After listening to our story, he fell silent for a while and then told us in deliberate tones that we should bring the patient to his house rather than carry him to the clinic and not breathe a word even to his compounder about the episode.

After removing the crude dressing we had put on the young revolutionary's injury, Dr. Kehar Singh declared that it would take at least 10 days for the wound to heal. He said that he would put up the patient at his residence and give the impression that he was his guest. He warned that nobody should get even an inkling of the injury and promised to look after the patient with all earnestness. To our enquiry about the expenses involved, he asked us not to give even a thought to it. We beat a hasty retreat from the doctor's residence and returned to Janga Singh's house and nonchalantly plunged in ceremonial recitation of the scriptures.

The two elder revolutionaries gave me two books, one of them in Punjabi entitled *Ghadar Dian Goonjan* (Echoes of Revolution) and the other in Urdu *Khoon-e-Shahidan* (Blood of the Martyrs). They also shared with me pamphlets, booklets and posters. I kept this literature very carefully with me for a long time. Now, most of our conversation at Janga Singh's house centred on the freedom movement. The earlier discussions on devotional themes gave way to enthusiasm for wresting freedom from foreign rulers. The news at that juncture of the executions of Bhagat Singh, Sukhdev and Rajguru in the Lahore Central jail fired our hearts further with patriotic fervour.

1 was told by Janga singh that lshar Singh camouflaged as a "saint" was in fact known as "Baba" in revolutionary circles. The other "saint" Amar Singh's popular name was Amar Singh "Tegh" (meaning "Sword"). And whenever there was a secret talk about him, it was asked, How was the sword? Was it quite sharp or otherwise?

After the executions of the trio—Bhagat Singh, Sukhdev and Rajguru—the two "saints" asked me, if I would stand by them. Most readily I replied in the affirmative. For this, they told me that I would have to pass a test. The time was fixed for the evening, when the Baba lit a candle and, putting it on the table, asked me to place my arm on it. Instantly, I placed my wrist on the flame and as the flesh started burning, the Baba suddenly extinguished the candle and calmly proclaimed that I had succeeded in the test. He explained that such a trial was given to a novice by a single person, lest the man undergoing the test was influenced by the presence of others and, to prove his courage, concealed his true reaction. The Baba declared with solemnity that from that moment onwards there would be no secret between the two of them and me. He promised regular contacts with me in future, and said that emissaries from both of them should keep on coming to me from time to time with cryptic messages from the "saints" for compliance of certain requests. After asking the names of my father and two brothers and their addresses and other particulars and reassuring himself of my sincerity for the cause, he gave me a pistol and some cartridges for use at the time of need. To my innocent query about the means to procure a licence for the weapon, he burst into laughter, and remarked that I was a simpleton. If I obtained a licence, he said, the police would summon me from time to time and keep an eye on the gun. He told me that the pistol was being left in my keeping for putting away any possible enemy of the country or a traitor. Any court witness against a freedom fighter would have to be wiped out. They had vowed, he said, to finish those who had given evidence against Bhagat Singh, Sukhdev and Rajguru during their trial.

Two days after the *Akhand Path*—ceremonial reading of the holy scripture—was completed, I came away and I did not know, where the two "saints" had disappeared. After some time, they surfaced at my village and took away the pistol and cartridges from me saying that they would give these things back to me after sometime. Their youngest companion, Jaswant Singh, whom we had left in the care of Dr. Kehar Singh of Muktsar, I gathered, left for China, where he got married and raised a family, only to return to India in 1949, two years after the country secured its independence. When, later, I became a Minister in the erstwhile Patiala and East Punjab States Union (PEPSU), he came to see me, and it took me quite a bit of effort to recognize him, as earlier I had known him as a man with a turban and beard, whereas now he was clean-shaven, and his face was crisscrossed with lines of worry and weariness. I never saw "Baba" again, but, of course, Amar Singh Tegh, who is about 95, is still around. Had "Baba" Ishar Singh been alive, he, in all probability, would have found a way of meeting me. There is a possibility of his having fallen a victim to the vicious killings during the partition of the subcontinent.

Though these "saints" had taken away their pistol from me, I was impressed by their devotion to the cause of emancipation of the country, and got convinced that without national independence, no religion could be genuinely free. Slavery was a curse and it was the sacred duty of every Indian to cast away the yoke of foreign subjugation.

Gradually I found my mind less inclined to attending religious congregations and more keen to listen to the views of political activists in their meetings. The intrepidation of the pioneers of the Ghaddar movement and the daring deeds of Sardar Bhagat Singh had left a deep imprint on my mind. At that moment my views were at variance with the ideology of Mahatma Gandhi. When Sardar Bhagat Singh and his companions were hanged, I was filled with grief and anger and felt a spontaneous surge of emotion for sacrificing everything to secure freedom for my motherland. I made up my mind to dedicate every moment of my existence to serve the momentous cause. My parents were opposed to my way of thinking, as to them concentration on religious thought and meditation on the name of God represented the highest state of piety and, to achieve this, religious service was of very great importance. I was setting out on war-path with the Government, and though my parents would not vehemently force me to stop, they had no mind to encourage me to take further steps on this uncharted course either. The martyrdom of Bhagat Singh and his companions had created a great awakening which resulted in frequent political meetings, to which I was naturaly attracted. There, I used to avidly listen to the speeches of the freedom fighters and the leaders.

During those days, in the Akali religious congregations, great stress used to be laid on the national cause. People were urged to participate in efforts to eliminate British imperialism from India. My frequent attendance of such religious-political sermons strengthened my resolve to launch myself on the turbulent waters of the national struggle. It was at that point of time, that Sardar Sewa Singh Thikriwala had sacrificed his life in a fast-unto-death in the jail in the Patiala State, which left a deep scar on my mind. I established contact with the members of the Parja Mandal movement, which was fighting against the autocractic rule. in princely States. One of them gave me a journal entitled "Desh Dardi' (Patriot), in which the eminent poet, Vidhata Singh "Tir' had published a poem in Punjabi steeped in patriotic zeal, .It read like this.

"O, the lion-hearted handsome hero of the nation, what is the use of your scintillating youth?

If you do not sacrifice yourself like a moth on the burning flame, what is the purpose of your lighting candles in temples?

Your country has been plundered by the foreigners. What is the use of your complacent living?

If in your heart there is no enthusiasm, no zeal, What use is it, if your chest is made of steel?"

I committed a number of such poems to memory, and I used to recite them on various occasions. I started discussing with friends the ways and means of making solid and meaningful contributions to the national movement. Long hours of contemplation and nascent effervescence marked that period of my life. Direction and guidance were my need. I often thought of Ishar Singh "Baba", if I could ever meet him again and seek his counsel. But since his whereabouts were not known, I started attending the meetings of the Parja MandaI activists and participating in their processions, but did not join the movement actively.

In 1937 a mass political meeting was held in the Harike-Kalan village of the Muktsar Tehsil, in which many eminent freedom-fighters took part. Among them were Gopal Singh Quami, Master Kabul Singh, Lala Chandi Ram, Lala Achint Ram and Munshi Ahmed Din. After listening to their scintillating speeches, I thought of setting up a committee of the Indian National Congress in Faridkot State. I broached the topic with Lala Chandi Ram, who was the President of the District Congress Committee of Ferozepur. He said, it was not permissible to set up Congress Committees in princely States, and it would be best, if we joined the Riyasti Parja Mandai, which was also known as the States People's Conference and was functioning in the States ruled by the Rajas, Maharajas and Nawabs. In spite of this, we were very keen on setting up a Congress Committee in our State being ruled by an autocratic ruler.

After some time a political conference was held in the Rode village, in which celebrated leaders like Doctor Gopi Chand Bhargava, Doctor Saifuddin Kichlew, Master Bachan Singh and many others participated. The proceedings were marked with seething national sentiment. I had occasion to talk to several leaders about our desire to set up a Congress Committee in Faridkot. They appreciated our keenness, and said that if an organisation started working) in our State, and if they were invited by it, they would be willing to come and encourage us. I had parleys with several prominent persons including Janga Singh, Baba Dyal Singh of Kotkapura, Sandhura Singh Manisinghwala, Rattan Singh Vandarjatana and Jathedar Nahar Singh Dansinghwala. It was decided to convene a meeting to consider the steps to set up a Congress Committee. It was thought necessary to associate members of all communities in this task. Janga Singh of Burj Harika village used his influence to recruit a shopkeeper, Lekh Ram, who, in fact, did not know the exact purpose of his alignment. Some friends from the business community were liberal in making monetary contributions to the committee, but were most reluctant to take active part in the work, as they were quite scared of the possible retributions. From amongst the Muslims, only Qazi Obedullah and Maulvi Sulaiman joined us. Muslim friends generally agreed that it was a noble mission and they promised all cooperation. Janga Singh was chosen President and I was made General Secretary of the Committee. Qazi Obedullah was named Vice-President and Lekh Ram became the Secretary. Posters were got printed, recruitment of workers got underway and excitement of this new activity caught up with many people.

Chapter 2

RUMBLINGS OF A REBELLION AGAINST THE RULER

In Faridkot city, a mosque was located in the middle of a big bazar. In a bid to beautify the area, the State government intended to demolish the mosque. As a preliminary step, they put a lock on it and promised to give an alternative site for construction of another mosque. This created widespread resentment among the Muslims, who started protesting against this unreasonable intrusion into their religious rights. We supported the Muslims and stood for the continuance of the mosque at its old location and the unalienable right of the Muslim community to say its prayers in its place of worship like any other community. In public meetings, voices were raised against the arbitrary attitude of the State authorities. The general din reached its crescendo, as a result of which the princely government abandoned its plans to remove the mosque from the middle of the road and assured the Muslims of non-interference in their religious practices. The Muslim community started joining us in greater numbers. They deputed Sufi Khushi Mohammed to our Committee, in which he was appointed as an office-bearer. We intensified our activities and started organizing meetings and processions more frequently. Promising youths like Jugal Kishore, Sammat Rai and Ram Chander of Kotkapura joined our movement and later went to jail with us. Jugal Kishore was a very handsome young man, who lost an eye in police brutalities.

The State Government started coming down with a heavy hand on our public meetings. In the meantime, Congress activities in the adjoining towns like Muktsar, Ferozepur and Moga were intensified, from which we received a lot of sympathy and support. The secret police in Faridkot State started functioning without any scruples and let loose a reign of terror. Our members were arrested, intimidated and mercilessly beaten. To avoid this repression, we shifted our meetings outside the State boundaries. Instead of road travel, we started undertaking rail journeys, as trains were outside the jurisdiction of the princely State Governments. These were treated as the British Indian territory.

One day, I received information about the serious illness of my father, which necessitated my return to the village. Finding my father in a grave condition, I decided to stay on at home for a few days. Though my companions had apprehensions of my arrest, miraculously I was left alone. Party members sent me a word for convening an emergency meeting, which, instead of a nearby town, was arranged in the cremation-grounds of Kotkapura. After the meeting, my companions boarded a train post haste and I beat hasty retreat to my village.

On my return, I found that the condition of my father had further deteriorated, as he had slipped into semiconsciousness. In that sombre atmosphere, my elder brother whispered into the father's ear that I had come back. Opening his eyes slowly, Father asked me where I had been. When I told him about the meeting, he remarked that the path on which I had set myself was full of obstacles and difficulties. I might have to suffer privations like imprisonment, he said. I remained silent, lest he asked me to give up this course. I heaved a sigh of relief, when he did not pursue the matter further. I got the satisfaction that he was not, after all, opposed to my decision.

My father's life seemed to be ebbing every moment, but he went on conversing with the relatives around him in his feeble and almost inaudible voice. I kept awake most part of the night, but the cool breeze lulled me to sleep. In the thin hours of the morning, I was suddenly woken up, as the flame of Father's life had started flickering. He looked towards a small book, *Sukhmani* (Psalm of Peace), a part of the religious scriptures and beckoned the earthen lamp to be brought near him. It seemed, he wanted to recite some holy hymns in the last moments of his life. Suddenly he felt darkness enveloping him. He asked for oil to be replenished in the lamp. We did his bidding, but, he said, the flame was flickering and the lamp was about to be extinguished. Holding the book in his hand, he said, he could not see its contents. The book fell from his hands. My brother started reciting the hymns, but I heard the following words drawling from my father's lips, while his eyes were shut:

Raj na koyee jivia, pahunch na sakia koye
Giani jivai sada sada, surtin hi pat hoye

(Nobody has ever been satiated with the years of his life, No one has ever been able to master his worldly existence. Immortal are those who try to seek enlightenment; and endeavour to reach supreme consciousness with all persistence).

These were the last words my father uttered; he folded his hands and his soul departed from his body's cage.

My foster-mother had undergone surgery in the eye and she was in the hospital. My sister and wives of my brothers tried reverently to shake my father's limbs to see, if a whiff of life still lingered, but he had travelled yonder to meet his Creator. My eldest brother's wife was the first to announce that Father had passed away, which plunged every one present in deep grief. This was the first time I had seen anyone dying. I felt a warm stream of tears trickling down my cheeks.

Chapter 3

A SHAM TRIAL AND JAIL SENTENCE

The fire of my political activities kept on invincibly burning. The series of meetings and conferences in Faridkot continued with ever-increasing zeal and earnestness. It attracted police atrocities with mounting fury and vindictiveness. The authorities gave a battle cry to stem the rising tide of nationalism.

The Raja of Faridkot, who was ruling the State with an iron hand like most other rulers in the princely States, was keen to keep the national movement away from his domain. He was alien to the principles of justice and fairplay. Levying taxes and raising revenues for filling his own coffers was his prerogative, which he exploited fully. Large parts of revenues were utilized by him for his personal aggrandisement and only a fraction was spent on the welfare of the people. Public oppression was the order of the day. A licence was needed to form an association. The burgeoning political consciousness for democratic rights was anathema to the ruler. No newspapers were allowed in the Faridkot State.

In 1933, for the first time I was arrested by the British while taking part in a march demanding democratic rights and put in the Lahore Central Jail. That was the time when Akalis, imbued with national spirit, were fighting the erstwhile Rajas and the British Raj, but when an understanding was reached between the Maharaja of Patiala and the Akali leader, Master Tara Singh, the attitude of the Akalis betrayed some change. I, therefore, found the Congress as a more stable and steadfast source of strength to continue the struggle.

To associate the masses with the movement, it was essential to establish wide contacts with them. Mammoth gatherings started replacing small village meetings to arouse the people's conscience and to create awareness and enthusiasm. But this could not have any effect on us. The State authorities asked me not to make any political speech, which might excite dissatisfaction against the princely family. A senior magistrate and a Superintendent of Police were deputed to watch the proceedings of a big gathering and to report to the State government after every two hours.

Over eight thousand people attended the meeting, in which the British were taken to task for allowing the Raja to oppress the poor masses, and the ruler was criticised for exploiting the peasantry for his personal edification. The ruler was called upon to grant civil liberties to the people and to keep his minions on leash, who were out to crush the common man.

On receipt of a report from his Chief Secretary, the Raja expressed his anger and ordered not to allow any such public gathering at all in the State in future. I was hauled up before the State cabinet and then before the Ruler in person, along with some others, and sternly warned to desist from such seditious activities.

With the efforts of the Congress Committee headed by Janga Singh of Burj Harika, the rural masses, and particularly the peasants, became the votaries of the Congress. It brought about a remarkable change in the oppressed and the exploited from sheer acquiescence to open protest. One Nand Singh, encouraged by the Raja, launched a frontal attack on me for having set up a Congress Party unit in Faridkot, which he said, was not meant for the princely states. I was singled out by the State authorities for the sacrilege of inciting the people against autocracy and repression. Undeterred, I enrolled many members for the Congress Party and continued to organize political conferences with the help of my colleagues like Janga Singh and Sandhura Singh.

The sixth session of the All-India State People's Conference was held at Ludhiana in February 1938 under the chairmanship of Pandit Jawaharlal Nehru, which boosted the morale of the people of the States in Punjab and other parts of northern India. It gave a big jolt to the feudal rulers and made them more uncomfortable. I participated in the Conference, which offended the Faridkot ruler.

Policemen in plain clothes started disturbing the peaceful Congress meetings and bashing up the participants. Some staunch supporters of the ruler took a lead in engineering disruption of the Congress gatherings. In June 1938 at the proposed site of a public meeting in Kotkapura, we erected a stage, which was demolished by the police. But it could not deter us from holding the meeting at that very spot, where we installed a public address system and started the deliberations. A large number of people had collected for the conference. No sooner had I started speaking, than an agent of the ruler embarked on beating an empty tin to drown my voice. One of my party colleagues snatched the tin from the intruder, but plain-clothed policemen pulled out the wires of the loud speaker. That prompted me to stand on a chair and to continue my speech without a microphone. An official agent pushed me down and hurled the chair at me. I suffered a severe injury and was stunned. A stampede followed and the meeting was dispersed. In the melee, several persons sustained injuries. I moved a resolution decrying the unfair tactics of the authorities and promising to continue to hold such political meetings.

The next meeting was organized in the market of Kotkapura, which was attended among others by a well-known patriotic leader, Jathedar Udham Singh Nagoke. There was stone throwing by policemen at that meeting. In the melee I was again injured and my spectacles were broken. Many of my comrades sustained cuts and bruises. The police went amok and thrashed everyone around.

I alongwith Sandhura Singh left for Vandar Jatana and went to the residence of Puran Singh. Some other party 'workers were also there including Janga Singh. We had planned to organize another meeting in that village. We were pursued by the police and ordered to report at Kotkapura. Immediately, on our arrival there, we were clamped in the lock up. After two days, we were shifted to Faridkot. A magistrate was summoned to the Police Station, who after peremptory proceedings, remanded us in judicial custody. Within minutes, we found ourselves behind the bars in the forbidding jail. We were locked up in separate cells, which in that part of the prison were ten in number, five on either side of a brick wall. We were not informed for a couple of months of the crime we were guilty of or the law under which we had been deprived of our liberty.

It so happened that before our arrest, when we were short of resources to organize political mass meetings, we had collected foodgrains from the peasantry for sale to raise some funds. This activity had been decided upon and undertaken by the Executive of the Congress committee. We were accused of criminal breach of trust and misappropriation of funds. The Raja had little difficulty in finding a few Akalis to give false evidence against us. The ruler used his legal machinery to muffle our voice of protest against his misdeeds.

The proceedings of the case went on for nearly 11 months during which we remained in custody. For the first five months, the magistrate used to hold his court in the jail, which evoked popular protest in the two market towns of Kotkapura and Faridkot. Strikes were observed by shopkeepers and the anger of people was aroused against the inequities of the legal process. Panic gripped the State authorities, who were afraid of setting us at liberty or holding an open trial. At almost every hearing, the magistrate would adjourn the case in the precincts of the jail, which created public opinion in our favour. But the government launched a subtle campaign projecting the Raja as a devout Sikh and a compassionate ruler with sympathies for the poor people at his heart. This propaganda initiative carried out with alacrity with the help of official funds was aimed at depicting us as hoodlums out to destroy the established social fabric and to bring about anarchy to the peaceful and prosperous populace. A major exercise of mudslinging was commenced with a systematic and sustained endeavour: I prepared a charter entitled *Parja di Pukar* (Cry of the People) listing our demands, which was printed under my name. But, paradoxically, some gullible people were taken in by the pernicious propaganda against us. The sympathy wave in our favour seemed to start waning. The popular enthusiasm appeared to be ebbing away. Some persons were purchased with money, some were frightened into silence and we continued to languish in the cages.

During the trial we were approached by one Kehar Singh, a Deputy Superintendent of Police, who had been honoured by the British Raj with the title of *Sardar Sahib* for his loyalty to the crown, who sought to talk to me alone. He reasoned that I was so young and had a fruitful career ahead of me, and since the government was determined to award me seven years' imprisonment through a court of law, I should try to rescue my youth from the ignominy of a sentence. He said that he was in touch with the other accused as well, but he felt more concerned about me, because of my spotless antecedents. The best course for me, he advised, was to ask for unconditional pardon from the Raja, whose benevolence could be invoked to withdraw all the charges against me. Finding me reticent, he left saying that I need not make any commitment in haste, and I could take my time to arrive at a decision. After ten days, Kehar Singh came again and, picking up the thread of our earlier conversation, pointed out that even my parents were not in favour of my coming into conflict with the Raja. Moreover, he warned that the warmth of public about the movement had cooled down and the struggle we had started against the Ruler was, in fact, a non-starter. It would be a better course for us to seek the clemency of the Ruler and get out of the State to join the Congress movement elsewhere. Since we were working for the ouster of the British from India, the Raja could not take our activities kindly, nor could he turn a blind eye to our blandishments. He tried to reinforce his plea for our seeking the indulgence of the Ruler with the observation that even our national leaders were not interested in intensifying the stir in the princely States. They were in favour of directing the national movement in British India at that stage, and we were unnecessarily trying to open another front, which was offending the Raja. The latter had otherwise no ill-will against us, we were assured by Kehar Singh. I thanked him for his sympathy and concern and promised to ponder over his words of advice and wisdom.

After five months the venue of our trial was shifted from the jail to an open court. Outside the jail, we felt that the intensity of the movement had suffered a setback. Curious people would look at us from a distance, but would not show courage to come near and talk to us. Only a couple of persons tried to draw closer, but were shooed away by the police. When we would return to the jail after the court hearings, before getting locked up in our respective cells, we would exchange notes with one another. We were convinced that the magistrate was interested only in issuing adjournments. We tried to find a good lawyer in Faridkot to plead our case, but failed to locate one, who would be willing to take our brief. Ultimately a well-known lawyer, Prithi Singh Brar of Ferozepur, agreed to be our counsel by charging travel expenses and a nominal fee, though, otherwise, he was a costly advocate. On the next hearing, he asked for a speedy trial or our liberty, as it was iniquitous to hold us in captivity indefinitely without the due process of law. The magistrate said that he was willing to set us at liberty on bail. But we were not willing to offer bail. Our counsel argued that since the case was based on a bundle of lies, we were not interested in seeking the bail. The magistrate promised to expedite the trial, and so on the next hearing the proceedings began. During the evidence by witnesses and the cross examination, the magistrate, instead of recording what was actually being said in the court, would take notes arbitrarily. When our counsel took serious objection to this unusual process, the magistrate, Sant Singh Dod claimed that it was his discretion, and he was under no obligation to record exactly what was being stated in the proceedings. Dod enjoyed some sort of notoriety for being a harsh judge, and in most cases, he convicted the accused. One day, he instructed the police to leave me alone with him in the court-room and everyone else was to withdraw. As I was handcuffed, the policemen suggested to the magistrate to hold the loose end of the chain in his own hands or allow one of them to do so, lest I played a trick to escape. But the magistrate insisted on being left alone with me for a talk. He ordered his clerical staff also out, taking personal responsibility of watching over me. When the court-room was vacated by everybody, he asked me why I was interested in an expeditious trial. The pace of the case would depend upon the pleasure of the Raja, he told me, and asked me not to waste our money on a lawyer, as it would be of no avail. Whatever he was recording on the file should not really matter, as it was obligatory on his part to make out a case against us. It did not mean, however, that a conviction was inevitable. Everything depended on the discretion of the Ruler—a conviction, an acquittal or the quantum of punishment. He advised me not to share this information with my companions. At the end of this conversation, the police and the staff were allowed to re-enter the court-room. Later, when asked by my colleagues, I told them that the magistrate had talked about the futility of incurring expenditure on a counsel, as the case depended on the discretion of the government.

In a further hearing, the magistrate ruled that we, the accused, were free to cross-examine the witnesses produced by the prosecution. Three separate cases had been filed against us. One witness, Giani Mehr Singh, after giving evidence in one case, took the witness box in the second case as well. Cross-examining him, I asked him if he had ever given evidence against me earlier, to which he replied in the negative. He failed to realize that he had given evidence against me in the first case as well. The magistrate understood the catch in my question, but was reluctant to record this episode. He refused to record it even on my insistence. He was seen scribbling something illegibly, though I had firm belief that he would not record anything that went against the prosecution and he would prepare proceedings of his own choice.

The same witness, Giani Mehr Singh, took the box in the third case against us. In the cross-examination, I asked him if he was ever ousted from the Akali Dal. When he replied in the negative, I further put the question, if he was ever suspended from that Party, which he also denied. Then my question was whether he was ever called upon to explain his position in any manner, while he was in that Party. He said, as far as he remembered, there was no such occasion. Then I reminded him that even in Akali Dal, he was charged with leaking secret information about the Party to the government, and though he was a member of the Executive Committee of Akali Dal, he was not trusted and was kept away from its meetings.

We kept on arguing our case without any expertise or material, which the authorities any way were never interested in providing us. Another witness against us, Kripal Singh, belonging to our village was at loggerheads with the whole village community, as he was a relative of the Raja and claimed ownership of all land under cultivation, condemning all the farmers as mere tenants-at-will. There were four other families, who were kins of the Ruler and all these five had been arbitrarily invested with overlordship, trampling over the rights of the toiling farmers. Actually this gentleman, Kripal Singh, had personal cordial relations with my family, but under duress from the Raja, he gave evidence against me in court, though his eyes were cast down and anxiety was writ large on his face. Obviously, he could not afford to sour his relations with the Ruler, his benefactor. My co-accused, Sandhura Singh, cross-examining him asked that since he belonged to my village, he must be knowing me very well, and if so, he should tell the court about my general character, whether he had ever found any blemish on me. The witness replied that he was happy to say that there was never anything adverse against me and, in fact, I was considered to be a noble and well-behaved young man in the. village and the neighbourhood. He said that to his personal knowledge, I was a man of character with no stigma of any kind. Kripal Singh also referred to my father respectfully and remembered his saintly qualities. Intervening, the magistrate asked how this question was relevant to the case, to which Sandhura Singh took the plea that it was connected with the character of Zail Singh. The magistrate chiding the witness remarked that he had pulled the rug from under his own feet,' as, in his evidence, he had accused me of collecting the foodgrains from the farmers, selling them and spending the proceeds on political work and then he gave me a certificate of impeccable character.

Our trial lingered on at a snail's pace. On conclusion of the marathon proceedings, the magistrate gave his verdict of guilty and sentenced me to rigorous imprisonment for two years in the first case, two years in the second case and one year in the third case, alongwith a fine of Rs.250 and, in default, a further term of 10 months in jail. In the absence of a counsel, we unwittingly asked the magistrate, if the sentences would run concurrently, to which he pronounced that these . vould run consecutively. Perhaps, had we not raised this question, the sentences would have been concurrent.

Some of our sympathizers in the jail advised us to go in appeal, as the cases were false, and then it might also provide an opportunity to the Raja to reconsider his attitude, as the movement had almost died down. Accordingly, we filed an appeal in the court of the District and Sessions Judge, Mehr Singh Sandhu, who was an obsequious servant of the Raja. We had the moral support of senior Congress leaders, who were convinced that we had been implicated in false cases in a political vendetta.

On the first hearing of the appeal, the Appellate Judge asked us, if we had a counsel. To our reply in the negative, he adjourned the case to another date. On the second hearing, he ordered another adjournment. Since he spoke in English, which then I did not understand very well, I asked him to speak in Punjabi, but the judge pronounced his ignorance of the Punjabi language. As it sounded rather odd, I asked him, if he meant business or was just interested in prolonging the case. He remarked that it was good for us after all to get an occasional exposure to the outside world, so that we could see the hustle and bustle of the town before returning to the sombre solitude of our cells. Of course, the judge added that we knew very well the course our appeal was most likely to take. He advised us not to bother about engaging the services of a counsel, as it would be futile, because of little possibility of our being successful in the appeal. The will of the Ruler was supreme and could not be thwarted, he said with a twinkle in his eye. He, however, made a sporting offer to devote some time to teaching us English after every hearing, if only we would agree to teach him Punjabi in return. He was a cultured and polished man, besides being vivacious.

In the meantime, we received a message on behalf of Dr. Gopi Chand Bhargava and a letter was sent to us by Dr. Saifuddin Kitchlew in Urdu language through Ralia Singh, which was read out to us in the jail, but not delivered to us. The letter eulogized our patriotic spirit and our will to fight for freedom, but it emphasized the resolve of the All-India Congress Committee to concentrate their efforts only on British India and not to intensify the movement in the princely States. It would be much easier to democratize the States after winning independence for the country. The letter added that the Akali Dal and the Punjab Congress Committee had passed resolutions proclaiming our innocence and deprecating the evil designs of the princely regime to implicate us in false cases. We were urged to acquire acquittals even by tendering apology, as it would cast no aspersion on our names or stigma to our integrity.

The State authorities made their own move in granting my mother an exclusive interview with me. In earlier interviews, intelligence men used to be present and they took notes on our conversations, but this time they discreetly disappeared and left the two of us alone. They had impressed on my mother to urge me to tender an apology to the Raja. My mother disclosed that they had brought her to jail at their own initiative, even though it was earlier than a month, which was the usual interval for interviews with prisoners. They had told her that since her son was heading for a long sentence of seven years incarceration, she could save him from th is tribulation by persuading him to apologize to the Ruler. But my mother confided that she had not come to ask me to apologize. Though she had not been in favour of my joining the crusade for freedom, yet, since I had launched myself on this unchartered course, there was no going back, and if I ever thought of tendering an apology, it would sadden her heart, besmirch my name and damage the prestige of the family. The abject act of apologizing would not only cause a stigma, ·to my person, it would also embarrass her mortally, for which she would never be able to forgive me. Whatever the difficulties and whatever the sufferings, I should never capitulate. I should not surrender my honour under any threat or temptation. She had come to avail of this opportunity of meeting me only to have an intimate conversation with me, which the regime had denied her earlier, she said, and I should be astute enough not to tell them that she had dissuaded me from tendering an' apology. I should inform them on the other hand that she had spoken to me and I had promised to think over her counsel.

This was my last meeting with my mother, when I could exchange a few words with her without anybody's interference. After that in spite of repeated efforts on my part and her behalf, no exclusive meeting between mother and son could take place.

After some days in the prison, I realized that the fire of our movement had dissipated and the embers had cooled down. We were being treated as common criminals. The District and Sessions Judge rejected our appeal and we returned to our dreary and desolate cells.

We were supposed to do rigorous physical labour. I had to work on ropes, which made my hands raw and bleed. I tore a piece of my turban and wrapped it on my lacerated hands to do the labour. My companions Janga Singh and Sandhura Singh, who had experience of earlier political imprisonments, advised me not to work full steam, but to adopt the tactics of slow rhythm. I should not refuse to accept the labour assigned to me, but I need not slog to complete the full quota. In defiance of the discipline imposed on us by the jail authorities, we communicated with one another talking loudly. We were taken out of our cells into the open only for half an hour daily. My companions advised me to work thick ropes instead of thin and fine ones to save time. The rough ropes made by me attracted the ire of the authorities. They put me on the grindstones to grind the foodgrains into flour within my cell. My task was to grind 16 kilograms of wheat every day. In case of a shortfall, I had to explain to the authorities. I often went beyond my endurance in labour which, of course, did not deter the authorities from making adverse entries in our records. On the other hand, none of us was keen to earn the approbation of the Raja's minions.

Chapter 4

WORKING AN OIL MILL LIKE AN OX

One fine morning I was yoked to an oil mill like a bullock to extract oil from the seeds. I felt indignant, but had no way out. Three prisoners were assigned to one oil mill to extract oil from the mustard in three rounds of 10 kilograms each. From 10 kilograms of mustard 21½ kilograms of oil could be extracted. I went on for several days acting a bullock, when 1 felt that my limbs were at the breaking point. The other two persons in my team were non-political prisoners and they were appreciative of the fact that I had been convicted for political activities. To prove their point, they offered me more time than my due for respite, which I politely turned down. In fatigue and desperation, I poured a bucketful of cold water into the mill, which ruined the mustard. When produced before the Jail Superintendent, I owned the responsibility and refused to give an assurance that such a peccadillo would not be repeated. This forced the jailor to keep me confined to my cell measuring 10' x 7'.

After the lapse of some weeks, I was put on the labour of weaving. They placed a weaving frame in the verandah outside my cell and started imparting me the training. Though I had very little interest in this task, to ward off boredom I soon learnt it and started making *durries, khes, khadi* cloth and even silken cloth. This gave me ample time to stay out of my cell during day time. After sunset, I had to step into my cage to spend the hours of the night in utter darkness.

Newspapers were a taboo in the jail. If some minor official was able to smuggle in an old newspaper, we used to compensate him with money. After avidly grasping the contents, we used to burn the paper to ashes. Quite often, policemen helped us getting money from our homes, keeping a sizeable cut for themselves. We were not allowed to read books on any political topic. We were permitted to have books only on religious subjects. My persistent efforts to procure publications on current affairs were seldom fruitful, as sympathetic members of the jail staff found it hazardous to smuggle them in.

1 was allowed to write only one letter a month. Pen, paper and pencil were out of reach. Even one letter that I had the permission to write, with the benevolence of the prison administration, was invariably censored, before it was posted. No wonder, I found it pointless to pour out my innermost feelings in such letters. I looked for other avenues to send out letters, for giving expression to my pent-up feelings. At times, I borrowed stubs of pencils from friendly policemen and scribbled letters on the blank leaves inside the covers of books allowed to me for reading. The letters would then be handed over to a warder, who would generally be a convict with good behaviour and had served a good number of years in the jail.

One day I wrote a two-page letter to my mother and handed it over to a veteran convict, Pritam Singh to take it out for posting. Being a devout Sikh, and very fond of reciting holy hymns, he used to keep a *Gutka* (a small book containing excerpts from the scriptures) in the holster of his small *kirpan* (sword). He placed the letter inside the holster, and coincidentally was not allowed to go out of the jail that evening. Two days later the whole barrack was searched and my letter was discovered. A horde of officers descended on my cell and questioned me about the letter. I admitted, I had written the letter. They interrogated me about the source of acquiring a pencil and paper, which I flatly refused to disclose. They taunted me for not telling the truth.

I told them not to ask any questions so that no lies would be told. They searched my cell and found that one or two blank leaves from each book had been torn out. They compared the paper on which my letter was scribbled with the pages of a book, which made it obvious to them that it was a tear-off from the book's inside cover. Instant orders were issued that no book with any blank page should be issued to me in future and 1 should not be allowed more than two books at a time.

To acquire a pencil was a herculean task. If and when I could get one, I buried it under the roots of a shrub at a measured distance from my cell. I would dig it out at an opportune time to jot down a few lines addressed to a relative or a friend. Since it was extremely difficult to keep money in the cell, it was interned in the ground at a few paces from the cell, to be taken out prudently and parsimoniously for the purchase of an old newspaper or an occasional glass of milk.

Sundays were credited to the prisoners' period of sentence. A remission of 27 days was granted on the birthday of the Ruler, as he had completed that many years of his age. The jail authorities gradually realised that it was rather difficult to repress my soul. Their attitude hardened and they came down with a heavy hand on me. They disallowed me the ordinary remissions and enhanced my imprisonment by a fortnight.

I was put in fetters. The attrition of the iron caused a wound on my ankle, and I started running high temperature. I was unfettered when taken to the hospital, but I refused to give a written undertaking not to seek a pencil and paper again to write letters furtively. I stressed my right to communicate with the outside world and not to mortgage my conscience. I was brought back to the cell and fettered again with recurrence of fever. The fetters were filed to widen the rings to avoid further attrition. After a couple of months they removed the fetters from my person.

When they started removing the blank leaves from the books before issuing them to me, I started using the reverse sides of pictures in the books for writing letters. When they found out my pencil and confiscated it, I got hold of a two-inch long lead of a pencil and hollowing a *datun* (a twig used for brushing the teeth after chewing it hard) inserted it in it. Using the twig as a peg, I fitted it in a wall of my cell and hung my clothes on it. My cell was searched a number of times over a few months, but they could not detect the twig. One fine morning an over-zealous warder rung the curtain down on the drama and deprived me of the lead of the pencil.

The jail administration would allow books only like *Bhagwat Gita, Quran,* excerpts from *Guru Granth Sahib* and *Ramayana* etc. Maulvi Suleiman was one of the prisoners convicted for active participation in our movement. He was a scholar of *Quran.* He agreed to teach me to read the Holy Book. We started discussions during the half hour daily recess in the open, which sometimes was prolonged thanks to some accommodating warder There was a drain running under the wall separating two rows of cells, which faced opposite directions. There was a hole in the common wall of my cell and that of Maulvi Suleiman. Due to heavy rain, the hole got widened, as one brick was dislocated from its place. We ourselves removed a couple of more bricks and the gap became wide enough for us to communicate with each other. As a Muslim, he had a copy of the *Quran* in his own right. I got one issued by the jail library for perusal for comparative study of religions. We used to place our copies on either side of the drain and he used to guide me in reading three or four pages every day. I used to repeat those pages over and over again in my cell, and if I needed any further help, it was provided by him the following day. It took me about six months to complete three rounds of recitation of the *Quran* with the help of Maulvi Suleiman. It motivated me to obtain a translation of this holy Islamic scripture to enable me to understand the intrinsic meanings and nuances of this great volume.

Nothing could be concealed very long in the jail. Our secret rendezvous was discovered by a warder, who noticed the wide hole in the wall with the open *Quran,* placed on a piece of cloth reverently.

The warden wondered at our inventiveness to pursue an intellectual objective, but being temperamentally harsh and strict, he got the gap in the wall narrowed to its previous width. With heavy downpour and the dampening of the wall, with overflow of the water in the drain, we were again able to pull out a brick to continue our study for another two months, before the Maulvi's jail term of three years ended and he was set free. Qazi Obedullah also completed his sentence. There was another Muslim inmate, who was undergoing life sentence for murder. He knew how to read *Quran,* but his knowledge of Arabic was so limited, that he was hardly of much help, except for pointing out my glaring mistakes. After his egress from the jail, my study of the *Quran* continued with the help of a book of translation.

By the time I completed about four years of my term, I started having a low-grade fever, which persisted for over a month. I had an apprehension of having contracted tuberculosis. When I told the doctor, he prescribed medicine No. 27 to be administered to me. He paid little personal attention to my suffering. Neither he got me X-rayed, nor did he test my blood.

In desperation, I sought permission to visit the *Gurudwara* in the jail daily, which was denied to me. Ultimately, I was allowed to go to the *Gurudwara* once a month. On the first day, I scooped the dust of the feet of the congregation and applied it to my body and miraculously, I felt relief. Perhaps, God heard my prayers to save me from that parasitic disease as I dreaded really to see my body shrivelling and being wasted away, before I could see the fulfilment of my dream of the country's redemption from foreign domination and the riddance for the groaning people of the capricious and suffocating role of the chieftains.

My companions were set free one after another after serving their sentences, which ranged from one-and-a-half year to four years. Jathedar Ram Singh and I had to complete five years. We were drafted as labourers for the construction of a cellar in the fort of the Raja of Faridkot. To excavate the earth for building of a veritable palace eighty feet below the ground level was a stupendous task, for which huge labour was required. For that I, along with a large number of convicts, was deployed. The Chief Warder was quite a tyrannical and sadistic person and ordered us to carryon our heads baskets full of earth from a hundred feet below up to the ground level. Taken to the site early in the morning, we started being brought back to the jail late in the evening. After some days, Jathedar Ram Singh was shifted to the task of breaking stones and my services were switched over to passing electric wires through the underground conduit pipes.

The Raja had started building this cellar in view of the Second World War for his and his family's safety. One day during a round of inspection, he chanced upon the spot when Jathedar Ram Singh and I were busy in our labour. The Raja asked the old political warrior questions about his physical well-being and the period of sentence still left to be served. The old man went on breaking the stones, while answering the Raja's queries.

The Raja asked him to suspend his work while answering. Ram Singh, mumbled that once he stopped the work, he would never resume it. The Raja then turned to me. He was earlier briefed by the Inspector about my identity. When he asked me about the period of sentence I was still to serve, I pleaded ignorance, as due to interception of the letter I had written for my people, the remissions had been cancelled, thereby enhancing the period of my imprisonment. The Raja then asked me, if I was feeling too uncomfortable, to which I replied that we were not looking for any comforts, while we had chosen this path.

To tell the truth, I told the Raja that, we had got used to the discomforts of the jail so much that there was hardly any inclination to complain. The Raja then left hurriedly after hurling a greeting. We were chided by the police officers later, that if we had sought the total remission of our sentences from the Ruler without even tendering formal apologies, the favour would most probably have been granted. But that was not in our reckoning and could never have been a part of our culture.

A fifty-five feet layer of earthwork was laid over the roof of the cellar to save it from a possible bomb attack by any foreign power during the War. Many years later, when I became the Union Home Minister, I visited the Faridkot fort and wanted to see the cellar. But I was told that since it had remained in desuetude for decades, the air down below had become polluted and poisonous and thus positively dangerous.

During the last few months of my jail term, I came to know that my mother's health was failing. Since I had to sleep on hard ground in my cell, my mother also left the luxury of a cot and started sleeping on the floor. A fellow prisoner, who had been set free, had gone and told her about the miserable quality of food we were served. She had started taking the same type of food at home. We were not given tea or any other beverage to drink.

My companion Janga Singh, who was very fond of tea, hit upon a novel idea. He used to beg a warder to spare a little kerosene oil, which he burnt under a small piece of pipe, over which he kept a vessel with a little water to boil. He drank that concoction without sugar and milk, but nothing could deter him from making this insipid beverage.

Our morning meal consisted of two hard chapatis, for lunch we were given parched grams (which were later substituted with a chapatti) and the dinner comprised three chapattis and a vegetable. The dough was made by some prisoners with their feet and the pulse was cooked without being sifted of pebbles. Handfuls of unground red chillies were thrown in the cauldrons of the pulse or the vegetable. A major part of the cooking oil meant for the prisoners was pilfered by the jail officials.

Jathedar Ram Singh's daughter died while he was in jail. He grieved mournfully over his loss. Tears never dried from his eyes. My mother was ill, but I was not allowed to go to see her. It was only a little over three months left in the completion of my sentence. My brother applied for my parole, but he was rebuffed and asked to persuade me to tender an apology, if I wanted freedom. My mother breathed her last and the family kept the news from me. One day while I was labouring in the exacavation work, one of the watermen engaged by the authorities to serve water to the prisoners, who hailed from my village, condoled me the death of my mother. That was the moment I came to know of the shocking event and my grief knew no bounds.

My sorrow was fathomless, as the floodgates of my tears opened and inspite of my best efforts, I could not stop the deluge. I was told later that during her last moments, the only word on her lips was my name. In her state of semiconsciousness, my brother's arm was placed in her hands and she was told that Zail Singh had come back from the jail. She felt the arm with her fingers and whispered that it was not true.

It was her last wish, that after her cremation, her ashes should be collected and kept till I came home, so that I could immerse them in the river Ganga at Hardwar. I fulfilled this last wish of my mother, who had nurtured me since my infancy, after departure of my mother who had given me birth and whom I did not remember.

Chapter 5

EMANCIPATION FROM INCARCERATION

After my return from the jail. perhaps due to long years of malnutrition, I suffered a serious digestive disorder, which wrecked my health. With months of treatment by an Ayurvedic doctor, I came on an even keel. At that point of lime, Kehar Singh, who had tried to persuade me to tender an apology to the Ruler during the trial of my case suggesting that I was marked for a seven years sentence, approached me again. He still owed unflinching loyalty to the Raja though at the same time he had some personal sympathy for me too. Later in 1946, he joined our movement. He calculated my sentence as seven years, recalling that the trial had lingered on for eleven months, and if my brothers had not paid a fine of Rs.250 imposed by the trial judge, I would have got an additional term of ten months. Thus it came roughly to seven years, he claimed.

My brothers had decided to pay the fine to save me from another ten months of jail. But when they could not muster this sum on demand, the officers of the Raja forcibly took possession of one hundred maunds of foodgrains harvested by the family. Kehar Singh once again counselled caution and tried to sell the idea, that if I did not get on the right side of the Raja, I might again find myself tied hand and foot and in jail. He pointed out the stark reality of desertions from the ranks of our sympathisers owing to pelf or pusillanimity and said, that only a handful of activists were left, who could also be nabbed any time. His thesis was that either I should mend my fences with the Raja or get out of the State for good.

Chapter 6

FROM FARIDKOT TO A WIDER ARENA

In the course of consultations with friends and companions, I met Jathedar Mohan Singh Nagoke a renowned Nationalist Akali Congress leader of the time, who advised me to work outside the princely State of Faridkot, which would give me greater freedom to pursue my goal. He anticipated early emancipation of the country from the foreign rule and hoped that after the exist of the British from India, it would need quite an effort to rid the princely States of the autocracy of Rajas and Nawabs. We should not lower our guards and try to keep our spirits high for a coup-de-grace.

I left Faridkot and went to Amritsar, where I came across Harchand Singh Jeji, a wealthy landlord of Patiala, who had fled his State in search of a haven. He was at daggers drawn with his erstwhile Ruler, but, ironically, later, with the efforts of the then well-known Akali leader, Master Tara Singh, his daughter, Mohinder Kaur was married to Maharaja Yadavindra Singh of Patiala. Master Tara Singh's inner sympathies were with the Parja Mandal movement, which was fighting against the autocratic and arbitrary rule of the princes.

He (Master Tara Singh) and Dr Saifuddin Kitchleu shared the opinion that I should shift the area of my activities from the narrow confines of Faridkot to the wider arena of British India. Master Tara Singh had a telephonic talk with Dr. Gopi Chand Bhargava, the veteran Congress leader of Punjab, at Lahore, who averred that the Congress Party wanted to go slow in taking on the State princes, till the country reached the goal of freedom. Even if I chose to lie low in my State, I would run the risk of being arrested. Expressing this opinion, he suggested to Master Tara Singh, to advise me to stay on in Amritsar.

In spite of the fact that Master Tara singh had innate sympathy with the Parja Mandal and that the Akali Dal, the Communist Party and others were inwardly united in their campaign against the whimsical rulers of the States, he asked me to hold my gun and stay put at Amritsar. It was suggested to Master Tara Singh that whereas Harchand Singh Jeji was an affluent farmer and the landlord of two villages and could afford to live comfortably outside his State, I was a man of very limited means, as my family consisting of three brothers owned only about sixty acres of land. I was asked not to shift my family to the city and to join the Sikh Missionary College.

Principal Ganga Singh was of the view that I knew all that his college could offer in instruction and that I could straightaway be drafted as a missionary. At the behest of Jathedar Mohan Singh Nagoke, I accepted the post of a Missionary at a consolidated salary of Rs. 81 per month, with my headquarters at Amritsar, but field work in various areas. It was in 1944-45 that I travelled to different districts like Lyallpur, Sialkot, Sheikhupura, Rawalpindi, Gujranwala, Jhelum, Ferozepur, Gurdaspur, Hoshiarpur and Ambala in Punjab for preaching religion at numerous congregations. Shortly, however, specific regions were assigned to the missionaries to enable them to make intensive and package efforts to preach religion and teach *Guruvani.* Dasuah in Hoshiarpur District was my first field posting, after which I went to Muktsar, where the President of Gurdwara Committee, Jathedar Harnam Singh Kabbarwachha also warned me of possible arrest, once J stepped on the soil of the Faridkot State. I reconciled myself to this voluntary exile from my home State to wait for the clarion call to rid the States of the oppressive rule and to usher in an era of democracy.

My campaign against the feudal rule continued. I went on

expressing my views on public platforms with the only difference that I was at a little distance from the State. At Dasuah in Hoshiarpur district, I ran into some active Communist workers. They were aware that I had become a missionary out of necessity, though I belonged to the Congress Party. Then the Akali and the Congress Parties were marching together in their struggle against the British. Twice I sneaked into my State to assist my brothers in ploughing the fields and reaping the harvests.

There were frequent contacts with the Communists, who too were working for the ouster of the colonial rulers. The intentions of all parties converged on this score. Simultaneously, I had to pay attention to my mission. There was hardly any tension or emotional chasm between the Hindus and the Sikhs. My task was to preach the qualities of the Sikh faith with a universal appeal of human fraternity, which attracted the attention of all Punjabis. I visited a village called Uchapind where I found an abandoned religious place and set up my camp there. The next day a score of people came to listen to me and soon they discovered about my political leanings and offered all help.

On 21-22 April 1946, a conference was organised by the Punjab States Peoples' Conference at Rampura Phul in Nabha State under the Chairmanship of Baba Kharak Singh, the eminent nationalist Sikh leader of the time. I, along with a large number of political workers, took part in the Conference. In his presidential address, Baba Kharak Singh expressed deep regret at the callous attitude of the Raja of Faridkot and his atrocities on the patriotic people.

It was decided in the Conference to hold a public meeting at Faridkot on 28 April 1946. A number of resolutions were passed. It was demanded that the British government, instead of writing the rules of the princely States for consultations regarding the transfer of power, should invite the real representatives of the people for negotiations."

The repressive measures of the Rulers of Faridkot, Nabha and Malerkotla were condemned. The Rulers of States were asked to provide essential commodities like kerosene, sugar and cloth to the public. Anguish was expressed at the incidents of repression at Faridkot, where a peaceful procession was lathi-charged and four young men were arrested and tortured.

In another resolution, the Governor-General and the States' Residents were called upon to appoint a Committee to look into the charges of corruption, nepotism and favouritism on the part of the State officials. Shock and sorrow were expressed for the atrocities perpetrated on the political workers in the States. An enquiry was demanded against the guilty. Proper medical treatment of the injured political workers was asked for.

Earlier, on 8 April 1946, a few young boys had tried to hoist the tricolour flag on a tree in the town. The police dealt with them violently and thrashed them badly. The flag was pulled down and destroyed. The following day I led a huge procession to protest against the police atrocities and demanded the establishment of a representative government. The police resorted to cane charge and injured many workers. Some were arrested. The next day a general strike was observed.

The public meeting on 28 April 1946, at Faridkot attracted a large number of people from all parts of the State as also the neighbouring States. Many eminent leaders including Brish Bhan, Hardev singh, Sant Ram Vakil and Seth Ram Nath attended. We raised our voice against the cruelties perpetrated by the Raja. We decried the absence of civil liberties and the stepmotherly treatment meted out to the peasants. They were being denied the proprietary rights, which were vested in the Ruler.

In the face of the repression let loose by the Raja of Faridkot and his tactics to get the public meetings of the peaceful agitators disturbed by hired goondas and the army personnel in plain clothes, I held discussions with the State officials asking them to refrain from disturbing peaceful public meetings, but without any positive result. The State Government persisted in its unholy acts and we decided to offer a Satyagraha.

Groups of four persons were asked to enter the State territory to defy the ban. Hira Singh Bhattal, who led the first group, was surrounded by the Raja's hatchet men and beaten mercilessly. Several other Jathas met the same fate. They were thrashed cruelly and put behind the bars. On 28 April a group led by Hardev Singh arrived at Faridkot to participate in the projected public meting. They were accosted by the Raja's musclemen and beaten brutally. More than a dozen men suffered severe injuries. Over 225 were arrested. The Tricolour was dishonoured. Gandhi caps were thrown about and destroyed.

At an emergency meeting held at Jaito, a unanimous decision was taken to launch a *Satyagraha* at Faridkot. I was made a member of the Executive Committee. Volunteers were recruited the very next day and despatched to Faridkot. As soon as the first group entered the State territory, the Tricolour was snatched from them. They were taken to the police station for a severe beating and later they were let off outside the city.

The entry of the *Jathas* and their merciless bashing by the police became a daily affair. The repression had a contrary effect. [athas from various parts of the State started entering the capital. I went from village to village and exhorted people to join the Satyagraha and to make sacrifices for the national cause. On 5 May 1946, a group of peaceful agitators led by Jiwa Singh of Malerkotla, on entering the Faridkot territory, was taken into custody. The members were assaulted, detained for the night and, later let off. The Punjab State Congress Committee lodged strong telegraphic protests to the Ruler of Faridkot and the Chancellor, Chamber of Princes to draw their attention to the atrocities being perpetrated by the Raja. They were asked to appoint an Enquiry Committee to look into beatings,. arrests, molestation of women and the desecration of the Tricolour. The Punjab State Congress Committee also decided to observe a Protest Day on 8 May 1946, as Faridkot Day. Thousands of people took partin rallies all over Punjab and Faridkot. The atrocities of the Faridkot Ruler were condemned.

Pandit Nehru sent a message stating that the peoples of the States had been following a policy of friendly approach to the rulers with the hope that fully responsible government would be possible for the States in free integrated India. This friendly approach and policy had evoked no practical response, though there had been expressions of goodwill about the future. We were on the threshold of changes and they would come, whether anybody wanted them or not. The next few months might well decide this question in the States as well as in India as a whole. The States being so numerous and various in India, it was difficult to lay down a hard rule as to when changes would come to them. But we could not have stagnant pools cut off from the rushing torrent of India's national life. In any case there had to be a measure of uniformity and democratic basis and progress all over India.

Small States, Pandit Nehru added, had a chance immediately to group themselves into efficient units of the Indian federation to come. Regarding events in Faridkot, Pandit Nehru said that the continuous hartal there showed the extreme resentment of the people.

The Faridkot State Administration threatened to arrest Dwarka Nath Kachru, Secretary of the States Peoples' Conference, if he dared enter the State. This annoyed Pandit Nehru, who reached the conclusion that sooner this incompetent and thoroughly out of date Administration went the better. Whatever the Raja and his administration might be doing, events were marching and we had to march with them.

Meetings all over Punjab and other States on 8 May 1946 were addressed by prominent leaders, who appealed to people to join the *Satyagraha*. I addressed several such meetings and exhorted people to preserve the honour and dignity of the national flag. The question of national honour was of paramount importance and no sacrifice was too great to defend it. Public opinion was mobilised to persuade the Faridkot Ruler to mend his ways. The latter, on the other hand, went berserk and he let loose a reign of terror, which shocked the conscience of the national leaders.

Pandit Nehru deputed Dwarka Nath Kachru to visit Faridkot

promptly to assess the situation. As a group of six persons led by Kachru arrived at Faridkot they were told that their entry had been banned. They were ordered. to leave the State immediately. That is how the recalcitrant Ruler refused the chance to the people to meet this group of national leaders.

Kachru apprised Pandit Nehru of the volatile and critical . situation. Pandit Nehru sent a telegram to the Faridkot Administration describing the behaviour of authorities as barbarous and scandalous. He asked them to withdraw the orders restricting entry and civil liberties in the State. Nehru also asked the Faridkot Administration to punish the guilty of the excesses. Faridkot had in his words become a symbol of degradation of some of the Indian States. The mighty popular movement everywhere in India, including the States, would not tolerate any oppression or insult to human rights. Those who thought that they were still in the medieval ages would havẹ to be swept away.

The State Administration started a counter-propaganda drive. They let loose a campaign of disinformation. They tried to tell people that outsiders had attempted to trespass into the State territory forcibly and when asked not to disturb the State's peace, they had become violent. They were arrested. therefore, without any physical harm' to them. The Administration also tried to play the communal card. The Satyagrahis were described as Hindus out to defame and weaken the Sikh power, who, in fact, was so popular among his subjects!

The whole country virtually condemned the Faridkot Ruler's attitude. Even the Shiromani Akali Dal called upon the Ruler to accept the genuine demands of the people: Babu Labh Singh, President of the Dal described the allegations that the Parja MandaI Movement intended to wipe out the Sikh Ruler, as baseless.

Dr. Saifuddin Kitchleu, President of Punjab Provincial Congress Committee, reminded the Faridkot Administration that suppression-of. civil liberties and the ban on the entry of the members of the Enquiry Committee into the State merited immediate enquiry. The Raja wilted under the sustained pressure of the nationalist forces. On 25 May 1946, he received a delegation led by Dr. Kitchleu for discussions. Members of the Council of Action also reached Faridkot. It was mutually agreed *inter alia* that all political prisoners would be released unconditionally, and enquiry would be held against the officials responsible for the repressive acts and the policy of revenge would be abandoned.

Before the ink on the compromise could dry, the Ruler's government went back on its word and tried to annul it. It caused great resentment among the people. The national leaders took exception to the Raja's perfidy. Pandit Nehru informed him that he was visiting Faridkot on 27 May. The Raja shot back a reply that his entry was banned and if he tried to set his foot on the State territory, he would be treated as a criminal.

Pandit Nehru reached Bhatinda by train from Delhi on the morning of 27 May to proceed further to Faridkot. As the train in which he was travelling steamed into the Bhatinda Railway Station, we joined him in his coach, as we had reached there in advance to meet him. This was the first time ever in my life to have a look into the First Class compartment of a railway train. Our group comprised Hardev Singh (President of the regional committee of Parja Mandal), Brish Bhan (President of Punjab State Parja Mandal), Seth Ram Nath (President of Nabha State Parja Mandal), and other leaders. As we went on narrating our tale of woes to Pandit Nehru, he lost no time pointing out our deficiencies and suggesting corrective measures.

As the train steamed into the Faridkot station, a milling crowd of thousands was present to greet Pandit Nehru. Though the State government had placed a number of restrictions, there was surging humanity to. have a glimpse of their beloved leader. Railway stations were outside the jurisdiction of the princely states and the State administration could not arrest anyone in their compounds. But no sooner had we crossed the boundary of the Railway station, than a magistrate served an order on Pandit Nehru not to enter Faridkot, otherwise he would be put under arrest.

Showing the contempt the order deserved, Pandit Nehru

mounted the horse, we had arranged for him and started towards the city, as we accompanied him on foot. Suddenly dismounting, Panditji took hold of the warrant from the magistrate and tore it into pieces. He asked the magistrate to tell the Raja to arrest him. He lustily patted my shoulder and asked me to lead the march. Thousands of men and women in a display of extraordinary enthusiasm heaved forward. The police lost nerve and did not have the courage to make any arrest. We took Pandit Nehru to the Grain Market near which the youths had earlier hoisted the Congress flag on a neem tree in defiance of the Raja. Panditji himself unfurled a Congress flag on that tree. The gate through which the throng entered is now named after Pandit Nehru, the idol of the masses.

In a thundering speech Panditji told the mammoth gathering that he would go to meet the comrades still languishing in the prison and would not seek any permission for the same. He would have to make it plain to the Ruler, he said, that the path the latter had taken to was disastrous. The voice of the people could not be suppressed. We were standing at the threshold of freedom and it would be imprudent to deny the rights of the citizens. It could be in the interest of the State, if erroneous paths were abandoned and the reality accepted. At the same time, he would advise the comrades in Parja Mandal to give up excesses and to adopt moderation in their conduct. He had received reports that some people had been indulging in the use of indecent language.

Since it was out of question for a room in the Government Rest House to be allotted to us for the sojourn of Pandit Nehru, we took him to the residence of a friend in Parja Mandai, Devi Lal, who owned a brick-house and gave quite a comfortable room for seating our honoured guest. Hardly had Nehru finished his bath and changed his clothes, that a messenger of the Raja came with a letter requesting him to visit him in his palace and indicate the time convenient to him. It was in the afternoon and Panditji gave time in the evening for the purpose. After his lunch, Panditji asked us to give him a copy of the charter of demands we wanted the Raja to concede.

Barring two villages, the Raja was the supreme landlord in all the two hundred villages in the State. No farmer could sell or mortgage his land without the approval of the Raja. Along with usual revenue, the farmers were bound to pay the Supreme landlordship tax to the Raja, which went into his personal coffers. In my village and another, the supreme proprietary rights of the land had been vested in the kins of the Ruler. We were considered as their peasants. This had made our position piquant and people outside had corne to consider us much inferior in status. This had brought us down in the social scale and the people outside shirked from entering in matrimonial alliances with people in these two villages.

The relatives of the Raja enjoying these superior proprietary rights in the two villages had imposed a tax of one-fourth of the produce from every crop, but, whenever they carne to the fields to demand this arbitrary share, the villagers got together and very often entered into altercations and bitter exchanges with them. We hardly had any other supporter in our resistance movement. There was zamindari system in the states like Patiala and Nabha, where ownership of the land vested in big landlords. We were decidely the underdogs.

When Pandit Nehru went to see the Raja of Faridkot, the latter's mother, in a show of supplication, placed her dupatta (the scarf used by ladies to cover their heads) at Panditji's feet and, after extolling his virtues and greatness as a popular leader, she asked him if it would serve any purpose demolishing the rule of her child. She pledged the Raja's allegiance and loyalty to India's great leader. The Raja too promised to mete out just and fair treatment to the people, but complained that the supporters of the Parja Manda] Movement often indulged in abusive language and indecent behaviour. After listening to the mother and son Pandit Nehru really carne to believe that the Raja was not such a bad person after all and, perhaps, the agitators should share the blame.

Pandit Nehru asked the Raja to institute a high-level Judicial enquiry against the officials responsible for excesses against and misbehaviour with the peaceful demonstrators, to release all political prisoners unconditionally, not to prevent the unfurling of the Tricolour, to allow freedom of speech, assembly of persons and processions, to withdraw the Registration of Societies Act, and to eschew feelings of revenge.

The Raja immediately released political prisoners and rescinded the Registration of Societies Act, under which it was obligatory to register any Association or Society and promised to institute an enquiry against officials responsible for physical assaults on the public. He also pledged to negotiate with the leaders of Parja Mandal about the land proprietary rights, but pleaded that he should not be coerced to implement all the decisions in haste. He demanded respite for two months for carrying out all his pledges and promises.

Pandit Nehru chided us for being tyros in the art of fighting political battles. It required prudence and foresight, he said. It is essential to notify the demands, give some time, negotiate and then, if necessary, take a stiff stand. He was impressed by the suaveness of the Raja and desired that we should provide proper justification for our demand for his removal from his princely position. We told Panditji that we had made no such demand, but we definitely wanted democratic processes to be introduced in the State.

Before Nehru returned to Devi Lal's residence, the released political prisoners had already trudged the distance from the jail. There were about forty of them. Their freedom and the end of bestial treatment they suffered in captivity was a blessing due to Nehru's visit to the State. But as Nehru turned his back on Faridkot, the Raja's solicitude evaporated in thin air. A few weeks elapsed, but no enquiry was instituted, nor did the Raja show any. enthusiasm for initiating talks. We were not allowed to unfurl the Tricolour at any place, though he did not disturb the flag unfurled by Pandit Nehru. He deputed special teams to villages to announce that a compromise had been arrived at with Pandit Nehru that apart from this flag, no other Tricolour would be unfurled anywhere, no political meeting or procession would take place and no political propaganda would be allowed. We were completely taken aback at this somersault, and we felt constrained to seek an appointment with the Raja. Receiving us in audience, he pleaded that he needed further time to lend practical shape to the commitments made to Panditji,

Thus being cold-shouldered by the Raja, we decided to convey our feelings of hurt to Pandit Nehru. Qazi Obedullah and I went to Delhi and made straight for the office of the Congress, where the Working Committee was in session. Top leaders like Sardar Vallabh Bhai Patel, Maulana Abul Kalam Azad, Khan Abdul Ghaffar Khan and Pattabhi Sitaramayya were attending the meeting. We were told to wait till the meeting was over. After a little while, Maulana Azad came out and entered another room to say his prayers. Pandit Nehru was informed about our presence outside. He soon emerged out of the Committee room and after giving us a patient hearing, dictated an urgent letter for the Raja of Faridkot pointing out the non-implementation of various items of the agreement reached between them. Pandit Nehru gave us a copy of the letter, which we delivered to the Raja soon after our return to the State.

The Raja in his reply denied this allegation and asserted that he stood by the agreement in letter and spirit. Pandit Nehru expressed his unhappiness for probable prevarication on our part, but we took pains to explain to him the insidious propaganda of the Ruler about the so-called understanding having been reached with him about the passive role of Parja Mandal and his complacency in implementing the agreement. Pandit Nehru felt disillusioned at the Raja's perfidy and quite sceptical about his credibility.

It was then that reports about the failure of what had come to be known as Nehru-Harindar pact started circulating. Pandit Nehru directed us to continue our movement with some restraint, as the Congress was locked in fierce struggle for gaining freedom from foreign rule and it was not possible to pay full attention to the princely States. But, the time would come, he said, when the Rulers of these states would be dealt with appropriately. Qazi Obedullah and I returned to Faridkot and earnestly engaged ourselves in the activities of our organization. The Raja in the meantime started adopting dubious tactics to damage our movement. He tried to give communal colour to our struggle and with the help of hooligans started harassing members of the public. I did my best to persuade the Raja to fulfil his promises, but he seemed bent upon overlooking the reality and sticking to his old postures. I called for a protest day to be observed on 24 November 1946, when public meetings were held at various important centres of the State. At these meetings, I urged the Raja to stop fabricating false cases against the freedom fighters, take steps to introduce representative government and grant ownership rights in agricultural land to the farmers.

The Raja made a clever move to announce his decision about the setting up of a Legislative Council, but the offer being vague and devoid of any mention about the composition and functions of the Council, we had no choice but to reject it outright. The Raja was also silent over the issue of universal adult franchise. On 18 December 1946 I led a delegation to the Chief Secretary, Faridkot government and protested against atrocities against Bhola Singh, President of the Parja Mandal, Virk Kalan and the hardships caused to certain shopkeepers, but we did not receive any satisfactory response.

In Faridkot, the masses missed no opportunity to convince the Raja about their determination to annul his anachronistic rule. The latter on the other hand seemed to be enamoured of the mirage of perpetual personal rule.

Chapter 7

INDIA GAINS INDEPENDENCE

India kept her tryst with destiny and became free on 15 August 1947. Of course, the trauma of partition and communal riots clouded the jubilations. The hearts of millions of people were filled with grief and sadness. About a million people fell prey to the communalism and fanaticism of the leaders of the Muslim League and many millions were uprooted from their hearths and homes resulting in one of the biggest and most tragic migrations in the world history.

Notwithstanding the sufferings and tribulations of the migrants and the stupendous problems of their rehabilitation, the multitudes were savouring their emancipation from colonial domination. People in the princely states were still groaning under the weight of feudalism. They were keen to do away with the suffocation under the Rulers and to join the national mainstream. The iron man of India, Sardar Vallabh Bhai Patel, called upon the Rajas, Maharajas and Nawabs to read the writing on the wall and to accede to the Indian Union. Patiala was the first to do so. Some States dithered and Faridkot was one of them. Though our morale was high, we continued to face repression. The Raja appeared quite slow in comprehending the reality of the situation.

In a public meeting at Kotkapura on 18 October 1947, the attitude of the Raja came under consistent criticism and his procrastination in implementing the Nehru-Harinder Pact was decried. I had to give an ultimatum to the Raja on 21 December

1947 to accept the people's demands or to face a non-violent agitation. There being no satisfactory response from the Ruler, we continued to educate the masses about the desirability and the need for a responsible government. We maintained our contacts with the national leaders and continued to apprise them of the developing situation.

On the fateful day of the assassination of Mahatma Gandhi, we visited him in New Delhi and told him about the repression the people in our State were facing and their democratic aspirations. I was accompanied by Brish Bhan, Pandit Sat Dev, Advocate, Seth Ram Nath and Inder Singh Chakravarty. The Mahatma was kind and gracious. He patiently heard our problems and asked us to meet him again after the prayer meeting. He also advised us to prepare a memorandum laying down our predicaments and our views in detail.

We were in the process of preparing a memorandum, when the assassin struck and the bullets rent the air followed by a serene cry of *Hey Ram* emanating from the lips of Bapu. The life of the Father of the Nation, the man who had moved millions in India and many other parts of the world with his message of love and non-violence, was snuffed out by the hands of bigotry and fanaticism.

The Raja persisted in his reluctance to see reason. On 29 February 1948, we were constrained to take out a procession in the main city of Faridkot. We launched a *Satyagrah* on 1 March 1948. For this purpose camps were set up at three places, viz. Mandi Goniana, Kotkapura and Faridkot. Under popular pressure, the Raja showed some signs of wilting, but as a face saving device, he went about proclaiming that he had reached an understanding with the Government of India, that his position would continue to remain as it was under the British regime, and that he would try to redress the people's genuine grievances.

Sardar Vallabh Bhai Patel, the Deputy Prime Minister and Minister for Home and the erstwhile States, started calling the Rulers advising them about the desirability of making Unions of States for greater cohesion and viability. Saurashtra in Western India was the first of such Unions to be formed, of which Jam Sahib of Jamnagar was designated Rajpramukh. Once, when I was in the waiting room of Sardar Patel, Ifound myself in the company of several erstwhile Rulers, who were awaiting their turns to go in and meet the iron man. Some went in and signed the covenants and some were perspiring in nervousness trying to calm themselves with glasses of cold water. Though the Rulers lost their domains, they gained privy purses free of Income Tax and several other perquisites like customs-free import of various items, the ownership of residences, free supply of water, electricity and free telephone connections, as also the privilege of flying their personal flags on their cars.

Chapter 8

THE LAST DITCH BATTLE WITH THE RAJA

In Faridkot, we were fortunate to have popular support of the people in spite of the fact that the Raja, being a devout Sikh, was trying to play on the religious sentiments of his subjects, eighty per cent of whom professed the Sikh faith. In about two hundred villages in his State, he knew several people personally and could address them by their names. But because of his unreasonable and imperious land management system, the wind was blowing against him.

As we announced the date of our satyagrah, we were advised by some leaders to take the Congress High Command into confidence. Pattabhi Sitaramayya, the President of the Indian National Congress, was also the President of the State People's Conference. Wherever the States Unions were being formed, the States People's Conference was giving way to the State Congress. In our meeting with Pattabhi Sitaramayya, he asked us to go ahead with our satyagrah plan, if we had the capacity to sustain it. I wanted to take the advice of Sardar Patel as well. My appointment with him was fixed for the next morning in the Lodhi Gardens, where he used to go for a walk. He asked me, if I had come alone to talk to him and why was not I accompanied by some elder leader from my State? I told him that I was the President of the State Parja Mandal and I happened to be alone at that particular hour. Sardar Patel remarked that he knew of my position and my passion for fighting for righteous causes, but he was wondering, if a delegation of our organisation had come to Delhi, or I was representing my people alone. Sardar Patel said that he was conscious of the plight of the people in the princely states and was very eager to ensure their emancipation. The process had started from the Gujarat region, and it was expected to be completed in the whole country in about a year's time. I pointed out about the unabashed personal rule of the Raja and our resolve to launch a satyagrah, to which Sardar Patel said, that by our rash actions we might get our skulls battered by the Ruler, who might stop at nothing. When I told the Sardar that I had already received the consent of the Congress President, Pattabhi Sitaramayya, for starting a satyagrah, he reacted rather strongly and said that, perhaps, Sitaramayya was not fully aware of the machinations of some obstreperous princes, and if we did not curb our impetuosity, we might be the losers. In a tone of finality, the Sardar said that he had expressed his opinion and that I could leave. His daughter, Maniben Patel, reinforced the verdict by telling me not to utter a word further and to take my way.

I found myself verily on the horns of a dilemma. The Congress President had approved of our proposed protest against the Raja, but the Deputy Prime Minister had sounded a note of sobriety and caution. I did not know what to convey to my companions back in my State, as even a date for the satyagrah had been decided upon. To get out of the impasse, I thought of seeking an interview with the Prime Minister, which I got the next morning. After listening to me patiently, Pandit Nehru said in a measured tone that being the Prime Minister, how could he advise a satyagrah, but if I thought we could muster enough strength to make the Raja see reason, he had no objection to a show-down. As he was leaving for the Secretariat, he stopped his car near the gate and, beckoning me towards him, said that there was no need to tell anyone that he had given me this advice, adding that I could see Pattabhi Sitaramayya once again. But I was too flabbergasted at the jumbled situation to be wanting to see anyone further. I left for Faridkot, where a meeting was already in progress. People were worked up. The previous day they had taken out a procession and, in front of the Secretariat, burnt an effigy of the autocratic rule. They had announced the end of the personal rule of the Raja and called for disobedience and defiance of his authority.

Perhaps, due to the suddenness of the mass action, the Raja's government was momentarily dazed and they did not make any arrest even in the face of this open rebellion. Seeing the seething mood of the people, and in deference to their decisive opinion to form a parallel government, I set about selecting seven persons to be the people's Ministers. It was planned that they would reach the Secretariat a few minutes before the office timings and would occupy the chairs of the government secretaries. The "Chief Minister" would occupy the office of the Chief Secretary. In case of their arrest, seven other representatives would take their places, and the chain would continue.

On 1 March 1948, in a public meeting, I enumerated the ills of the autocratic rule. Most of the present Rajas were staunch henchmen of the foreign rulers and, if at all, they should visualise their role as constitutional heads and not the feudal lords. That was the call of the time, which they could not ignore anymore. My 45 minute speech on the public address system was quite audible in the Secretariat. I was told later by my comrades that my words had enough fire to influence some top brass in the Raja's courtiers.

The army commander pledged his allegiance to the People's government. A superintendent of Police, a sub-judge a magistrate and a Deputy Superintendent of Police promised their loyalty to the government of the people. Anyone refusing to sign was not allowed to leave, and was pushed back. The police and the army personnel remained silent spectators. A Commissioner and a Judge of the High Court walked into our camp. The imbroglio went upto nine at night, when the Raja, who had gone to Malerkotla to attend a function, returned home and saw the siege of his Secretariat. I had just left the place for Kotkapura for a little rest.

Chapter 9

PARALLEL GOVERNMENT

> In my absence, the Raja's minions started attacking the freedom fighters with their batons with an intent to teach them a real lesson. Over seventy persons sustained serious injuries including fractured limbs, two of them with both legs broken. One of the volunteers had both his arms fractured and another turned up with both arms and legs chipped at many places.
>
> About 500 persons, injured and groaning in pain, were thrown into jail. Several hundreds were left writhing in agony at the scene of the barbarous attack. One, Mehr Singh, who was nominated Horne Minister by the party, slipped away and another man, his namesake was caught and he received severe beating at the hands of the Raja's forces, though he was not even a member of the Parja Mandal movement.

A party member rushed to Kotkapura to inform me of the ghastly incident. I immediately reached the scene of the mayhem and saw the terror let loose by the armed personnel on the hapless people. The whole atmosphere in front of the Secretariat was drowned in the screams of the injured, some of them almost half-dead. One could hardly conjure up a vision of hell worse than the one witnessed then.

I was ordered by the police to alight from the car. Seeing me, quite a few persons carne closer, but in an instant they were made to run helter-skelter under the raining blows of lathis. In spite of indiscriminate baton-charge, about a dozen men stuck to their ground and did not move. I saw a jeep rushing at me from a distance, but since I did not make any attempt to step aside, the driver, applying full brakes brought the vehicle to a screeching halt with the fender almost touching my thighs. Obviously, it was an attempt to scare me out of my wits. They shouted orders at the freedom fighters to get into the jeep, but as we were clambering up, they changed their minds and once again resorted to beating mercilessly. I cannot say whether it was due to a coincidence or design that I did not receive many hard blows.

They got hold of me, snatched my turban and tied my hair to the rear bumper of the jeep. I was ordered either to tender unconditional apology or be prepared to face death. I was prepared for death, I told them. Then the officer shouted the order that I should be dragged on the roads of the city for the crime of having masterminded the formation of the People's Government. I deserved to be taught a lesson of my life, he added. I felt totally helpless and was reconciled to my fate. But as the engine was ignited and the vehicle ran for a few feet, I heard the voice of the Senior Superintendent of Police commanding the driver to stop.

As the engine was switched off, they untied my hair from the jeep and asked me to stand up. I could discover a glint of hate in the eyes of the SSP, who was known for his ruthlessness and his third degree methods on the suspects and the convicts alike. Spitting venom from his tongue, he announced that death for me would be of little avail. I deserved deterrence, which should be in the form of a thorough thrashing. To my utter surprise, they did not carry out this threat then, and returning my turban, they shoved me into the jeep along with others and made for the jail. I tried to tie my turban in the running vehicle. I thanked the Almighty for having given me the strength to withstand the ordeal.

We found a large number of our companions thrown into the cells, almost all of whom had received serious injuries and were groaning in pain. Their broken limbs were secured in tight bandages and some were plastered, but without proper

X-ray process' and without having been administered any painkiller or other medicines. I was rudely pushed into a cell behind the row of cells, where I had served a five-year sentence. Some state officials, who had revolted against the Raja were also thrown in the jail and treated like common criminals without any facility.

That night, without a wink of sleep, reflecting on the recent events, I remembered the advice of Sardar Patel and felt contrite. Had we heeded his counsel, innumerable people could have been spared of these indignities and suffering. The next morning, freedom fighters still in agony and the atmosphere full of anguish, we started hesitantly asking the warders, if any of our companions had lost his life. They feigned ignorance, and were non-committal, but some asserted that a few persons had died, and the authorities were concealing the truth.

The Raja toured the State and warned the people of dire consequences, if they supported the national movement. Panic was created among the people, but patriotic persons remained steadfast in their resolve to continue the fight. Satyagrah continued and volunteers kept on pouring from the neighbouring towns. They were arrested, beaten mercilessly and then released outside the State. The shopkeepers were not allowed to close their shops in protest. They were asked to continue with their vocations, without even a whimper. There was complete chaos in Faridkot. The autocratic rule of the Raja went on merrily, though India had become independent eight months earlier. The conditions in Faridkot continued to be inhuman and barbaric.

After initial stiffness, the State government started gradually releasing the detenus from the prison, while keeping about 175 persons, including myself, in jail for one month. During this period, our party members maintained contacts with national leaders like Pandit Nehru, Sardar Patel and Pattabhi Sitaramayya, reminding them about the refractory attitude of the Raja. It was due to the influence, these leaders brought to bear upon the unmending ruler, that he felt obliged to order our release. We heaved a sigh of relief to know that no death had occurred due to the brutal attack by the Raja's forces on the agitators.

After our release from the prison on 20 March 1948, we found that about seventy of the freedom fighters were still in bandages and plasters. It was decided to take them to Delhi for the national leaders to see for themselves the bestial treatment meted out to them. With prior appointment, we reached Prithviraj Road, New Delhi where a meeting of the Congress Working Committee was being attended in the building now housing the Kashmir Emporium, by Pandit Nehru, Sheikh Mohd. Abdullah, then Prime Minister of Jammu and Kashmir and President of the All India States Peoples' Conference among others. We positioned the injured, swathed in bandages and plasters in rows.

Our delegation included some of those senior State officials who had shown the courage to defect from the Raja's service to the ranks of the nationalists, comprising an Excise Commissioner, two sub-judges, a Superintendent of Police, a High Court Judge and Major Harpal Singh. I requested that one of them should speak, as they were certainly more educated and could explain things better. But they insisted that I should be the spokesman.

When Pandit Nehru emerged from the room, I tried to explain the plight of the injured. At such a ghastly sight, Panditji seemed to be perplexed, as any civilized individual would have to stretch his credulity over the savagery responsible for such mayhem. Pandit ji wanted to satisfy himself about the genuineness of the injuries, because though a month had passed after the incident in Faridkot, these persons were still in plasters. As he shared his thoughts with Sheikh Mohd. Abdullah, the latter, after having satisfied himself, convinced Pandit Nehru of the facts. Nehru and others present there expressed their deep disgust and indignation over the Raja's excessive cruelty.

When they conveyed their impressions to Sardar Patel, he told them about the advice he had rendered to us not to unnecessarily involve ourselves in a headlong collision with the Ruler and that we had ignored that advice, resulting in this miserable situation. There were heated exchanges in the meeting of the Working Committee. Pattabhi Sitaramayya who had conveyed his concurrence to the launching of the agitation, pointed out that Panditji had acquiesced. The latter observed that he had really believed in our political prowess, which could have brought the Ruler to his knees.

Panditji took a strong plea in our favour and said categorically that there was no question of our remaining under the Raja's heels any longer. Sardar Patel was prevailed upon to divest the Raja of the powers of governance. It was meant to be a strong blow to the Raja, who was aspiring to become the Rajpramukh of the Union of Phulkian States, in case it was decided to give Patiala a separate identity.

I described the situation prevailing in Faridkot in these words:

> "I was released from Jail along with three ministers of Azad Government and 250 prominent Parja Mandal workers. I am of the opinion that it is my humble duty to bring to light the repressive measures adopted by the Ruler of Faridkot against the workers, progressive elements in the State and some senior State officials, both inside and out of the jail.
>
> We started a movement for the establishment of a Panchayati Raj and restoration of liberties to the people on 1 March 1948. The movement was peaceful and the people who joined it were ninety per cent Sikhs. The atrocities committed on our workers cannot be described in words. It was an awful state of affairs. The cruelties were of the worst type. No other State ruler has resorted to such measures so far.
>
> In free India, nobody can resort to such barbarities to crush people's movement. Five hundred peaceful and disciplined satyagrahis were lathi-charged and were badly injured. The injuries were so severe that even after 20 days of merciless beating, 45 of our workers are not out of danger. Many have broken limbs and fractured arms. Sacrilege was committed against the Sikhs as they were dragged by their hair and their beards were pulled.
>
> The officials who showed sympathy with the people's movement were imprisoned, kept in solitary confinement and treated brutally. They were forced to clean the excreta of other prisoners. They were paraded on the streets of

Faridkot with baskets full of garbage on their heads. The Raja himself beat them from time to time and forced them to sign incriminating documents. The police and army officials indulged in inhuman acts. They were more loyal than the king and in their overenthusiasm they committed brutalities.

The underwears of old and respected leaders like Jathedar Nahar Singh were removed and they were beaten mercilessly. State officials committed such obscene acts that even to describe those is not considered respectable. Satyagrahis were forced to lay prostrate on the ground and iron rods were used to beat them. Sand was put in their hair. Their private parts were injured.

We withdrew the people's movement on the appeals made by national leaders. The States Ministry directed the Raja to release all political prisoners. When those prisoners were released they were forced to sign apologies and those who refused were brutally beaten. Indignities were unbearable. The Raja's intrigues and plots hatched to humiliate the workers were nullified by the patriotic acts of our workers. Some of the satyagrahis were abandoned at lonely places miles away.

At the instance of the Congress High Command, we suspended the satyagrah, but the Raja became more vindictive and resorted to all sorts of inhuman acts. Nobody's life, honour and property is safe. We obeyed the orders of the High Command.

We are confident that Pt. Nehru and Sardar Patel would understand our problems and fix responsibility on the Raja and his officials. There is no law and order in the State and complete chaos and confusion prevails. Impartial enquiry should be ordered into the misdeeds of the Raja. I strongly appeal to the Home Minister that an administrator be appointed immediately and the people's grievances be redressed."

Our agitation in Faridkot and the Raja's cruel reaction were cogent factors in Sardar Patel's decision to merge all the States in the Punjab region into one single Union with the Maharaja of Patiala as its constitutional Head. The Sardar definitely had a soft corner for the Maharaja of Patiala, as he was the first Ruler to have acceded to India after the partition of th» sub-continent. He commanded great respect among the masses. He had rendered great service to the refugees from Pakistan, who had been uprooted from their hearths and homes. He had helped in their rehabilitation. He had also contributed his forces for the defence of Kashmir from the marauding hordes from Pakistan. He had also stood solidly against the intrigues of certain Rulers of States, who were keen on remaining independent and were thinking of creating a 'Third Force'.

The Sardar told the Maharaja that it would be of no practical advantage to him to maintain a separate identity for Patiala, because the Centre wanted to make him the head of the entire Patiala and East Punjab States Union. The Sardar deputed Balbir Singh Garewal, a member of the Indian Civil Service to take over the administration of Faridkot with the Raja discharging only constitutional functions. Thus we were assured of a new era free of suffocating, exploitative and barbaric feudal system. But, unfortunately, for us that very Garewal turned out to be a relative of the Ruler of the neighbouring State of Jind with feelings of sympathy towards the Raja of Faridkot, with the latter wielding vicarious ruling power.

Chapter 10

A NEW DAWN

With the announcement for the formation of the Patiala and East Punjab States Union (PEPSU), there was a flurry of activity for introduction of a popular government. The Union consisted of the States of Patiala, Nabha, Jind, Kapurthala, Malerkotla, Faridkot, Nalagarh and Kalsia. Whereas Brish Bhan was the President of the Punjab States Parja Mandal, I was the President of the Faridkot organization. In the meeting of the Executive Committee of the Punjab Parja Mandal for election of a leader to head an interim government, the name of Brish Bhan was proposed, to which Harcharan Singh took serious objection on the plea that Brish Bhan lacked the leadership qualities. As a compromise, Brish Bhan and I were elected joint leaders to conduct negotiations with the Central leadership, for the formation of a popular ministry.

In July 1948, Sardar Patel went to Patiala for inauguration of the Union, accompanied by V.P. Menon, a highly competent Secretary to the Ministry of States and close confidant of the Sardar. He called our joint meeting with the Maharaja of Patiala and said in a tone that would leave no one in any doubt that he valued his statesmanship and sense of patriotism and that his opinion would be given great weightage in the selection of a Prime Minister, though our views would also receive his consideration. We had already apprised V.P. Menon of our line of thinking that we would prefer Brish Bhan for the coveted post, as he was the President of the Punjab States

Parja Mandal. Sardar Patel declared his intention to return to Delhi the next day and advised us to reconsider our stand. In fact Brish Bhan had an overwhelming desire to be the Prime Minister, unmindful of the aspirations of his party colleagues to find berths in the cabinet. Another claimant was Colonel Raghbir Singh, leader of the recently formed "Lok Sabha Party." The third party in the fray was the Akali Party, which it was also difficult to ignore.

On the advice of Sardar Patel, we had invited the veteran leader, Giani Gurmukh Singh Musafir in our confabulations, who strived for a consensus. More than one formula was discussed. I was keen on at least one leader of Parja Maridal in each constituent State to be included in the Council of Ministers, as this party had faced the fury of the feudal-lords and had made maximum sacrifices. Sardar Patel was reluctant to exclude the Lok Sabha Party, as it had the patronage of the Maharaja of Patiala. Brish Bhan had strong views against it for that very reason, though he was not averse to the inclusion of the Akalis because of their active participation in the struggle against the autocratic rule of the princes.

V.P. Menon took pains to explain to Brish Bhan that he should give up his claim to be the Prime Minister, as that position had necessarily to be given to a Sikh and that too who was acceptable to the Maharaja of Patiala. Our night-long deliberations proved fruitless. In the morning, Sardar Patel expressing his disappointment, remarked that though he had come from Delhi to transfer the power from the hands of the princes to the popular political leaders, it appeared to him that we lacked the necessary statesmanship and sagacity. Brish Bhan took it as a mere outburst of the otherwise quiescent Sardar, but the latter advised the Maharaja to appoint Gian Singh Rarewala as Prime Minister, and promised to send a Chief Secretary, a Finance Secretary and another officer, who would all constitute a Council for the governance of the States Union.

On 15 July 1948, the Sardar in his historic address in the Darbar Hall at Patiala said that a new chapter in the history of India was opening before us. We had reason to congratulate ourselves that we were all participating in such an auspicious event. We had also the justification to be proud of it. But alongwith this pride we should not be unmindful of our duties and obligations. We must cleanse our hearts and purify our minds and resolve to do sensible deeds by ourselves, by the new Union and by our country. We should harbour no evil, we should reflect on who we are, what we have inherited and what we have achieved. History showed that for centuries India had been steeped in slavery. We had to face onslaughts, had to make sacrifices and had to put up with sorrow to rid India of that centuries-old malady that had eaten into the very vitals of its nationhood.

A great change, rather a revolution had been brought about. The greater the change, the more comprehensive the revolution and the more were the travails through which the country had to pass. We had already more than our due share of troubles and turmoils. We were lucky to have survived so many of them, but many were still to be overcome. If we faltered or failed, we would have to consign ourselves to eternal shame and disgrace.

The Sardar referred to the gravity of the situation and wanted everyone to consider the position in the light of the legacy which we had inherited. He wondered if anyone could dream a year or two earlier whether one-third of India would be integrated in this fashion. This was the first time in history after centuries that India could call itself an integrated whole in the real sense of the term. But we must resolve, and whatever mistakes we might commit, we should do nothing which would be calculated to send India back into the slavery of the past. It was the duty of India's valiant sons to see that the clocks of progress were not put back, but advanced forward. We had to take due place in the comity of nations and it would not come to us for mere asking. We would have to strain every nerve for it.

The Sardar reminded the parties to the new Union that it was easy to rule by one's will, but difficult to rule by consent and jointly, particularly when administrative experience was lacking. We should tread the ground cautiously. The Sardar urged for a secular approach to the Indian problem. There was no question of the Central Government attacking any religion or placing any religion in danger.

Sardar Patel made a particular mention of the notable contributions made by the Maharaja of Patiala to the unity and integrity of India. He had taken up the cause of the country at a time when there were a few friends amongst the princely order and when serious attempts were being made to balkanise India. It was his patriotic lead that had contributed in a large measure to a change in the attitude of the princes to the problem of accession to the Indian Dominion.

The Sardar described the inauguration of the Patiala and East Punjab States Union as the corner stone of an arch which the Government of India had built with the cooperation of the Rulers and the States' people to contribute to the stability of the country's structure. It was now for the people to utilise the tremendous opportunity that lay before them. The future was now in the hands of the people; they themselves could make or mar it.

The Sardar was unhappy at the uncompromising attitude of the political parties and announced the formation of an interim government under the Maharaja of Patiala as the Rajpramukh and the Raja of Kapurthala as the Deputy Rajpramukh. He appealed to the people to extend their support to the new administration. He described the Patiala and East Punjab States Union as a homeland for the Sikhs. He made a passionate appeal for the strength and prosperity of the new Union and held the promise of elections at an appropriate time, asserting that only the deserving political parties would find their way to victory.

After this announcement, the Sardar returned to Delhi. On 22 August 1948, a caretaker Government was formed with Gian Singh Rarewala, as the Chief Minister and B.R. Patel as Chief Secretary. A Finance Secretary and an Advisor were also appointed. The Parja Mandal, the Lok Dal Party and the Akalis were left in a lurch. The Akalis could not conceal their jubilation that the Parja Mandal was excluded. My friend, Seth Ram Nath, told Brish Bhan that our Party's exclusion might lead us to political wilderness. In an impetuous moment, Brish Bhan authorized Seth Ram Nath, in writing, to restart negotiations on his behalf. I was asked to hold parleys with the Maharaja Patiala, but I preferred to talk to Sardar Patel and came for the purpose to Delhi.

Seth Ram Nath and I camped in a Dharamshala (Community Centre) in Ballimaran in Old Delhi and rented a dormitory accommodation for a quarter of a rupee each. On the date of our appointment with the Deputy Prime Minister, we hired a *tanga* (horse-driven cart) to reach his residence, but the skeletal horse pulling the cart at a snail's pace caused us a delay of five or six minutes. As we reached the Sardar's bungalow, his daughter, Maniben Patel, took us to task asking us sarcastically, if we had sought an appointment with the Deputy Prime Minister or a shepherd. We, the penniless politicians, with ambitions to form a Ministry mumbled our apologies. But she asked us to turn back. When we summoned up enough courage to ask for another appointment, it was refused, though she relented to the extent that we could leave a written request for consideration. We approached V. Shankar, Secretary to Sardar Patel, expressing our predicament. He told us of the contempt the Sardar had for those, who did not observe strict punctuality. We were given an appointment for five days later. When we met the Sardar at the appointed time, he was calm and businesslike. He said that he did not like the bureaucrats to govern PEPSU, but since we were not amenable to reason and did not grasp the reality, there was no alternative. If we did not assume power, albeit jointly with other parties, our chances in the popular elections would be dim. Seth Ram Nath held Brish Bhan responsible for the impasse and assured Sardar Patel of unconditional compliance of his wishes. Seth Ram Nath told him that he was the President of the Nabha State Parja Mandal, I was the head of the Faridkot Unit and Sunder Lal was leading the movement in Patiala. We were all united and Brish Bhan, who was the President of the Punjab Parja Mandal, had authorized him to reach a settlement. I emphatically told the Sardar that his wishes would be carried out.

V.P. Menon advised us to consider carefully the views of Sardar Patel and to come again after about ten days. At our next appointment, we were accompanied by Giani Gurmukh

Singh Musafir, .who made a fervent plea to the Sardar about our case on the basis of our sufferings and sacrifices, which Sardar Patel said, he was fully aware of Pointing towards me, he recalled that he had asked me not to cross swords with the Raja of Faridkot, but I had not abandoned my plan. He asked for a reassurance that we would be able to shoulder the responsibility of administration with reasonable efficiency, which we readily offered. Giani Gurmukh Singh Musafir expected jubilation and illuminations at homes of the people in the event of transfer of power to us. That was the popular appeal and the influence we had over the public mind, he asserted.

Sardar Patel issued instructions to V.P. Menon to put him in contact with the Maharaja of Patiala, to summon Colonel Raghbir Singh, President of Lok Sabha Party and, as suggested by us, to call Pratap Singh Kairon, a Minister of Punjab and Member, Congress Working Committee as well.

After discussions among Sardar Patel, Colonel Raghbir Singh and Pratap Singh Kairon, we were informed of the Sardar's decision to instal an interim popular government in PEPSU. Kairon suggested the inclusion of two representatives of the Lok Sabha Party of Colonel Raghbir Singh, one nominee of Sardar Bahadur Ranjit Singh, four representatives of the Parja Mandal along with one Prime Minister, in the cabinet. If Maharaja Patiala would agree to Colonel Raghbir Singh becoming the Prime Minister, there would be a seven member Ministry, otherwise he could nominate any other person, but the post of the Prime Minister would positively go to a Sikh. From Parja Mandal, I suggested four names, but refrained from including my own name in the belief that I did not have the requisite ability to be on the Council of Ministers. Kairon disagreed with me and insisted on including my name, which, as revealed later, was done on an indication from the Prime Minister, Jawaharlal Nehru.

On 20 January 1949, a seven member Cabinet under the leadership of Gian Singh Rarewala was sworn in. It consisted of myself, Seth Ram Nath, Nihal Singh Takshak, Harcharan Singh (all Congress), Colonel Raghbir Singh, L.D. Kaushal (both Lok Sabha Party) and Ajit Singh (nominee of Sardar

Bahadur Ranjit Singh). It caused pique to Brish Bhan, who got a resolution passed by the PEPSU Provincial Congress Committee, calling upon the party representatives in the cabinet to resign, which they did not accept. In February 1949, the Provincial Congress Executive Committee served a show-cause notice and then expelled Seth Ram Nath and Harcharan Singh from the Party for two years. Since I and Nihal Singh Takshak were members of the All India Congress Committee, our cases for similar action were referred to the Congress High Command. The PEPSU Congress Committee's move was, however, decried in a gathering of over 200 Congress workers, at Patiala.

This Ministry stayed in office for a little less than a year. More or less it was free of tensions within and it put up a united front outside. The Ministers worked with sincerity and solicitude but while taking progressive measures, they faced resistance from the lobby of landlords. I was holding the portfolio of Revenue, Excise and Taxation. I proposed an amendment to the Criminal Tribes Statute removing restrictions on people on the basis of their birth. No one should be considered criminal just because he was born in a particular tribe. This would give relief to a sizeable population in the Bhatinda and Barnala Districts and the Faridkot State who had this stigma attached to them for eight decades. The cabinet agreed to accept it for one year, to be reviewed later. But pressing my point, I was successful in getting the measure carried through. I contacted the Punjab government also, which considered the proposal with due despatch and alacrity and freed a large number of people from the ignominy of being called members of criminal tribes.

Chapter 11

PROPRIETARY RIGHTS TO TENANTS

As the constituent states of PEPSU were being governed by divergent tax policies and laws, it was considered more pragmatic to integrate such laws, though the laws of the Patiala State were in preponderance of-those selected for promulgation throughout the States Union.

A major subject on our agenda was to grant proprietary rights to the tenants, who had been groaning under the burden imposed by Rajas and landlords. Though the question of land reforms had been agitating the minds of people throughout the country, it was of particular concern to the farmers in princely states, where pressures had been building up constantly, In Faridkot, superior ownership vested in the Raja in all the two hundred villages barring two, where his kinsmen ruled the roost. The biggest state of the Union, Patiala, with a population of two million was the bastion of overweening landlords. Just as I rivetted my attention on the solution of the problem, Patiala proposed to grant ownership rights to the tenants by transferring two-thirds of land to them with one-third remaining with the landlords.

We decided to let the tenants have three-fourths of the land with one-fourth remaining with the landlords. The latter approached me and expressed a grievance that we were hostile to them as a class. I held that the landed gentry commanded great resources. They had means to get elected to State legislatures. It was surprising that they were clinging to predatory tendencies and were not inclined to let the sons of the soil, the toiling tenants live with dignity and honour. Impervious to this advice, they launched an agitation with, of course, little chance of success. In Faridkot, I got the proprietary rights transferred to the tenants through a notification issued on 7 September 1949. By the abolition of superior proprietary rights of the Raja, four hundred thousand acres of land reverted to full ownership of the tenants. I withdrew the concession given to the *biswadars* to file suits *forma pauperis* against tenants for recovery of arrears of rent. Any tenant or his heir, who had been dispossessed of his land during nine months before August 1949 for non-payment of the dues, could now reclaim the land from the landlord on payment of the due amount. A nine-member Land Tenure Committee was constituted under my chairmanship to examine various systems of land tenure, revenue assessment and water rates, etc., prevailing in the constituent States and to recommend a suitable system.

The just claims of tenants were accepted in a manner that would end the repression and high-handedness of the landlords. Three-fourths of the land was given to tenants with a right to buy the remaining one-fourth from the landlord on cash payment, but this right was not conceded to the landlords.

While our government was busy chalking out plans to compensate political sufferers, whose properties had been confiscated and who were subjected to miseries in a myraid ways, we came to face serious opposition from Akalis and the Congress faction led by Brish Bhan. In collusion with his friends among communists, Brish Bhan created a plethora of problems for the government. Baldev Singh, then Union Defence Minister also showed prejudice against our government, since it had been formed with the cooperation of Par tap Singh Kairon, with whom he did not see eye to eye. When Maharaja Patiala also showed inclination to the dissolution of the government, Sardar Patel gave in to these diverse pressures and decided to dissolve the interim cabinet, which tendered resignation on 19 November 1949, less than a year after it had assumed office. The President's rule was promulgated.

Our group suffered certain disabilities in the State Congress elections. I had to boycott the elections and my group was christened "Patiala and East Punjab States Union Congress." It also came to be known as "Zail Singh Congress." Though the Congress High Command appointed Ram Sahai, an AICC member and Speaker of the Madhya Pradesh Assembly to look into our complaints of irregularities in the elections, we were disappointed at his biased attitude. Our separate group came into existence on 20 July 1950, with many a veteran freedom fighter on our side.

Pratap Singh Kairon, the intrepid crusader against communalization of politics in Punjab, convened an anti-Punjabi Suba Convention at Amritsar in December 1950, to which he invited me. As a true well-wisher of Punjab would do, I too was not in favour of reducing the size of Punjab by re-delineating the State map on narrow considerations.

In the meantime, an interesting episode was witnessed on relations between Sardar Patel and Brish Bhan. During the election for the President of Indian National Congress, Sardar Patel was in favour of Purushotam Das Tandon. Though Pandit Nehru never took sides openly, his predilection for Pattabhi Sitaramayya was well known. Brish Bhan sought the instructions of Sardar Patel and voted for Tandon accordingly. This softened the edge of Sardar Patel's indifference to Brish Bhan, who was actually averse even to meeting the latter, earlier.

The Sardar thought of formation of a Ministry in PEPSU. Though he had started thinking well of Brish Bhan, he would not ignore us. He sent for Brish Bhan and myself and asked us to sink our differences to pave the way for a Ministry to be formed. He advised me to dissolve my Congress and told Brish Bhan to recognise all members of my group as members of the State Congress, and to absorb them at various levels in different committees. Sardar Patel called upon Colonel Raghbir Singh to wind up his Lok Sabha Party and to persuade his members to join the Congress. The pragmatic Secretary in the Ministry of States V.P. Menon suggested parity between the group of Brish Bhan and myself on the basis of forty per cent of each group and twenty per cent of Colonel Raghbir Singh's party in the cabinet, with the Colonel as the Chief Minister.

After some wrangling, a cabinet was formed on 23 May, 1951, with three members of the Brish Bhan group, two of my group and one Minister of State of the choice of each of us with Col. Raghbir Singh as Chief Minister. I was given the portfolio of Revenue, Agriculture and Public Works Department. Throughout this period, the Akalis were out of power, who tried to keep the political heat on with their agitations. The Congress Ministry did not lack in steam to offset the communal stance of the Akalis.

Nevertheless, the Congress Party could not keep the necessary inner cohesion, which led us to present separate lists of candidates to the centre for the first general elections in 1952, Brish Bhan's group was given twenty nominations, my group got seventeen and an equal number was allotted to others. The main consideration with the Congress leaders was to give preference to winning horses and to brush aside the considerations such as service, sacrifice or sincerity to the ideology. I was really dismayed at the turn of events, but was in no position to change their course.

Strangely enough, in the elections, the combined efforts of Colonel Raghbir Singh and Brish Bhan were successful in engineering my defeat, though eight candidates of my group made to the legislature. The very first day the Legislature held its session, the ruling party suffered a defeat on 16 April 1952, with the defection of Kahan Singh, a Deputy Minister, to the Opposition, to be elected Speaker with their support. The majority of Congress turned into a minority and Gian Singh Rarewala, an independent legislator, with the help of other independents, entering into an arrangement with the Akalis, formed a United Front Ministry with himself as the Chief Minister on 22 April 1952. With this a new chapter came to be written in the political history of free India, when the first non-Congress government came into existence in one of its States.

Democracy in PEPSU being in infancy faced a lot of teething troubles. Efforts ensued to topple the Rarewala Ministry, in which the erstwhile Raja of Faridkot played quite a prominent role. He flew to Patiala in his private plane to pitch a pavillion in front of Colonel Raghbir Singh's residence and tried to lure the legislators with money, asking them to defect from Rarewala's United Front. They succeeded in securing the support of a few members reducing the ruling group to a minority. But sudden floor crossings from the Congress including that of Nihal Singh Takshak and three other legislators, gave a new lease of life to Rarewala group. Colonel Raghbir Singh and Brish Bhan went to Pandit Nehru and accused me of allowing the defections from the Congress, but the allegation being baseless and rather puerile, Pandit Nehru did not pay any attention to it. The position being uncertain and mercurial, the Rajpramukh sent a report to the Centre recommending dissolution of the Assembly and promulgation of the President's rule. Rarewala resigned on 1 March 1953, and PEPSU came under the President's rule on 5 March 1953.

The mid-term assembly elections slated for February-March 1954 generated a great deal of political heat. D.K. Barooah, the Assamese leader, deputed by the Congress High Command as observer for selection of party candidates, told Colonel Raghbir Singh to win the confidence of the Maharaja of Patiala, if he wanted victory at the hustings. I did not contest the mid-term elections and the Congress ticket in my constituency went to the brother of the erstwhile Raja of Faridkot. A large number of Congress candidates ironically were scions of feudal and princely families and as they wielded influence, most of them were returned, which led the Congress to victory. I was approached by the Akalis to contest as an independent candidate, but I could not even think of shifting my loyalty from the Congress, under whose banner I had spent so many years struggling for national freedom. I helped the Congress Party to the best of my ability and capacity in the elections personally as well as through my Punjabi Daily *Khalsa Sewak,* which I had started from Amritsar. I could not continue the venture of running a newspaper for long, due to financial difficulties. I did not have the knack of securing advertisements from the Punjab government and others to provide monetary support and the journal had to fade away.

The new government formed by Colonel Raghbir Singh on 27

March 1954 decided to nationalize the transport, to which most of the transporters in the States Union were opposed. They sought my help inspite of my cautioning them that my intervention might have an adverse effect. In the firm belief that they had a just and legitimate cause, I told the government to desist from nationalization, otherwise we would be forced to start an agitation. The Congress High Command, when apprised of my stand, were of the opinion that a person having served the national cause and the party faithfully and having helped the party candidates in the elections without contesting himself, had every right to express independent opinion on economic and social matters. I was summoned by the General Secretary of the All India Congress Committee, who, after listening to my arguments, was convinced of my stand and averred that no mandate had been given to the State government to effect nationalization.

Chapter 12

A NEW TURNING

In the party elections, I found my name missmg from the list. In fact, my active membership form was nowhere to be seen, thanks to the furtive attempts of my detractors. This would have debarred me from seeking election to the State Congress Committee. The game was to deprive me even of primary membership of the Congress. My appeal to the Congress Working Committee was not expected to bear any fruit. Therefore, under the advice of Bhargava, a permanent Secretary in the party office, I approached the Congress President, Pandit Nehru, who again came to my rescue. He had just finished his breakfast, when he saw me at the door and asked me, if I would like to have some breakfast. When I fumbled for words that I wanted to discuss something with him, he chuckled and asked how I could force myself on him for a discussion without a prior appointment. He washed his hands, straightened his Gandhi cap on his head and walking up to the staircase asked me to go on talking.

Climbing down the stairs with Nehru, I told him that 1 attached the highest importance to my membership of the Congress, but, unfortunately, I found my name missing from the list and he, in his capacity as the President of the organization, alone could help restore my membership. Pandit Nehru retorted by suggesting that he did not think I attached so much importance to the membership of the Congress. When I started protesting, he flashed his characteristic benign smile, and in a tone clearly laced with indulgence, asked me to go and see the Congress General Secretary, Balwant Rai Mehta.

When I told him that I had met Mehta the previous day without any hope of redressal, Pandit Nehru asked me to meet him again. As I entered Mehta's room, he was looking through the files and papers received back from Pandit Nehru. He was full of surprise that I could see Pandit Nehru without previous appointment. He was curious to know, how it had been managed. I politely explained that I had gone to Panditji on my own, and it was at his behest that I was approaching him (Mehta) again. The application, which I had previously sent to the Congress President, was before Mehta with Nehru's express directions for restoration of my membership.

Mehta dictated a letter for the President of the State Congress and endorsed a copy to Prakash Chand Sethi, who had been deputed as an observer by the Central Committee for the State party elections. He also gave a copy of the letter to me to carry it personally. Jagan Nath Kaushal, Member of Parliament, on being told by me, rang up Brish Bhan not to create any further obstacle, which could boomerang on him.

The restoration of Congress membership to me changed the atmosphere in PEPSU in my favour, as the impression overtly created in the State about my ineffectiveness was promptly dispelled and I was elected to the Pradesh Congress Committee without contest. Without much persuasion, my opponent withdrew from the election, which saved me quite a lot of botheration. Though in the forty member Pradesh Congress Committee, my group was the smallest, yet without my support Brish Bhan could not compete with the group led by Colonel Raghbir Singh. On the other hand, my support to Colonel Raghbir Singh could have reduced the Brish Bhan group to a minority.

Jagan Nath Kaushal suggested unity between my group and that of Brish Bhan. It was also his view that I should be made President of the Pradesh Congress, which, to start with, was not palatable to the Brish Bhan supporters. They floated the idea that the Congress High Command would countenance my becoming General Secretary, instead of the President and in spite of Jagan Nath Kaushal's exhortations, the

Brish Bhan group would not yield any ground. In fact, Brish Bhan phoned me up to say that it was the wish of the Congress High Command that I should be the General Secretary.

I talked on phone to Shriman Narayan, General Secretary of the Indian National Congress, to inquire if the High Command or Pandit Nehru personally had any reservation about my contesting for the top post in the State Congress. After a few minutes, he rang back suggesting postponement of election of President for a day, as he himself would come to Patiala to sort out things.

The next day, on their arrival at Patiala, Shriman Narayan and D.K. Barooah declared that there was no restriction on my contesting the election to the office of the President of the Pradesh Congress. Barooah was pro-landlord, but Shriman Narayan had obviously received blessings from Nehru about my election. His behind the scene consultations with Colonel Raghbir Singh and Brish Bhan ensured my unanimous election as President on 6 January 1955. I was authorized to constitute an Executive Committee. I thought it prudent to take Colonel Raghbir Singh into confidence, who was seriously ill. At his residence, he promised to offer his suggestions after his recovery, but, unfortunately, he breathed his last the next morning.

When the news about his demise and my election as the State Congress President were published side by side, people started speculating that his death was due to the mental shock he had received. The Colonel had enjoyed the support of leaders like Jathedar Udham Singh Nagoke and Partap Singh Kairon. Extremely shrewd and tactful, he had remained President of the Golden Temple Committee at Amritsar and was the founder of the Lok Sabha Party, which was called the King's party, though Maharaja Patiala had no soft corner for him. He had also no love lost for Gian Singh Rarewala, the erstwhile United Front Prime Minister of PEPSU and an uncle of the Maharaja.

After observing a ten-day mourning on the death of Colonel Raghbir Singh, I constituted an Executive Committee including the representatives of his faction as well as those of Brish Bhan.

The latter, being second in seniority in the cabinet of the late Colonel, became the interim Chief Minister, for which he had my support.

The most important task facing the peasantry, which formed a vast majority of the population, was the land reforms. The yawning gap in prosperity between the rich landlords and the toiling tenants was too spectacular to be ignored. As the State Congress President, therefore, I addressed myself to the problems of the common man. Inspired by the *Bhoodan* (land donation) movement launched by the devout Gandian, Acharya Vinoba Bhave, we pressed the opulent landlords to donate one-sixth of their estates towards this movement. The gentry not possessing land should donate one-twelfth of their income towards *sampattidan* (assets donation). The Gandhi Samarak Nidhi were good enough to allot a sum of rupees eight lakhs for implementation of Gandhian programmes in PEPSU.

It was my firm belief that dissensions and lack of unity among workers were a major cause of slow development. But frequent strikes and demonstrations were not conducive to our nascent democratic country's progress either. The working class no doubt had to safeguard its rights against exploitation by the rich and the avaricious, but I counselled them to adopt peaceful methods to redress their legitimate grievances, instead of such means as would jeopardize the State's economy.

On 27 February 1956, I got nomination of the Congress Party and was elected unopposed to the Rajya Sabha (Upper House of Parliament).

—

Chapter 13

LINGUISTIC STATES

During the freedom struggle, the Congress Party had made a commitment to the Nation for creation of States on linguistic basis. The haphazard demarcation of boundaries of the Provinces by the British rulers was not found congenial to the development of various regions on the basis of linguistic homogeneity. In pursuance of the assurances given to the people by national leaders, the government set up a three-member States Reorganization Commission on 27 December 1953, comprising Syed Fazal Ali, Pandit H.N. Kunzru and K.M. Pannikar. They submitted a report to the government on 30 September 1955, which was formally released to the public in October 1955. The Commission rejected the demand for creation of a State of Maharashtra by bifurcating the Bombay State, which caused widespread resentment among the Marathi-speaking people. They also declined to accept the demand for a Punjabi-speaking state and recommended the then existing state of Punjab to be bilingual. They recommended PEPSU and Himachal Pradesh to be merged with Punjab. The Brish Bhan group took a lead in supporting the merger of PEPSU with Punjab, though the group led by Colonel Raghbir Singh was opposed to this move.

At the time of my election as President of the State Congress, a debate on this issue had already begun. In the general body meeting of the State Congress held at Bhatinda, there was an overwhelming opinion in favour of the merger, which I accepted and supported, but pleaded for Patiala to be the capital of the larger state of Punjab.

The Congress leaders of Himachal Pradesh were never in favour of merging their territory with a population of 1.1 million, in Punjab, lest they were overshadowed and entirely dominated by the volatile Punjabis. Himachal's pleas were accepted and it continued to have a separate entity. After the merger of PEPSU with Punjab, Himachal Pradesh asked for the popular hill station of Simla to be transferred to them from Punjab, where they could set up their capital. It went to the credit of Y.S. Parmar, the Himachal Pradesh leader to get the Union Territory of Himachal Pradesh upgraded to a full-fledged State of the Indian Union. Any leader who would not plead the cause of his own State would soon lose ground. An astute politician as he was, Parmar remained Chief Minister of his State for almost eighteen years, though he had no personal sacrifice to his credit.

My plea to make Patiala the capital of Punjab did not carry weight with Partap Singh Kairon, who was of the view that PEPSU being a citadel of big landlords would not be an ideal place for smooth democratic functioning of our polity. Chandigarh, the new capital of Punjab under construction should not be abandoned midstream, which plea was supported by the Central Government. However, they assured due importance for the city of Patiala. This importance could have been enhanced further, had the Brish Bhan group not shown aversion to it. The only concessions given were that the Public Service Commission and the Irrigation Department were retained in Patiala. The Language Department and the State Public Works Department are still functioning in that city. The Central Government planned to start an electric train between Patiala and Chandigarh, which never materialised. No rail link has so far been established between these two important cities hardly 65 kilometres apart from each other.

Kairon exerted all his influence to ensure non-inclusion of my supporters in the cabinet. I espoused the cause of Raja of Nalagarh, who was an educated Hindu, non-communal in outlook, honest and popular among people. He had been returned to the State Assembly in elections from his constituency and enjoyed a reputation for his integrity. Kairon showed little regard for these attributes of that youthful aspirant, as he was related to the Maharaja of Patiala, the fact he did not relish because of the admiration Pandit Nehru and Sardar Patel had for the latter.

As Akalis did not see any hope of achieving a *Punjabi Suba* in 1955, they resolved to work only in the religious, educational, cultural, social and economic fields and advised the members and supporters of the Akali Dal to join the Congress. I welcomed this move, as I did not see any role for communal organizations in the politics of a secular India. The Akalis accordingly decided to adopt the political manifesto of Congress as their own. Any member of the Akali Dal could be a member of the Congress Party.

The Regional Formula was adopted in February 1956. After the political merger of Punjab and PEPSU, Kairon mooted the idea of merging the Congress bodies of the two erstwhile States, to which I agreed. In a combined meeting, it was decided to treat the members of the two Executive bodies as members of the common Executive till such time as new elections were held. In the combined Executive Committee, I would be the Vice-President, while Giani Gurmukh Singh Musafir, veteran of the freedom struggle, poet and literateur, would be the President. I assumed the post of Vice-President on 26 October 1956.

In the General Elections of 1957, I was put incharge of the Congress electioneering in Punjab. To buttress the party campaign, Pandit Nehru and Pandit Govind Vallabh Pant visited the State, when I accompanied them to various places, to which gesture Kairon did not take very kindly. He also did not relish my suggestion to campaign for Brish Bhan, who was locked in a contest with Shivdev Singh, a kin of Maharaja of Patiala. Dexterous political games as Kairon was accustomed to playing, he worked secretly against Brish Bhan. In fact he was bent upon erasing the Congress leadership of the erstwhile PEPSU personified by Brish Bhan and myself. I was slightly out of his target, as I was in the Rajya Sabha, but Brish Bhan was vanquished at the hustings.

From the constituency in Kotkapura, where I used to fight my political battles, Kairon put up the brother of the erstwhile Raja of Faridkot as a candidate for the Assembly elections, who was stoutly opposed by his wife, and was routed in polling by her. The Raja himself suffered the same fate, when he was defeated by one of my keen supporters, Mehr Singh. The debacle of both the brothers did not really disappoint me, because of the dig of the Raja's brother at the Patiala Club that people like him should have been taken in the committees appointed to provide relief to the freedom fighters, as they were equipped with better information of the beatings they had given to these barbarians.

I found the attitude of Partap Singh Kairon quite lukewarm. Perhaps, it was a bit odd, but I preferred to be aloof for about a year or more. In the Presidential election to the Punjab State Congress, Kairon put up Devi Lal as his candidate putting Giani Gurmukh Singh Musafir in the cold storage. Devi Lal won in opposition to Brish Bhan and in a clever move, Kairon proposed my name for Vice-Presidency, which resulted in my victory with complete unanimity. The Congress High Command did not take Devi Lal's ascendancy to the top party post in the State with favour.

Seven members of the Working Committee including myself tendered our resignations. Kairon tried to persuade me to withdraw my resignation as Vice-President, but I could not oblige him. Kairon was compelled to put Darbara Singh in the Presidency in place of Devi Lal. That was a crucial point in my political career. Had I accepted the overtures of Kairon, I could have easily bagged the Congress Presidency of the Punjab. In the elections to the All India Congress Committee, I openly faced the opposition of Kairon, but he could not design my defeat, though many of our supporters could not withstand the hostile volleys of Kairon and fell fighting politically in the election arena.

A great deal of my time began to be occupied with frequent meetings with a larger number of visitors bearing political burden, and the chasm between me and Kairon went on widening.

At the session of the All India Congress Committee at Chandigarh, when Indira Gandhi was the Congress President, I spoke critically about the Congress Government policies in various States, where the voice of the poor and the downtrodden was not heard properly. I did not particularly mention the Punjab Government or the Central Government in my speech, but, perhaps, due to my plain-speaking in bold language, it evoked general interest among the delegates and attracted warm applause.

So absorbed was I in my speech that I did not notice the unconcealed disapproval of Pandit Nehru, at whose instance Mrs. Gandhi rang the bell warning me of crossing the time limit of my speech, but unmindful, I continued. The audience expressed their approbation with renewed clapping, but as soon as I sat down, Pandit Nehru told me in obvious anger that he would oppose me. I was not happy with the Punjab government or the Punjab Congress, he said, and that was why I had chosen the occasion to criticize the Punjab affairs in an All-India Forum. In his speech, Pandit Nehru mentioned about my observations and remarked that local or State differences need not be highlighted in such big gatherings which were attended by the world press and others.

In the evening at a Reception hosted by the Chief Minister, Kairon he accosted me and, patting my back, sarcastically acclaimed my stand at the session and lauded my courage for openly taking on a national leader like Nehru. After a while, when I came face to face with Pandit Nehru at the Reception, he smilingly said that in his speech he had spared me, but had opposed only my observations. Never then or later, did Pandit Nehru give me any impression of his annoyance or disaffection towards me. He would not mind a discussion in private, though he would not relish public exposure of party matters reflecting on its integrity or cohesion.

Once at a meeting with Pandit Nehru of Abdul Ghani, Prabodh Chander and myself, the other two made highly critical comments about Partap Singh Kairon. Though I had political differences with Kairon, I had never attacked him or his family personally. The next morning news of this meeting was splashed in the newspapers. At 9.00 a.m., I received a letter from Pandit Nehru saying that we had breached his confidence and we had no right to give such a news item to the press, which could do incalculable harm.

I felt upset over Pandit Nehru's displeasure; and since I was reluctant to show this letter to anyone, I scribbled a reply in Hindi, which I wanted to get typed in Connaught Place. There I ran into a close friend, whom I did not have any hesitation in taking into confidence, and he promptly translated my reply into English. In my letter, reminding Pandit Nehru that no such indiscretion had ever been committed by me earlier, I regretted that such a version of our meeting should have found its way in print, and I assured him that I was trying to ascertain who was actually responsible for it.

Reaching Pandit Nehru's official residence, I discovered that he had left for Hyderabad for a Congress Session. Since I was also supposed to attend the session, I reached Hyderabad by the next flight. Pandit Nehru was staying with Bhim Sen Sachar, then Governor of Andhra Pradesh. With the purpose of handing over the letter to Pandit Nehru before the start of the session, I reached the Governor's residence early next morning. While I was sitting in the waiting room, I found Pandit Nehru and Sachar strolling leisurely in the verandah, after breakfast. Sachar saw me and asked me with a welcome smile, if I had had my breakfast. Pandit Nehru butted in saying that Sachar was a clever person. If he wanted me for breakfast, he should have had invited me earlier. Replying, Sachar said, that had he known where I was staying, he would have certainly asked me over. When I explained the purpose of my visit, Sachar offered to leave the scene, but both I and Pandit Nehru asked him to stay on.

I told Pandit Nehru that I had brought a reply to his letter, in which I had denied having approached the Press about what had transpired in our meeting with him. Without a hint of anger in his voice, he said that whosoever had done it, it was undesirable. His quiet advice was not to bring persons of such nature to him .for meetings, as had little regard for propriety. He conceded that they were good Congressmen, but they were not capable of being taken into strict confidence. As for my letter, Pandit Nehru said, there was no need for reading it, though he kept it with him, asking me not to carry burden of any kind on my mind.

I do not remember a single occasion when Pandit Nehru did not extend his support to me or did not try to help me improve myself. But for his helpful, objective and fair attitude, the senior Punjab leaders, who, of course, did not share his great qualities, would have tried to keep my stature to the level of a local party functionary. Later, that day when in an encounter with Prabodh Chandra, I told the latter what had transpired between me and Pandit Nehru, he remarked that there was little surprise in the Prime Minister losing his poise, though his anger was transient and he cooled down as easily as he flew into a temper. Had the news of our meeting him not appeared in the press, we would not have come into limelight, observed Prabodh Chandra. Because of this, the whole of Punjab was agog with the talk that Pandit Nehru had started listening to things hostile to Partap Singh Kairon. The intention of Prabodh Chandra, of course, was to spread the impression that Giani Zail Singh had launched a campaign against Kairon.

Prabodh Chandra followed it up with a charge-sheet against Kairon listing his misdeeds and those of his sons. It was signed by about eight persons and he tried to persuade me to sign it too, but I asked him to leave the papers with me for an in-depth study, which he did not, because he was aware that though Kairon could be my political adversary, I would not indulge in personal accusations against anyone. In meetings, we would naturally discuss political indiscretions of Kairon, the wind of which reached Pandit Nehru, and it was near the close of 1961, when one day he asked me why I had joined the battle against the Punjab Chief Minister.

People like Abdul Ghani and Prabodh Chandra belonged to the Congress Party no doubt, but they did not have the competence of holding the reins of the State. As such, Pandit Nehru declared that he would be firm in his support to Kairon at the helm of Punjab, and he would ask him to carry me with him. I told Pandit Nehru not to take the trouble of speaking to Kairon for me, as one reason of his estrangement with me had been my access to him (Nehru). His mediation could compel Kairon to put up a show of reconciliation towards me, but in his heart, he could still harbour hostile feelings.

One day, Giani Gurmukh Singh Musafir went to Pandit Nehru to unburden his mind of the grievances he nurtured against Kairon, but Pandit Nehru, looking into the vacuum remarked philosophically, that the world was like that. Pandit Nehru had a good measure of affection for Musafir and he did not want any harm to come to Prabodh Chandra either, but he did not deviate from his resolve to keep Kairon in power in Punjab.

A week later, Kairon visited my residence at Ferozeshah Road in New Delhi and in the evening met me at a reception. Conversing lightly about my attire, he touched a button on my long coat, when a photographer took a snap. It found its way into newspapers the next morning. It set off widespread comment of our reconciliation and camaraderie.

At our next meeting, Kairon complained that I had tendered resignation from the office of Vice-President of the State Congress against his will. Had I not done so, he would not have been obliged to offer an important position to Darbara Singh, in whom, he said, he did not have much faith. Nevertheless, he would like to bury the hatchet, he said, and start a new chapter of understanding and friendship with me. Though we shook hands, I realised later that his conciliatory gestures were generated only by the chastening counsel of Pandit Nehru.

Chapter 14

ELECTION WOES

For the 1962 general elections to the Lower House of Parliament and the State Assembly, I made no effort to seek a nomination. Kairon seemed to intend keeping me in the Upper House of Parliament, if he could do so, and did not want me to secure a seat in Lok Sabha or the Punjab Assembly. But, as a pleasant surprise to me, the Congress High Command told Kairon, that I must be accommodated in the party nominations. Neelam Sanjiva Reddy, later President of India, was then presiding over the Indian National Congress. When Kairon insisted on my seeking re-election to Rajya Sabha only, Neelam Sanjiva Reddy intervened and emphasized that I should at least contest election for an Assembly seat.

Consequently, I accepted nomination from the Faridkot constituency, although I had been out of touch with those people for about ten years. I was being opposed by the wife of the younger brother of the erstwhile Raja of Faridkot, who had been put up as a candidate by the Akali Party. She was the one who had trounced her husband at the hustings in the previous elections. As I jumped in the election arena, I started getting a comfortable feeling that I had stepped into an amiable atmosphere. The Presidents of Municipal Committees and Block Samitis were showing helpful leanings.

Pratap Singh Kairon, visiting Faridkot, asked me to respond favourably to an invitation for breakfast by the erstwhile Ruler. At the breakfast meeting, he urged both. of us to forget the past bitterness of the era of freedom struggle and to see things in a new perspective in the sunshine of freedom and democracy. The Raja recalled my incarceration in his jail for five years and wistfully felt that it might have left scars of anger in my heart. But I thanked him for whatever he had done to me. Had he not clamped me in jail, there could have been a possibility of my forfeiting my life in violent revolutionary activities. During my days in prison, I could study a lot about Gandhiji's creed of non-violence, which had helped me change my outlook. Addressing the Raja, I said that he could as well have done away with me physically or maimed me, if he had so chosen, but the fact that he had not resorted to any such drastic measure bespoke his basic mild approach.

Now our opposition was based on political differences, as I subscribed to the Congress ideology and the Raja's creed was different. Latching on to this observation, the erstwhile Raja said, that he had no mind lending his weight against me. Perhaps, to confirm this statement, he visited me in the Rest House, where I was staying and made an offer of putting at my disposal vehicles for the election campaign. I politely thanked him and took my leave stating that I would probably avail of his offer, when needed.

I started my campaign with full gusto, trundling through villages talking right upto dusk with the rural folk, bathing in cold water on chilly wintry mornings and leaving it to the discretion and judgement of the electors, if they would vote in my favour. Some of them pledged support, while others conceded my right to fight the election without firm promise to cast their votes for me at the hustings.

I managed to get hold of some vehicles for my campaigners, being aware that if I did not arrange a mount for them, they would jump on to someone else's bandwagon! Some people must join the fray without caring whose side they would be ultimately on. I was wary about the erstwhile Raja's help of any kind, lest his detractors turned against me in the belief that I was acquiescing in his machinations. For a month I lived on raw carrots and plain water, completely immersed in the campaign right from 5.00 a.m. till 9.00 p.m. or even later in the night.

Five or six days before the date of polling, the erstwhile Raja put his whole fleet of vehicles at the disposal of his sister-in-law, my opponent in the election, with all the manpower to back her. Big landlords and money-bags joined hands to defeat me in the polling, which included some close relatives of Kairon, and, to my utter surprise, the latter did not restrain them from their course. The joint endeavours of the erstwhile Raja, his brother, the Akali Party and the feudal lobby tended to become a formidable challenge to my campaign.

A feeble effort on the part of Kairon to enlist support for me was obviously aimed at reassuring Pandit Nehru of his genuine intentions, and in case of my ultimate defeat, the entire blame could have been laid at the door of the crafty ex-ruler for his perfidy. But inspite of all alignments among my opponents and their patrons and all pernicious propaganda unleashed by feudal forces, the people elected me to the Punjab State Assembly.

It is, perhaps, a coincidence that wherever I contested the elections, I was subjected to assaults by unruly elements. My opponents gave vent to their frustrations with unmerited violence. Soon after the declaration of the result in my constituency, the losers resorted to vandalism, severely damaging my vehicle and causing serious misapprehension about my personal safety. The victory procession taken out by my partymen and supporters, eliciting scenes of irrepressible jubilation, had to be heavily escorted by the law-enforcing authorities to ward off danger of attack from the frustrated opponents.

Since I had held ministerial positions in PEPSU twice, my successful election to the Punjab Assembly weighed iri my favour for my inclusion in the Council of Ministers. But instead of Cabinet rank, I was offered a post of Minister of State with independent charge. I was persuaded by my friends to accept the post, as in the government, I would be in a better position to help the depressed and the deprived sections of the society. I was also conscious of the promise I had made to Pandit Nehru to get along with Kairon without any squabble or bickering. Besides me, there was one more Minister of State with independent charge, "Niranjan Singh, whereas all others were attached to the Cabinet Ministers.

Chapter 15

EXIT FROM THE CABINET

At the time of the Chinese aggression on our borders in October 1962, the Punjab Council of Ministers comprised 31 persons. I supported Kairon's proposal to reduce the number of Ministers as an economy measure and suggested to him to secure resignations from all Ministers to use his discretion for retaining some of them. I tendered my resignationon the spot. On the New Year Day 1963, the Chief Minister decided to limit his cabinet only to nine members, dropping the rest.

In the light of the prevailing emergency due to the Chinese invasion, Kairon proposed to assign special activities to the persons dropped from the Council of Ministers. As a result I was appointed an Honorary Commander of the Home Guards and I helped in drafting Kairon's public and Radio speeches full of patriotic fervour, which he was so fond of delivering with great frequency. We worked in very close cooperation in the spirit generated by the Chinese betrayal of our friendship, that galvanised the whole nation into action.

In 1964, some legislators submitted a memorandum accusing Kairon and his family of corruption, with, reference to which Kairon announced in the Assembly that he was prepared to face an inquiry by a Commission. Taking him at this word, Pandit Nehru appointed a one-man Commission consisting of Justice Das, whose findings went against Kairon. Unfortunately, Pandit Nehru breathed his last on 27 May 1964, and after a short spell of interim Prime Ministership held by

Gulzari Lal Nanda, Lal Bahadur Shastri took over the reigns of the Union government.

Kairon resigned the Chief Ministership of Punjab on 15 June 1964. Darbara Singh harboured a strong ambition to be the Chief Minister, but at that point of time could not enlist the Centre's support. Surprisingly, Kairon announced my candidature too, the news about which I read in the newspapers. Kairon brought my name in against the opinion of General Mohan Singh of the Indian National Army, who himself was an aspirant to the coveted position. Kairon admitted to General Mohan Singh that my candidature was to stall the chances of Darbara Singh, and in the eventuality of my success, the cohesion of the majority group would not be lost.

Shastri deputed Swaran Singh, a veteran Congress leader from Punjab to the State to assess the situation. Kairon pleaded with him my case as a freedom fighter, a political prisoner, who had suffered severe persecution, and my record as a successful Minister. But Swaran Singh was aware of Shastri's inclinations. Shastri had not taken kindly to Kairon's style of functioning. Some people were apprising Shastri of events which tainted Kairon and his family members with corrupt practices. The Prime Minister was aware of my penchant for defending Kairon on the ground that he could not be blamed for the actions of his progeny, who were engaged in business and were alone responsible for the lack of scruples. My this stance displeased quite a few.

Kairon had to advise Swaran Singh to propose someone of his own choice. They jointly decided upon the candidature of Comrade Ram Kishen. In the meeting of the Congress Legislature Party, Swaran Singh, declared, as observer, that he would prefer unanimous election of a leader. Discounting complete unanimity on such an issue, some members suggested that the observer himself should assess the situation and choose a person acceptable to the Congress High Command, who would be adopted as Leader by the legislators.

Swaran Singh named Comrade Ram Kishen, who became the new Chief Minister of Punjab on 7 July 1964. The Comrade included Darbara Singh and Prabodh Chandra, among others, in his Council of Ministers to the exclusion and chagrin of the Kairon supporters. At the time of expansion of his cabinet, he asked me to accompany him to New Delhi for the High Command's approval for my inclusion in his Ministry.

I had a strong feeling that Prime Minister, Lal Bahadur Shastri, would not oppose my induction in the Punjab Cabinet, but I was told that he was not inclined favourably in the belief that the presence of a strong Kairon supporter might lead to tension and strife in the cabinet. Another reason for Shastri's indifference was the reminder of Kairon's support for Morarji Desai in the contest in the Parliamentary Legislature Party for the Prime Ministership of the country.

Though at that point of time I was considered to be on the side of Kairon, I was not a supporter of Morarji Desai. In fact I was not in any reckoning, as I was not a member of Parliament. I saw Mrs. Indira Gandhi, who was a Minister in the cabinet of Shastri. She offered to talk to the latter, but expressed a doubt about evoking a positive response in him.

While I was descending the stairs of the Central Secretariat, after taking leave of Mrs. Gandhi, she recalled me to her office and suggested to speak to Kamraj, then President of the Indian National Congress, who, she thought, would be more receptive. I insisted that Mrs. Gandhi should not do anything for me which she would not consider totally appropriate or would find even a little embarrassing. As Kamraj was not available on telephone, she decided to speak to him later.

In the meantime, Comrade Ram Kishen started finding the going quite tough in the company of some of his chosen cabinet colleagues and he twice came to my flat to express disenchantment with those rather over-assertive ministers. He nominated me as a permanent invitee to all meetings of the Executive Committee of the Congress Legislature Party. I also became the chairman of the Punjab Branch of Indo-Soviet Cultural Society, earlier having held that position in PEPSU since 1952. On 3 November 1964, I went on a tour of the Soviet Union in a delegation visiting several important centres in that country for about three weeks, where I got glimpses of the life in the leading socialist State.

Comrade Ram Kishen submitted his resignation on 20 June 1966, and President's rule was promulgated in Punjab on 6 July 1966.

Chapter 16

PUNJABI-SPEAKING STATE

In Punjab, a powerful movement took birth for the establishment of a Punjabi linguistic State, which was spearheaded by the Akali Party. The movement was based more on sentimental than logical grounds. When the government had redemarcated boundaries of various states in the country on linguistic lines, people of Punjab and Bombay had been left out in the cold. In Punjab, however, in most part the agitation was confined to the Akali Party, which came to be considered as militant exponent of Sikh interests.

I was of the view that the existent Punjab was itself a Punjabi-speaking state and it would be more pragmatic to attach such areas, as claimed to be Hindi speaking, to the adjoining Hindi States. This view was shared by Gian Singh Rarewala and Niranjan Singh Talib, and all the three of us met Pandit Nehru to explain our point of view. I also suggested that Himachal Pradesh and Punjab could be merged, the language of the former being a dialect of Punjabi.

Over ten members of the Legislative Assembly issued a public statement suggesting delineation of three regions-Punjabi, Hindi and Pahari (hill dialect) with a common High Court and a joint Public Service Commission with one Chief Minister and the portfolio of Home Minister to be rotated among the three regions. Now that Lal Bahadur Shastri had assumed Prime Ministership, after the demise of Pandit Nehru, with Gulzạri Lal Nanda as his Home Minister, he did not show much inclination to consider this proposal.

The Home Minister announced in Parliament the setting up of a Committee under the Chairmanship of Hukum Singh to go into the question of establishment of a Punjabi lingual state. In a bid to boost their claim, the Akalis made overtures to leaders from the Hindi-speaking areas of the then existing Punjab to pitchfork a demand for creation of Haryana.

The establishment of the Hukum Singh Committee took the wind out of the sails of the Akali agitation and peace descended on the strife-torn region. Sant Chanan Singh, 'an Akali leader, saw me at Chandigarh pleading for my support for the creation of a *Punjabi Suba* (State). My stand on the subject was well known, but to my dismay, no one heeded my views. The Akalis were keen to have even a small State with a majority of Sikh population, which they could use later as leverage for acceptance of some other demands.

Hukum Singh Committee's Report recommended the carving out of a Punjabi-speaking state. A Committee set up by Prime Minister Lal Bahadur Shastri under the chairmanship of Mrs. Indira Gandhi, with the Home Minister, Y.B. Chavan as Member, examined the Report.

On 9 March 1966, the Congress Working Committee passed a resolution that "out of the existing State of Punjab, a State with Punjabi as the state language be formed". As per recommendations of the Hukum Singh Committee, the other areas' of Punjab should constitute a state of Haryana. The Report also recommended the setting up of a Commission to determine the boundaries of these States.

A clash of interests between the protagonists of Punjab and Haryana set in. The Justice Shah Commission came into being for deciding the boundaries, which was quite an astounding decision, as Justice Shah had hardly any knowledge of the linguistic situation or political ethos of the region. There is always an overlapping of languages in certain areas. The language of the Haryana region can hardly be called Hindi. In fact, it is Haryanvi. The language of Rajasthan cannot also be termed Hindi in the true sense, as mostly it is Rajasthani. The division between Punjab and Haryana created a wedge between the people on communal lines. The Akali leaders were obsessed with a State with Punjabi language and a majority of Sikhs. The sectarian undertones were visible on the other side too. The Punjab Congress was divided in two parts-one for either State. Bhagwat Dyal Sharma, who was the President of the undivided Punjab State Congress, became Congress Chief of the Haryana State, while Giani Gurmukh Singh Musafir was made the head of the Punjab State Congress.

The Akali leaders failed to put forward a well-reasoned and cogent case for demarcation of the boundaries with the result that several Punjabi-speaking villages were included in Haryana. The Haryana leaders were much more meticulous in presenting their case. Large chunks of the undivided Punjab territory were given to Himachal Pradesh, while demarcating boundaries of the newly formed linguistic states of Punjab and Haryana.

On the back of the lack of interest or complacency on the part of the Akalis was their contentment in the culmination of their long-cherished desire to achieve a state with Punjabi as the dominant language, however, small or circumscribed it might be. The distinguished exponent of the Punjabi Suba, Giani Kartar Singh had once declared that the Akalis would go on striving for such a State, even if it was confined to the District of Amritsar. Their dream was to use it as a springboard to achieve a Sikh State.

The present states of Punjab and Haryana came into existence on 1 November 1966. It was decided by the Central government to induct the legislators originally elected from the constituencies now forming part of either state to the new Legislative Assemblies of the respective states. The decision to instal Bhagwat Dyal Sharma, the Haryana Congress President as the Chief Minister of the nascent State presented little difficulty. No such easy decision seemed possible for Punjab.

There were sharp differences among the Punjab legislators, as support was divided among Major Harinder Singh, Comrade Ram Kishen, who had earlier held the office and myself. My supporters met Mrs. Indira Gandhi, who had taken over as Prime Minister, after the death of Lal Bahadur Shastri in Tashkent in January 1966. She expressed her fullest satisfaction at the move, but naturally said, it should depend on the support I could muster among the Party members in the Assembly. Twenty-four legislators assured the Prime Minister of their support to me.

Dinesh Singh and I.K. Gujral, members of the Council of Ministers of Mrs. Gandhi, who enjoyed her confidence, sent for me and told me that my candidature for Chief Ministership was being considered, but wondered, if I would be in a position to muster the majority support. Gulzari Lal Nanda, Minister for Home Affairs, had clear predilection for Major Harinder Singh, a highly opulent landlord. Swaran Singh showed unusual neutrality. Mrs. Indira Gandhi, though very much inclined in my favour got around the view expressed by I.K. Gujral that Giani Gurmukh Singh Musafir, the State Congress Chief, could be drafted for the post of Chief Minister to avoid dissensions in the party.

Mrs. Gandhi had pointedly asked me, if I had strong feelings for becoming the Chief Minister, to which I had replied in the negative. I was later told by Dinesh Singh that this was my undoing. It was my mistake not to show my complete willingness to Mrs. Gandhi for wearing the mantle of leadership. Now that a decision had been taken to bring in Musafir as leader of the Congress legislature party, I expressed my deep satisfaction to Mrs. Gandhi over her choice.

I was then General Secretary of the State Congress and I extended wholehearted support to Musafir. I exhorted him to prepare for the Party's victory in the general elections in 1967, which were just a few months hence. Musafir approached Mrs. Gandhi with the proposal to elevate me to the post of the State Congress President, but the latter wished to leave it to me either to accept this exalted position in the Party or to join the Council of Ministers. I told Mrs. Gandhi of my preference for the party position.

I found to my dismay the dilatory methods adopted by Musafir and some others to fix a date for election of the State Congress President. It was their desire to let Musafir combine the two offices of the Chief Minister and the Congress President in himself till the distribution of party tickets to candidates. It was an obvious attempt to keep me out of the process of choosing party candidates for the general elections.

When I insisted on fixation of an early date, they persuaded General Mohan Singh of the Indian National Army fame to oppose me in the election. Simultaneously they tried to convince Mrs. Gandhi that factionalism had crept into the party on this issue. But she observed that no power could stop me from becoming the Punjab State Congress Chief. She upbraided Musafir for unwanted vacillation, who duly informed General Mohan Singh of the Centre's feelings. In the election held on 17 November 1966, General Mohan Singh proposed my name, but Seth Ram Nath another colleague, became a contestant, who in the election, had to be satisfied with very few votes in his favour.

With the corning into being of a Punjabi-Speaking State on 1 November 1966, a setback was caused to the Congress Party. In the elections held in February 1967, it was for the first time that Congress could not romp horne with a majority in the legislature. Giani Gurmukh Singh Musafir, the Chief Minister, lost his election with a big margin. The Hindu voters, generally alienated from the Congress, cast their lot with the Jana Sangh, besides acute factionalism in the Congress ranks.

The Akalis forged an alliance with the Jana Sangh, both the Communist parties and some independent members to form a United Front, and with this, the heterogeneous group could muster a very slender majority in the House of 104. The United Front government headed by Gurnam Singh, former Chief Justice of the Punjab High Court was sworn in on 8 March 1967, with hardly any common ideology among the various constituents.

An unprecedented horse trading followed with some Congress legislators defecting to the United Front to give it a transient feeling of comfort. Some people always crave to be on the winning side. Those crossing the floor were among those who had obtained the Congress tickets after entreaties and tall claims of loyalty. Though the Akali strength in the legislature was only 24, they attracted a motley group of anti-Congress elements, which gave them a chance to rule the State. Frequent defections created a good deal of uncertainty, leading to numerous expansions of the Council of Ministers to accommodate the mercurial members.

The Chief Minister was obliged to expand his Council of Ministers five times in the first two and a half months of his stewardship. As for the Congress party, some supporters of Musafir mooted the idea of electing him the leader of the Legislature party, inspite of his defeat in polling, but that was not to be. The Congress Legislature party balked at electing its leader for four or five days, which caused it considerable damage. It was short of only three members to gain a majority, though quite tenuous.

I was not in the Assembly, as I had refrained from contesting in the elections, the fact rued by my friends. The sole reason for my doing so was my desire to devote all my energy and time to work for the Party, instead of concentrating on my own individual constituency.

Since the Gurnam Singh Ministry was in doldrums most of the time during its nine months' tenure, the Congress Party could have easily toppled it with the help of some of the nine independent members including Yadavendra Singh, the erstwhile Maharaja of Patiala, but they remained on the sidelines watching the situation. Out of 57 MLAs of the ruling alliance, 17 defected and on 22 November 1967, the Gurnam Singh government fell.

The Congress Legislature Party asked its leader, Gian Singh Rarewala and myself to take suitable action and we decided to support Lachhman Singh Gill to form a new Ministry. In a discussion with the Union Home Minister, Y.B. Chavan, I had to tell him that since the Akali legislature party had split, it was not for the Congress to stop their quarrels. They themselves should keep their house in order. Lachhman Singh Gill formed a minority government on 25 November 1967, and gave ministerial posts to all the defectors. There was only one honourable exception in his Council of Ministers without taint of being a defector.

Lachhman Singh Gill was being supported by the Congress Party from outside, without forming a coalition. Quite adroitly he got a bill passed for introduction of the Punjabi language with the support of the Congress legislators, but took the entire credit for himself to the exclusion of the Congress party.

There was no better example of the power going to the

head of an individual than the Chief Minister, who very often started indulging in braggadocio belittling the Congress as well as his Akali detractors. He publicly ridiculed the top Akali leaders like Sant Chanan Singh, then President of the Shiromani Gurdwara Prabandhak Committee and Sant Fateh Singh, the Akali Supremo, much to their chagrin and the amusement of the Congressmen.

Following one of his diatribes, I questioned him about his following in the Assembly, but he could not show even one more than seventeen, who had defected from their parent body to share the spoils of the office. As was his wont, Gill asked me to swear on The Holy Book of our continued support to him, but I had to remind him that politics could not be enforced with religious fealties.

Gill somehow seemed to be deceptively convinced that the salvation of the Congress Party lay in lending its unstinted support to his minority government, and without much circumspection, he started granting favours to the officers close to him and taking punitive action against those refusing to play his tune. He took the sizeable gatherings managed by sycophantic officials as genuine mass adultation. The paranoia led him to attempt sowing dissensions in the Congress ranks, which proved to be the proverbial last straw.

I suggested to my Party to withdraw support from Gill, though a handful of Congress members were keen on continuing the arrangement to embarrass Rarewala, their leader in the legislative wing, who was being spoofed unsparingly by the minority Chief Minister. Along with Rarewala, I met Prime Minister, Mrs. Indira Gandhi on 20 August 1968 and also the Congress President S. Nijalingappa to apprise them of the situation. I again met Mrs. Gandhi and a decision was taken to withdraw immediately the Congress support from the splinter group of the Akalis. No party being in majority, the Centre decided to place the State under the President's rule on 23 August 1968, dissolving the Legislative Assembly.

The President's rule lasted six months, with the political parties plunging headlong in hectic electioneering campaign. Following a High Command fiat not to give party tickets to those, who did not strictly adhere to party discipline, the candidates proposed by Rarewala were ignored, which caused him enough pique to resign from the Congress and to join the Akali Dal. Rarewala had made a curious attempt to constitute an ad hoc committee to choose party candidates, which was not accepted. Nijalingappa, the Congress President had to tour the State himself, after which the Congress Parliamentary Board appointed Mohan Lal Sukhadia, Chief Minister of Rajasthan as an observer to supervise the selection of party candidates.

In the midterm elections on 9 February 1969, the Akalis emerged as the single largest party in the Assembly, but failed to gain an absolute majority. The Akali Dal had entered into an understanding with the [ana Sangh which resulted in the Akalis winning 43 seats with Jana Sangh getting 8. The Congress tally was 38, though they secured over three lakh more votes than they had been able to get in the 1967 elections.

A coalition government consisting of the Akalis and the Jana Sangh came into power with Gurnam Singh as Chief Minister on 17 February 1969. Very soon the Akalis started engineering defections from the Congress ranks. As many as ten Congress members crossed the floor over to the United Front, which swelled the latter's pride only to be deflated shortly afterwards, when a sizeable number of Akalis abandoned their leaders to cause the fall of the government.

An ego conflict arose between Gurnam Singh, the Akali Chief Minister, and Sant Fateh Singh, the President of the Akali Dal. A bizarre spectacle of open dissensions came to be witnessed on the floor of the House, when Balwant Singh, the Finance Minister, refused to rise to present the Appropriation Bill. When it was moved by the Chief Minister himself, it was defeated by 44 votes to 22. Gurnam Singh found himself in an uncomfortable minority. The Congress party declined to extend support to Gurnam Singh.

One of the main reasons for Gurnam Singh's debacle was the rift between him and Sant Fateh Singh over the selection of candidates for Rajya Sabha elections from the State on 25 March 1970. The forces of communalism and opportunism were having a field day in the State with the law and order situation dipping low. There were a large number of complaints from members of the Harijan community, especially from the Bhatinda district, of harassment, because of their support to the Congress party during the mid-term elections.

Following withdrawal of support to the Chief Minister by some Akali members, the Gurnam Singh government fell. He sued for the Congress help. In the interest of stability, the Congress Parliamentary Board took a decision on 25 March 1970, to extend support to the beleaguered Chief Minister, but the breakaway Akalis with the help of [ana Sangh formed a government with Prakash Singh Badal at the helm, on 27 March 1970. However, the legislators threw their scruples to the wind-and defections started taking place in a stream, thereby making a mockery of the moral standards professed by them. During Badal's tenure, there were as many as 59 defections.

The Jana Sangh withdrew their support from the Akalis reducing the Badal government to a minority, leading Badal to seek the Congress support. We decided to act as constructive opposition, at the same time supporting Badal to escape another spell of the President's rule. Gurnam Singh compromised with Badal to pre-empt an understanding between the latter and the Congress. As a result, the Akalis became a majority Party and they chose to adopt a stiff attitude towards the Congress Party.

However, Gurnam Singh was restive as ever before and could not accept the leadership of Badal. Due to defections, Badal lost the majority and on 13 June 1971, advised the Governor to dissolve the House, which was accepted by the Governor. The President's Rule was imposed. It dashed the hopes of those Congressmen for getting ministerial positions, who had jettisoned their party to join the bandwagon of the Akalis.

Chapter 17

RIFT IN THE CONGRESS

In 1969, a rift took place in the Central Congress leadership, leading to the defeat of Neelam Sanjiva Reddy in the Presidential election and the victory for V.V.Giri. Consequently, Mrs. Indira Gandhi was expelled from the Party on 12 November 1969, by the Syndicate. I expressed great unhappiness over this development and pledged my firm support to Mrs. Gandhi. I had met her on 1 November 1969 to reassure her of complete following of the Punjab Congress in her hour of trial. Mrs. Gandhi represented the progressive forces in the country as against the conservative stance adopted by the Syndicate.

I did not find any justification in the appeal of Nijalingappa to the members of the All India Congress Committee to boycott the meeting convened by the pro-Indira group on 22-23 November 1969 in New Delhi. My support to Mrs. Gandhi was unqualified, but I would like to deal with the subject a little later. I, Kamlapathi Tripathi and A.P. Sharma, State Congress Presidents, were expelled by the Syndicate. Jagjivan Ram and Fakhruddin Ali Ahmed met the same fate.

I contested a by-election to the Punjab Assembly from the Anandpur Sahib constituency, in December 1970 and in spite of intimidation and harassment of voters, particularly the Scheduled Castes and Backward Classes by the Akalis, I won the election with a comfortable margin. It was a pyrrhic victory for the Congress.

In March 1971, the rout of the Akali party in the Parliamentary elections demoralized it completely. I was the President of the Punjab Pradesh Congress Committee and I tried my best for the Congress win. Out of 13 parliamentary seats from Punjab, the Congress won 10, the Communist Party of India 2 and the Akalis could get only 1 seat.

In the State Assembly, the inimical attitude of the Gurnam Singh and Badal factions towards each other vitiated the atmosphere in their Party further, resulting in the resignation of the Badal Government on 13 June 1971. The President's rule was promulgated in the State on 15 June 1971. Badal recommended dissolution of the Assembly. Because of uncertainty and corruption during the Badal regime, the morale of the people suffered a great setback, and it was an herculean task to restore the people's confidence in the political system.

A large number of meetings had to be organized, where people gathered and discussed their grievances. The State Congress called upon all secular and national forces to make collective efforts to face and defeat the communal and reactionary elements. I tried to organize the youths to make united endeavours to frustrate communal forces.

A political conference was held at Ludhiana in September 1971, which passed a resolution to set up a Commission to investigate the charges of corruption against the former Akali Ministers. In my presidential address, I emphasized the need for economic, cultural and social progress to make political freedom meaningful. Exploitation by a few of the common man had to be mitigated, if not altogether eliminated. During the Akali rule, reactionary, corrupt, communal and feudal forces had flourished resulting in people's misery and humiliation. The common man had to be liberated from the stranglehold of the exploiting landlords.

In the State Assembly elections, held on 11 March 1972, the Congress won 66 seats, while Akali Dal could get 24. CPI got 10 and CPM won 1 seat. The Jana Sangh, and other minor parties could not succeed even in one constituency. Three independent candidates were elected. In the Congress Legislature party meeting on 15 March 1972, I was unanimously elected its Leader and was sworn in as Chief Minister of

Punjab by Governor, Dr. D.C. Pavate on 17 March 1972. I was reliably told that even while election preparations was being made, the Prime Minister Mrs. Indira Gandhi, had noted on a Party file that the Congress victory was certain and that Giani Zail Singh would be the appropriate person to be the party leader in the Assembly.

Following declaration of the result from my constituency, where I was locked in a serious contest with a candidate supported by almost all Opposition parties, I was told telephonically by Yashpal Kapur, Private Secretary to the Prime Minister, of her views about me for the post of the Chief Minister. While I took over as CM of Punjab, Bansi Lal took up the reins of the government in the neighbouring State of Haryana.

Chapter 18

TIME FOR ACTION

I had never overestimated my abilities to carryon the onerous duties of the Chief Minister. Predictions and prognostications started making the rounds about the maximum life of the Ministry, which was put at six months to the maximum. My non-jat status was cited as another factor for the possible ephemerality of my office. With quite a bit of trepidation, I set out on the arduous course and decided never to look back.

The first task before me was to alleviate the abject poverty in which lakhs of rural folk had been wallowing. Over five Blillion peasants were having a per capita annual income of Rs. 335 only. They were virtually crushed under the burden of indebtedness. Over 43 per cent of the rural population was living below the poverty line, which meant that they were existing in inhuman economic conditions, The consumption level of the urban population was only marginally higher.

This was the image of the Punjab inherited by me from the feudal-oriented rule of the Akalis, whose main contribution was to play on the communal sentiments of the gullible people of the State to perpetuate their rule. To take Punjab on the road to progress by pulling it out of the slush of poverty was a colossal task. I formulated a twelve-point programme and vowed to implement it at the fastest possible speed. Its main objectives were:

"To ensure the upliftment of members of the Scheduled Castes, to transfer surplus and government land to the landless labourers, to provide avenues of employment to the poor and the needy and to work for the development of the border and backward areas of the State;

Constitution of Committees for speedy development, especially of semi-hilly areas, where canal water could not reach; To link all villages by metalled roads within a period of two years;

To get adequate tenancy laws passed to plug loopholes in the existing laws and to impose a suitable ceiling on land holdings and urban property;

To streamline the cooperative and *Panchayati Raj* movement; To set up heavy industries and to encourage and assist Punjabis living outside the state to invest capital in the development of the State;

To provide a fair deal to the working classes;

To ensure payment of remunerative prices to the farmers and to supply foodgrains at reasonable rates to the consumers; To simplify tax structure;

To remove genuine grievances of the government employees;

To rehabilitate the people uprooted by the December, 1971 war and to take special care of the dependents of the martyrs on high priority basis;

To pay special attention to social measures like old-age pensions, primary education, health and medical care and to take steps to nationalise transport".

This programme was targeted for a five year period, but its implementation took a little over half that time and the fourth year saw completion and even exceeding of the targets fixed. Electrification of villages in Punjab was accomplished by 1976. Each village in the State got electricity and the hamlets and homes were lit by electric bulbs.

A large number of villages had already been provided with primary schools, but we ensured a school in each and every village. We decided to provide two primary schools in a village with a population of more than one thousand and five hundred. A population of more than four thousand would get three primary schools and that of more than six thousands would be given four primary schools. A large number of middle and high schools were also opened. About 98 per cent children in the age group of 6-11 years were enrolled in schools. A large number of scholarships for professional and technical courses were provided, besides making a special provision for the handicapped children.

Some leaders including politicians within the Congress Party tried to incite members of the Scheduled Castes against my government for the lack of adequate social welfare measures. They hardly realised that my foremost priority was to raise the standards of living of the backward communities. As such I conceded all reasonable demands of the Harijans and, if I could not do something beyond the pail of possibility, I explained it to them, readily winning their understanding.

It was not that these leaders were genuinely interested in the welfare of the backward class people. Their obvious aim was to use these vulnerable sections against the government, but instead of succeeding in their designs, they had feigned happiness at the acceptance of the demands of Harijans. In fact, I made twentyfive per cent reservations for Harijans in employment, which in the given situation was quite a substantial measure.

I received repeated complaints that certain politicians and civil servants had grabbed the government land. It was decided in a party meeting to set up a committee comprising some members of the Legislative Assembly to investigate these complaints. Accordingly a committee headed by Harchand Singh, a member of the Scheduled Castes was appointed on 4 July 1972, which submitted its report indicating some prominent Ministers and some other public men for grabbing the evacuee land.

Some Ministers resigned on their own but Darbara Singh, Speaker, Vidhan Sabha, was one of the persons named. He initially hedged on submitting his resignation, but subsequently wilted under the admonition of Mrs. Gandhi. Kewal Krishan Deputy Speaker was elevated to the position of the Speaker. I had to resist powerful attempts at absolving the guilty of the taint of land-grab, and in the process earned the displeasure of some senior leaders like Swaran Singh.

In a students clash at Moga, two students and two others lost their lives. Their agitation concerned the hike in rates of cinema tickets. The violence spread to many parts of the State for incitement of which some members of my own ruling party played a notable part. Inspite of the advice of entire administration to the contrary, owing to widespread violence, I went to Moga to meet the students. They asked for a private meeting with me. I called them to the Jagrawan Rest House, in spite of the police reluctance, when I told them about my orders for a judicial enquiry. The investigating officer held the District Officer and the Superintendent of Police responsible for lapses, which triggered a demand for their transfer and the continued closure of the cinemas. I conceded the demands and sent for the two erring officers to tell them about their transfer.

In November 1973, I reconstituted my cabinet including ten new members raising the number to seventeen. One of the major steps taken by my government was to enhance the minimum wages of unskilled workers. This affected workers in most occupations including those employed in agriculture and industry. Assiduous implementation of these measures subscribed to a considerable extent to the amelioration of the lot of a large number of neglected workers.

To provide shelter to poor people, over three hundred thousand free housing plots were allotted to those living in rural areas. The urban improvement trusts and urban estates were asked to reserve two thirds of the developed residential plots for persons in lower-income brackets. To assist the weavers' community, interest-free loans were granted with a view to improving the hand loom industry. A textile development corporation was set up with an authorised capital of ten million rupees for marketing the hand loom products.

A decision was taken to link all villages with metalled roads. Four hundred and twenty million rupees were spent in two years on this project. Out of a little over twelve thousand villages in Punjab, nine thousand were linked with metalled roads and the work in over one thousand villages was going apace.

My government introduced the Punjab Land Reforms Bill (1972) in the Legislative Assembly on 14 December 1972, which was passed in spite of stiff Akali opposition, fixing land ceiling of *barani* land and land with assured irrigation.

Though there was a provision for inclusion of Harijans in the Municipal Committees, no such arrangement existed for other backward classes and the women. We ordered the co-option of at least one sweeper, two women and one member of backward communities in each Municipal Committee and if the civic body failed to do so, then the government would nominate them. No Municipal committee could elect its President without participation in voting by these four persons. The elected member of the Legislative Assembly from that area would be ex-officio member of the committee without the right of voting. We made it incumbent on each Panchayat to have at least one woman member, which was later raised to two. We gave varied facilities to ex-service men as a mark of the nation's gratitude for services rendered by them, to impart a sense of pride and self-respect to our soldiers and officers.

Besides material development of the State, we were determined to provide encouragement to intellectuals and literateurs. Environment had to be created for human values to proliferate. I convened meetings of journalists, historians, authors, playwrights and others to ascertain the facilities needed for gaining further proficiency in their respective fields. My government believed in maximum freedom of the Press. The memory of my, own days in journalism provided me enough momentum to see this fraternity flourish. We helped in the establishment of Press Clubs. Awards were instituted by the Language Department for excellence in works in the Punjabi, Urdu, Hindi and Dogri languages. Dogri, though the language of Jammu in the State of Jammu & Kashmir, has close kinship with the Punjabi language. Competitions among musicians gave them impetus. The poor and indigent writers could get financial aid for publication of their books. The families of the deceased writers were provided financial assistance.

I pleaded for remunerative prices to the producers of agricultural commodities. Finding the recommendations of the Agricultural Price Commission rather unrealistic and inadequate for the farmers, I took up their case for ralsmg the procurement prices of rice and wheat commensurate with the cost of production. My government made special efforts to ensure supply of essential inputs like fertilisers.. seeds and insecticides, besides providing incentives to wheat growers. The per acre production of wheat in Punjab became almost the highest in the world.

I was in favour of taking over by the government the trade in essential commodities like sugar, edible oil, diesel, kerosene and pulses to check rise in prices. In October 1973, my government decided that the bonus vouchers worth one hundred thirty five million rupees issued to farmers could be converted into cash from the Punjab State Co-operative Bank or used for the purchase of necessary inputs. Committees of representatives of people were set up in all the big markets to ensure that the farmers got reasonable prices for their cotton produce. We introduced a scheme to levy tax on rich farmers on a selective basis. My government drew a comprehensive plan to reclaim 26 lakh acres of land for cultivation. Eightysix per cent of the total geographical area of Punjab was under cultivation as against an average of fortynine per cent for the whole country. The cropping intensity as well as the cropped area increased. Fertiliser consumption per hectare went up. By the end of 1975, about fortysix thousand farmers in Punjab owned at least one tractor each.

Whereas on all-India basis about twenty five per cent of the total cultivated area was under irrigation, in Punjab, because of the intensive irrigation schemes, it went up to seventy two per cent. By the year 1975-76 four hundred and fifty thousand tubewells were installed in the State. My government adopted various irrigation schemes such as the use of surplus Ravi-Beas waters and the extension of perennial irrigation in the Upper Bari Doab canal tract. The Bhakra and Sirhind canal systems were remodelled, the Shah Nahar canal system was improved, the lining of channels was undertaken and a large number of tubewells were installed near the banks of the canals to augment the canal water for channelization to the deficient areas. On 16 January 1976, the foundation stone of the Shah Nahar feeder project was laid to regulate the irrigation water to about twenty-two thousand hectares. By March 1976, the production of food grains went up to nine million tons. The net value of farm produce increased to Rs. 1204 crores.

The community development package programmes saw their implementation at a rapid speed including education, health, sanitation, agriculture, dairy farming, animal husbandry, soil and water conservation, rural communications and welfare of weaker sections of the society. These and other measures brought prosperity to the rural folk on an unprecedented scale. The most important need of the rural people-the supply of drinking water was ensured for about one thousand and five hundred villages. The network of health services was expanded so as to provide protection against common diseases to 15 million people in over twelve thousand villages and over a hundred towns of the State. The life expectancy in Punjab went up to 58.6 years for females and 63.5 years for males.

Industries were set up in backward areas of the State. The agro-based and electronic industrial units were given a boost. An Electronic Nagar was set up at Mohali. About thirty-seven thousand small scale industrial units and one hundred and sixty medium and large industrial establishments were working in 1976-77. Hundreds of thousands of people got employment opportunities and industrial production increased by over two hundred per cent.

The poorest of the poor were given special attention to rise to reasonable positions. To encourage members of the Scheduled Castes and backward communities to gain self-respect, self-esteem and to attain competitive capabilities, they were given special coaching and free board and lodging facilities. Books were provided free of cost to the students of medical and engineering disciplines.

My aim was to transform every piece of agricultural land into a green field flowing with crops, to bring prosperity to every household and to see the face of every Punjabi villager and worker to be fresh as a pink rose.

Senior citizens—both male and female in indigent circumstances were granted old age pensions. Arrangements were made for the deserted, disabled and mentally disturbed women for free lodging and a subsistence allowance.

Rickshaw (passenger car) pullers were a highly depressed and exploited lot. They plied these contraptions owned by others, for which they had to pay daily hire charges. A scheme was introduced under which they could own rickshaws purchased on loans granted by the government, which they could repay with their earnings at the same rates at which they were paying hire charges to the exploiting owners. This scheme helped thousands of rickshaw pullers to have their own vehicles in a short time. Rickshaw *chalaks* became Rickshaw *malik.*

My twelve-points programme for the upliftment of the poor people in Punjab provided ample base for the 20 point socio-economic programme initiated by the Prime Minister. The implementation of the scheme of national permits for road transport helped facilitate the inter-state movement of essential goods, which contributed to checking the price rise. Cheap cloth was made freely available to rural masses to meet this primary need.

The setting up of production and work councils, greater participation of workers in production and management, formation of district level industrial production committees and a state-level tripartite committee contributed a great deal to homogeneous industrial relations and higher production with much lesser loss of mandays due to strikes or lockouts. The designation of Backward industrial areas gave great fillip to production, especially in the traditionally neglected areas.

The State government enacted the Dowry Prohibition (Amendment) Act in February 1976, making the existing law more stringent. Important steps were taken to implement the Apprenticeship Act, 1961, and to provide avenues for employment to those who had received training. Sports were made compulsory in schools and colleges. Students were encouraged to help farmers in reaping their harvests. Bureaucrats and Ministers including myself provided a helping hand in these operations. Road-building was made a co-operative enterprise between Panchayats and the government. Marketing committees were allowed to raise funds and gradually their area of contribution extended to paving streets, building guest houses and farmers' lodges. The marketing committees shared the funding of metalling roads with the government.

A code of conduct for Ministers prevented them from accepting invitations to functions arranged in their honour. To curb atrocities on women, the disposal of the mortal remains of a lady dying within five years of her wedlock was prohibited till the arrival of her parents. The investigation of such deaths could be conducted by an officer of the rank not less than that of a Deputy Superintendent of Police, and two doctors were required to conduct an autopsy in such cases instead of one.

Mindful of the need for creating high standards of teaching the graduate and post-graduate courses, my government looked after the interests of the University and college teachers. We revised their grades as per the recommendations of the University Grants Commission with retrospective effect. For teachers working in non-government affiliated colleges, the Punjab Affiliated Colleges (Security of Service of Teachers) Bill was passed by my government.

Chapter 19

GURU GOBIND SINGH MARG

It was the privilege of the Punjab government that the construction of Guru Gobind Singh Marg (Highway) stretching from Anandpur Sahib to Damdama Sahib, covering a distance of 640 km was completed. The life of Guru Gobind Singh, the Tenth and the last guru is a saga of sacrifice, valour of the highest order, bravery, courage, struggle against oppression, against religious fanaticism and exploitation and his deep love for the suffering humanity. In a brief life span of forty-two years, the tenth Guru achieved successes in various aspects of life unparalleled in human history. He was a great leader, an erudite scholar, a poet and protector of the poor, the helpless and the down-trodden. He created a new order, converting the meek and the weak into intrepid soldiers ready to make the supreme sacrifice in the noble cause of protection of the kingdom of God. He infused a new life into those who were considered members of low castes. He obliterated the distinctions between the high and the low and preached complete equality of status among all men and women. He combined compassion with courage and sacrifice with heroism. In homage to this unique personality, who changed the course of history in India, this immortal memorial was set up in the form of a Highway known after him, which connected ninety-one historic spots associated with him. The small town of Anandpur Sahib, the starting point of the Highway, is a picturesque place situated at the foot of the Shivalik hills. It was founded by the Ninth guru, Guru Tegh Bahadur in

1665 AD and began to be identified with the highest type of human bravery and sacrifice. Guru Gobind Singh spent almost three-fourths of his life-span of 42 at this spot. Here he initiated a sustained struggle against all kinds of inequities and discriminations. It was here that he wrote the most memorable verses embodying mystic visions and ethical values. To perpetuate the memory of the stirring saga of sacrifice of the Tenth Guru, the Punjab government decided on this enduring monument.

On the completion of the Highway, a big procession on the Marg was organised, which started from Takht Kesgarh Sahib on 10 April 1973. It included the sacred arms of the Guru and the horses, descendants of those used by the Guru .

These were brought especially from Nanded, a town in Maharashtra, where the Guru had breathed his last and where a magnificent memorial, Gurdwara Sach Khand Huzoor Sahib is situated. The procession was about 21 km. long. The enthusiasm of the people was boundless, as they were paying homage to a great soul, the one whose baptism administered to the helpless and hopeless people had wrought a miracle in the psychological make-up of those condemned to slavery and humiliation. They had earned a new self-respect and self-confidence and then challenged the armed might of their overweening and haughty rulers. The people now were only expressing their deepest gratitude to the saint-soldier, the hero and the saviour, who had given them a new dream and a new destiny, who had lent them pride and power, who had invested them with a voice and a will for victory. They now considered this road as trodden by those blessed feet and hallowed by the hooves of his spirited steed. I personally felt gratified to see the dream take a concrete and palpable shape. The procession culminated three days later on 13 April 1973, at Talwandi Sabo. Never before had the land of Punjab witnessed a concourse of pilgrims on such a massive scale. A sea of humanity surged in mighty waves over twenty-one kilo metres, which moved in ardour and ecstasy, bound together by a nostalgia of the Guru's grace and divine benediction. The Guru had chalked out noble ideals for the whole humanity, freedom from fear, renunciation and greed and avarice, protection of the poor and the oppressed, taking up the sword only in the defence of righteous causes and submission of self to the will of the Lord of the Universe. The Guru had sacrificed his father and all his four sons, so that people could live with dignity and honour.

As the mammoth crowd reached the first pillar, a Harijan worker, Bhajan Singh, who had laboured in the construction of the highway, was asked to unveil it. This mass of humanity entered Damdama Sahib on April 13. It was the first of Baisakh of the Bikrimi Calendar, the day when in 1699 Guru Gobind Singh had given first baptism to and was himself baptised by the Five Beloveds. Singh Sahib Sant Singh, a descendent of the legendary Akali Phula Singh presented me with honours, which I accepted with reverence and respect for the great Guru as a servant of the people and trustee of their progress and development, as an aspirant for their peace and prosperity.

Many Sikh and non-Sikh Organisations participated in the festivities. The Sanatan Dharma Sabha, Arya Samaj, Muslim Majlis, Jains, Buddhists, Christians, the Shiromani Gurdwara Prabandhak Committee were all partners in this procession, the soul-stirring pilgrimage. Mrs. Indira Gandhi in her message on the occasion, described Guru Gobind Singh as one of the most eminent heroes of our history, who by his spiritual attainment and faith, became a great personage. By his courage and fight against injustices, she said, he became an inspiration to all Indians. The prominent Christian leader of Amritsar, the Rev. George Harish paying tributes on behalf of the Christian community said that according to the Guru's teachings, true religion lies in resisting tyranny and oppression, in serving humanity, in mutual love and help to each other. The Nawab of Malerkotla said that Guru Gobind Singh was venerated not only by the Sikhs, but also by the Muslims.

Chapter 20

AMITY AND GOODWILL

The foundation of the freedom movement in the country had been laid on the concept of human equality and secularism. These principles were sanctified by the Constitution given by the people of India unto themselves. To strengthen and promote this spirit, my government took several steps to assist in various ways the followers of different faiths to flourish in their religious pursuits. Ram Tirath is a sacred spot of the Hindus, about seventeen kilometres from Amritsar, where the majestic Golden Temple stands in he middle of a magnificent tank. According to legend, when Sita, the consort of Lord Rama left her kingdom, she came to the abode (ashram) of Rishi Balmiki at this spot and stayed there for long, where her sons Luv and Kush were brought up under the benign care of the great savant. The Rishi imparted all the training in scriptures and weapons to them befitting royal princes. I was fascinated by the hoary past of this temple and my government sanctioned twentyfour lakhs of rupees for its renovation and construction of approach roads and the lodging of pilgrims. It was here that Luv and Kush, having grown into strapping youths, had stopped the horses of their father, resulting in a show of strength, in which they had the upper hand.

Luv and Kush established their own kingdoms and founded the cities of Lahore and Kasoor respectively. Guru Gobind Singh has recapituated in his writings the great conflicts that arose between the descendants of the two brothers resulting in the victory of the dynasty of Luv and defeat of the family of Kush. The vanquished retreated to Kashi (Varanasi), where they studied the Vedas and came. to be known as Vedis (Bedis). After a lapse of time the Vedis were summoned by the King of the Luv dynasty to recite the Vedas to propitiate the gods with a promise to ask for anything they cherished as recompense. They pleaded for the domain of their forefathers to be redeemed. The ruler of the Luv dynasty readily agreed and handed over his kingdom to the Vedis who were overjoyed and blessed the descendants of Luv with the promise of reincarnation of a spiritual king in another millennium. As per legend, Guru Nanak descended from the Bedi dynasty and the fourth guru, Guru Ram Das was a descendant of the Luv family of the Sodhis.

I set up a Trust for the Ram Tirath temple. Some scholars are of the opinion that Lord Rama and Lord Krishna were more of leaders of cultural renaissance than religious preceptors. My government made a firm resolve to preserve the common Indian cultural heritage. We were guided by the same concept in constructing the Guru Gobind Singh Marg.

We set up a stadium naming it after the great martyr, Baba Deep Singh. Such endeavours met with some opposition from our political detractors, but received unqualified support from the common man. Encouraged by mass approbation, we continued our crusade to preserve our cultural inheritance. A hospital was set up in Bhatinda named after Bhai Mani Singh, the scribe of the Adi Granth at Damdama Sahib, who was later martyred for his refusal to pay an unfair monetary tribute to the then rulers. A hospital was set up at Dasuha in the memory of the five Pandavas, eminent characters of the Mahabharata, and named after the most famous of them, Arjuna. In Amritsar, a school was established after the name of Swaroop Rani, the mother of Pandit Jawaharlal Nehru. In Patiala a colony in the memory of the child martyr Haqiqat Rai was set up. Similarly Sahibzada Ajit Singh Nagar was raised in the memory of the eldest son of the tenth Guru.

The title of Punjab Mata (Mother of Punjab) was given to the mother of Martyr Bhagat Singh, besides providing her with a car, a sizeable monthly pension, and certain other privileges. She was honoured in a gathering of representatives of all communities and political parties.

With the help of the Central Government, we repatriated the mortal remains of the martyrs Udham Singh and Madan Lal Dhingra from the United Kingdom, and cremated them with State honours.

I participated in the celebrations of the tricentenary of martyrdom of Guru Tcgh Bahadur. Mrs. Indira Gandhi accompanied me to this great event. In a mass gathering of about one and a half million people, she paid homage to the Guru as a martyr to the cause of the whole of India. She exhorted the countrymen to revere the memory of this great martyr, who made supreme sacrifice to defend the basic right of every individual to profess his own faith and creed.

After consultations with leaders of all affiliations like Arya Samaj. Sanatan Dharma, the Jain, Muslim, Sikh and other faiths smoking in all government offices was prohibited, as it is highly injurious to health. It was hailed as a right step by everyone. We named schools, libraries and link roads after those members of the Armed forces, who had laid down their lives defending our borders. We decided to hold commemorative functions in the honour of national martyrs.

Chapter 21

THE EMERGENCY AND THE OPPOSITION

In the wake of the emergency imposed by Mrs. Indira Gandhi, the Akalis in Punjab decided to launch an agitation, which proved to be a long drawn affair. Despite my reasoning with them not to use gurudwaras as a base for political agitations, they announced a Morcha, for which they had the support of Jana Sangh, Janata Party and other political parties in opposition to the Congress. I ordered the arrest of about one hundred and fifty activists and five hundred others. But the Akalis continued sending groups of volunteers to court arrest for about nineteen months. Throughout this period my emphasis was on the fact that it was sacrilegious to use holy places like gurdwaras for political purposes. Later, I ordered the release of members of Jana Sangh and other parties, barring a few [ana Sangh activists in Ludhiana and Amritsar. Anyone seeking pardon was released. When the Akalis refused to relent in sending their volunteers, I adopted the policy of apprehending them in the morning and releasing them in or near their own villages at dusk. This process went on for nineteen months. The stubborn were sent to the jails. In over a year and a half the Akalis mustered about fortytwo thousand volunteers and though they had tried to invest their movement with religious fervour, it had hardly anything religious about it.

My government granted parole to a large number of detainees. I did not allow more than five thousand detenus in jails at any point of time, as the excess would have led to the need for accommodating them in jails outside Punjab. One day, while I was passing through Amritsar, someone pointed out to me the residence of the leading [ana Sangh leader, Balram Tandon, who was on parole for three weeks. I visited him and extended his parole. Once I visited the hospital to see an ailing Congressman, where, I was told, the wife of another [ana Sangh leader, Dr. Baldev Prakash, who himself was in jail, was admitted. At the request of the sympathisers of the family, I granted parole to Baldev Prakash and extended it later at their behest. Lala Jagat Narain, who was in the Patiala Jail was sent to the hospital. Like him, the Akali leaders such as Jagdev Singh Talwandi and Jathedar Mohan Singh Tur were looked after very well in the hospitals, Any detainee, who felt indisposed, was provided prompt and specialised treatment. The emergency was opposed by political detractors of Mrs. Gandhi along with intellectuals, but the common man felt relieved, because of the discipline it generated in public life and the laxity in behaviour it checked. It was a mixed blessing in some ways. The mishandling, over-enthusiasm and the imperious attitude of its protagonists including some of the Chief Ministers were responsible for the large scale aversion to the Emergency witnessed in the country.

The opposition went full blast against Mrs. Gandhi. Jai Prakash Narayan spearheaded a strong campaign against the ruling party. Holding of public rallies exposing the Congress as a morally bankrupt organisation and thus unfit to govern the country became a frequent sight. In a speech, Narayan called upon members of the police and the armed forces to disregard unfair orders issued by the authorities. This sent shock waves in the ruling party and galvanised them into hasty action.

Though I was present in one of the meetings in which the possibility of declaration of Emergency was discussed, the timing of its actual proclamation was kept a closely guarded secret. I and some other Congress Chief Ministers were told to return to our respective States. At 8 p.m. that day, we were asked to introduce censorship of the press. Internal emergency was declared on 25 June 1975. A fierce agitation ensued in Punjab, though the edge of the protest was not as sharp in other states. Jai Prakash Narayan and Morarji Desai were detained in Haryana. Owing to illness, Narayan was got admitted to the Post-Graduate Medical Institute in Chandigarh.

I met the Sarvodaya leader, Acharya Vinoba Bhave, who felt cut up with and disapproved the detention of Jai Prakash Narayan. But he extolled the virtues of the general discipline generated by the emergency. One of the prerequisites of the successful implementation of the Emergency Rule was to strengthen the intelligence machinery to keep the finger on the pulse of the people. My experience had shown that even the Intelligence personnel often exercised too much of caution and entertained reservations in presenting a true picture to the leader, and fed him on the information he was eager to get. I, therefore, checked every piece of information with a second line of intelligence, I specially set up for the purpose with utmost secrecy. I warned the officials against the indiscriminate censorship. They were told to use their discretion to the utmost extent possible and to be liberal. Constructive criticism was not to be discouraged, but encouraged. Only malicious, mischievous and provocative comments were to be disallowed. Owing to this approach, I did not have any serious difficulty with the press. As I believed in taking the bureaucracy and the people into confidence, I did not have to face much alienation from the masses either.

I was constrained to make it clear to Mrs. Gandhi that I being the Chief Minister and the first servant of the people of Punjab, I could not accept any injustice to the people of the State with regard to the river waters. As the level of the sub-soil water was going down and the tube-wells were being affected, any discrimination to the peasants and farmers of Punjab would lead to the impoverishment of agriculture and result in undesirable situation.

But I did face alienation from another unexpected quarter. It was Sanjay Gandhi. On differences about the river waters and the future of Chandigarh I had a tough time. Bansi Lal, the Chief Minister of the neighbouring Haryana and

Sanjay Gandhi developed a close rapport between themselves. Had Bansi Lal not manipulated things at that juncture, perhaps, the river waters dispute between Punjab arid Haryana would not have assumed the proportions as it did later. It was, believed that Bansi Lal had ingratiated himself with Sanjay Gandhi by selling land in the Gurgaon district of his State adjoining Delhi for Sanjay's Maruti factory at a throw-away price, He thus commanded great influence with the Gandhi family,

I liked Sanjay Gandhi for his dynamism and youthful energy, He was quick at taking decisions and was an untiring worker. He was shrewd and intelligent, extrovert but over-ambitious. He was easy to be pleased and more easy to be annoyed. If happy with some one, he would go all out to benefit him, but if angry, he would know no limits of harm he could inflict on his adversaries. He attended the All India Congress Committee session in 1975 at Chandigarh, where he was pushed into prominence.

Mrs. Indira Gandhi was very keen to reshuffle her cabinet. In fact she wanted to ease out Swaran Singh and Jagjivan Ram, Their ambition to wear the mantle of Prime Ministership, by advising her to resign from the post following the Allahabad High Court judgement, rankled in her mind, She was quite aware of my rapport with Jagjivan Ram, She, therefore, asked my opinion how to proceed about it. I advised her against the ouster of the veteran Harijan leader, who had a considerable following in almost every region of the country. About Swaran Singh, I told her that as far as I knew, the gentleman had really not entertained a concrete desire to occupy the chair, though it came to be widely known that at the time of her adversity, he had failed to come and commiserate with her. Mrs. Gandhi gave up the idea of taking action to drop either of them from the cabinet at that stage.

I was elected to the Working Committee of the All India Congress and so was Bansi Lal, Chief Minister of Haryana.

Mrs. Indira Gandhi announced fresh elections to the Lok Sabha in January 1977, though one year was still left in the term of the House, I was not a party to this decision. To oppose her, the Opposition parties joined together to form the

Janata Party. Mrs. Gandhi and her son, Sanjay suffered defeat at the polls. In a massive anti-Congress wave, the Party was swept away from power in many States like Punjab, Haryana, Uttar Pradesh, Himachal Pradesh, Rajasthan and Madhya Pradesh. In Punjab, Congress could not capture even one of the thirteen seats for the Lok Sabha.

The stalwarts like Swaran Singh, Darbara Singh and G.S. Dhillon all lost at the hustings. In the Haryana state, only 17 per cent votes were cast in favour of the Congress, with many candidates losing their security deposits, whereas more than 36 per cent votes in Punjab went to this Party and no security deposits were forfeited. The Congress and the Opposition candidates had run a neck and neck race.

After Mrs. Gandhi's debacle, her close associates like D.K. Barooah, Congress President, and Y.B. Chavan, the senior Union Minister, turned their backs on her. It was a somersault least expected of friends, followers and fellow-Congressmen. Mrs. Gandhi told me that in Y.B. Chavan's reckoning, she had become a liability to the Congress. Swaran Singh was mooting the idea of collective leadership.

The lukewarm attitude of the Congress leaders like Brahmananda Reddy, D.K. Barooah, Y.B. Chavan and Swaran Singh towards Mrs. Gandhi and to persons like me, became evident at the time the Faridkot Lok Sabha seat fell vacant, after the election of Parkash Singh Badal to the Punjab Legislative Assembly. Taking advantage of the baseless allegations levelled against me by the Akali-Janata regime, the above mentioned Congress leaders resisted the efforts of Mrs. Gandhi and Kamlapati Tripathi for the issue of a Congress ticket to me for contesting a by-election. I was also asked by the Punjab Congress Chief telegraphically to withdraw from the Anandpur Sahib constituency. The blatant discrimination against persons owing allegiance to Mrs. Gandhi compelled them to call upon the Congress President Brahmananda Reddy to summon a meeting of the Congress Parliamentary Board to consider the matter, but he failed to oblige. The aggrieved supporters of Mrs. Gandhi, therefore, called a convention for unity on 1-2 January 1978. I was keen to make the convention successful, but my efforts were sabotaged by some prominent persons.

Swaran Singh sought to haul me up for criticizing Brahmananda Reddy and demanded disciplinary action against me. The two-day convention of the pro-Indira segment declared itself as the real Congress and Mrs. Indira Gandhi was named its President. In a resolution, she was authorised to reorganise the Party in consultation with seven members of the Congress Working Committee present at the convention. I extended my full support to the resolution, as a result of which I, along with 26 others, was expelled by the Punjab Pradesh Congress on 4 January 1978. It only inspired me to work for the Congress (I) with greater zeal. I campaigned for the party candidates in elections in Andhra Pradesh and Karnataka for the State Assemblies. On 16 February 1978, while I was addressing a public meeting along with Dev Raj Urs, then Chief Minister of Karnataka, at Bangalore we were attacked with stones. 1 was hit on my head and chest resulting in a long and painful hospitalization.

Chapter 22

PERSECUTION

After the dismissal of my government by the newly elected Akali-Janata regime, I was faced with a serious problem of residential accommodation. With quite a bit of difficulty, I was able to rent a small house at Chandigarh, where I stayed up to October 1978, but due to stringent surveillance by the police, and harassment of the hapless house-owner, I virtually felt suffocated, and consequently had to shift to my daughter's house. Other house-owners were scared to rent out their accommodation to me due to the dread of the police.

After about four months of its formation, the Janata Government at the Centre appointed a Commission comprising Justice J.C. Shah to inquire into the excesses committed during the emergency imposed by Mrs. Gandhi. The Chief Minister, Badal announced in the State Assembly on 11 January 1978, the appointment of a one-man Emergency Excesses Enquiry Authority consisting of Justice Gurdev Singh, a former Judge of the Punjab and Haryana High Court to look into the matters covered by the terms of reference of the Justice Shah Commission. Badal announced that 30 of the 120 complaints referred by the Shah Commission would be investigated by the Authority and the remaining complaints would be put before a Sessions Judge.

Persons close to me were subjected. to physical and mental torture. Onkar Chand, Secretary, Punjab Congress Committee was arrested and assaulted. He was hung upside down.

Tirath Singh Sobti, Chairman, Marketing Board was put in manacles so that he could not sit. Swaran Singh, my car driver's legs were pulled apart. He was not allowed to sleep for several days. My personal attendant, Shalig Ram Bhardwaj had to run for his life and he had to remain underground for a considerable time. My Personal Secretary, Kulwant Singh was harassed and badly insulted. An Act was amended by the State Assembly to remove my son-in-law Surinder Singh Virdi from his job. They intended to put him to physical torture too, but he escaped to Siliguri to spend some time with his brother, to thwart the efforts of the State government.

On 12 January 1978, I was intensively interrogated by the Punjab Vigilance Bureau at Chandigarh about the collection of funds for the Congress session in Mattaur in 1975 and amassing of wealth. I told my interrogators that I had not collected any money for myself or my family. The Akali-Janata Government in Punjab vied with the Centre in hauling the Congress (I) leaders over the nails.

I was summoned by the Authority to appear before it regarding the appointment of one Zora Singh Brar to the post of Chairman of the PEPSU Road Transport Corporation. In a procedural wrangle, I sought adjournment of the proceedings to enable me to appeal to the High Court against its rulings. As I came out of the Authority's office, I was arrested by the police. I complained to the Authority against this action. I had to furnish a personal bond and execute a surety to gain freedom.

Breathless efforts were seen being made to institute as many legal cases against me as possible in a bid to find some chinks in my armour. Yet another summon was issued by the Enquiry Authority for my appearance on 20 September 1978, to probe the appointment of Ajaib Singh Muchaki, an Advocate, as an Administrative Member of the Punjab State Electricity Board. To express my resentment against such frivolous cases, I did not appear before the Authority, which resulted in many a summons and bailable warrant being issued for my arrest. I opted for arrest and was taken in custody on 9 October 1978. Three days later, on re-appearance before the judge, I declined to furnish bail or a personal bond. But, surprisingly, I was set at liberty.

Still in another case, this time about the appointment of Kailash Chand, as Chief Engineer, I was constrained to tell the Commission of the extra-ordinary procedure adopted by it in framing its rules. Since it was- clear as daylight that laboured attempts were being made by the Government to implicate me in cases of favouritism as Chief Minister, I chose to register my protest by boycotting the Commission.

I approached the Supreme Court with the plea to transfer certain criminal cases pending against me from courts in Punjab to courts elsewhere, as the atmosphere in the State was hostile to me, thanks to the inimical attitude of persons holding high positions. The Supreme Court issued stay orders in some cases, which irked the State Government. They lost no time in contemplating alternative means to cause me inconvenience. Then about thirty criminal cases were filed against me and five erstwhile members of my Council of Ministers, and the State Government thought of trying us in a special court.

I was summoned by the Gupta Commission to answer the allegation about the illegal help extended to Sanjay Gandhi for purchase of fifteen Maruti road rollers, for which, it was said that I had put pressure on the concerned Departments of the Government.

It gave me no surprise when the Emergency Excesses Enquiry Authority indicted me for favouritism in appointments. These proceedings had been conducted ex-parte, but not a single charge of corruption or malfeasance against me could be substantiated.

The efforts to drag me from one court to another and from one Commission to another, were quite obvious. I was being denied any respite and at the same time the endeavour was to pull me down in public esteem. Being a member of the Congress (I) Working Committee, 1 had often to visit Delhi for consultations with Mrs. Indira Gandhi and to attend to party work.

The Akali-Janata Government was good to CPI(M), but quite hostile to CPI. The workers of the latter Party were subjected to a baton charge, which was quite unwarranted. I demanded a judicial inquiry against this excessive action. The policemen in the State launched an agitation, to curb which the State Government came down on them with a heavy hand. I could not put up with the vindictive attitude of the State Government and, therefore, met the President, Neelam Sanjiva Reddy to seek his intervention in the matter.

As the Chief Minister, I had taken several measures to improve the quality of life of the weaker sections of the society in the State, especially the Scheduled Castes, Scheduled Tribes and Backward Classes. For obvious reasons, they were not getting a right dispensation from the Akali regime. I could not ignore their plight and, therefore, I had to organise their conventions to seek for them fair and just treatment. The teachers and students also started an agitation and I urged the Governor to direct the Government to enter into a dialogue with the aggrieved parties.

The Punjab Akalis had been insisting on the enactment of an all-India Gurdwara Act for management of Gurdwaras by a single body, which undoubtedly would establish their domination over gurdwara management all over the country. The Gurdwaras have enormous financial resources contributed mainly by offerings made by the devout in many ways. An All-India management of the Sikh holy shrines would turn them into a hot bed of struggle for political influence. To ensure the utmost sanctity of the gurdwaras and to spare them of unnecessary interference, I took the stand that historical gurdwaras in other States should better be managed by the people living in those regions.

One incident of boisterous behaviour of some Akali leaders occurred in August 1978, during my stoppage at Sirhind, while on my way to Chandigarh. Accompanied by Beant Singh, Member of the Legislative Assembly and Darbara Singh Bhullar, Managing Director of the Faridkot Cooperative Bank, I sojourned at the residence of Vaid Harkishan, a Congress(I) worker. One Gurdev Singh Khalsa, an Akali activist alongwith his cohorts came and attacked the place. The local police were contacted, but they were indifferent. The Akali workers wanted me and my companions to come out and face their wrath. Their intent was to kill. They threatened to set the premises on fire. My companion, Darbara Singh Bhullar went out, but he was attacked and seriously injured. One Akali worker, Davinder Singh Pappu fired shots from his revolver in the presence of the local police officers, who stood as silent spectators. The hooligans then started biickbatting and damaging our cars. Some personal effects, books and documents were looted trom my vehicle. Darbara Singh Bhullar barely escaped with his life. His fingers were fractured. Beant Singh, MLA contacted the Inspector General of Police and the Deputy Commissioner, Patiala telling them of the grave situation. I contacted the Governor of the State, and then after a few hours the Senior Superintendent of Police reached the spot. During all these hours we were virtually made prisoners by the hooligans, while the children of our host were crying their lives out in fear of violence and death.

The business community in Sirhind observed a strike the next day in protest against this outrage. I sent a telegram to the Prime Minister, Morarji Desai, apprising him of the high-handed attitude of the ruling Akalis in Punjab. While a few workers of the Akali Dal and the [anata Party were apprehended, ironically an Akali worker lodged a report against me and some other Congressmen for an attempt to murder. It was alleged by him that he was physically assaulted with intent to murder at Sirhind. Several Congress (I) leaders lodged their protests against hooliganism and the attack on me and demanded a judicial enquiry. Unfortunately, no action was taken on these complaints.

In November 1978, Mrs. Indira Gandhi was elected to the Lok Sabha from the Chikmagalur constituency in Karnataka, but the House took a decision to deprive her of her seat and charged her with a breach of privilege and contempt of the House. She was arrested and taken to the Tihar Jail. It caused a shock and widespread resentment among her party men, who courted arrest in many parts of the country. In Punjab, over three thousand workers went to jails. I visited' a number of jails in the State to meet these prisoners of conscience, who had volunteered to go through the ordeal of imprisonment to express their anger over the persecution of their leader. On 3 January 1979, I and some other Congress leaders organised a protest against the vindictive attitude of the Punjab

Government resulting in our arrest near the residence of the Chief Minister for violating prohibitory orders. We were remanded in judicial custody for two weeks. Gurdial Singh Dhillon, former Speaker of the Lok Sabha was one of us. On the day of hearing in the court, we did not put up any defence, as we expressed concern over the suppression of civil liberties, undue repression of the peaceful Congress (I) workers and the cruelty perpetrated on the volunteers by the State machinery. We were sentenced to ten days' simple imprisonment, but since we had already spent about two weeks in jail, we were set free. The Punjab Pradesh Congress (I) Committee took a decision to continue the agitation against the Government's apathy in ordering a judicial enquiry over the excesses committed against the Congress (I) volunteers by the police. So vigorous was the popular sympathy for the aggrieved Congress (I) workers that the Akali-Janata Government was compelled to withdraw all cases against them. Consequently, we withdrew our agitation on 24 February 1979.

There were tremors of dissensions among the Janata leaders in the Central Government. Morarji Desai was replaced by Chaudhury Charan Singh as the Prime Minister. Raj Narain, the stormy petrel of the Socialist Party had quite a conspicuous role to play in the dividing game. Because of Congress (I)'s refusal to extend its support to the Charan Singh Ministry, the coalition formed by the Janata and Congress (S) fell on 20 August 1979. The Lok Sabha was dissolved by the President with orders for fresh elections later in the year. It provided great relief to the Congress (I), which had been at the receiving end for two years. In Punjab, Congress (I) contested from all the thirteen constituencies. It was suggested by Sanjay Gandhi that I should have an election duel with Swaran Singh, who was then leading the rival Congress, from the Jullunder constituency, but the latter decided to stay away from the hustings, whereupon I accepted a ticket for the Hoshiarpur constituency. The Akali Dal supported Balbir Singh Chaudhari, the Lok Dal candidate. Yagya Dutt Sharma was the Bharatiya Janata Party nominee. In the polling held on 3 January 1980, I was declared elected with 223,976 votes, whereas the Lok Oal and the Bharatiya Janata party candidates received 98,790 and 95,660 votes respectively. A whole chapter on the vicissitudes of Congress (I) and Mrs. Indira Gandhi personally was over and a new era of rehabilitation of the Congress (I) Party dawned over the Indian horizon.

Chapter 23

UNION CABINET

Congress (I) emerged winner with a thumping majority. Its ignominious defeat in 1977 was avenged thoroughly and it was catapulted back into power and also in public esteem. Mrs. Indira Gandhi was savouring her victory and did not seem in any haste to form a cabinet. For good ten days, names of persons to be inducted into the Council of Ministers were being discussed. The Punjab hopefuls were camping in the Punjab Bhavan. My political detractors tried to make full use of their leisure, working against my possible inclusion in the Central cabinet. I happened to meet Mrs. Indira Gandhi every now and then. One morning I reached her residence while she was dictating some notes to R.K. Dhawan, her Special Assistant. She called me in and there was a brief discussion about Punjab. Taking me aside, Sanjay Gandhi whispered in my eat that I should not talk to his Mummy about myself in the context of the Council of Ministers. I told him that I had no such intention. Joining in the discussion then between me and Mrs. Gandhi, Sanjay asked me, if it would be feasible to choose a Speaker for the Lok Sabha from Punjab. The name of Balram Jakhar was mentioned. I expressed my support and felt that he could be suitable for this job. Mrs. Gandhi agreed.

The day Mrs. Gandhi's cabinet was to be sworn in, I visited her residence in the morning. She casually told me that the members selected would be reaching the President's House by 10.00 a.m. and that I should also make it convenient to be there. She gave me no indication whatsoever, that I would be a member of her Council of Ministers. I took it easy and sauntered away. Quite disinterestedly, I made for the Rashtrapati Bhavan, where I was slightly late to reach. Almost every person of consequence was there. Members were being called to take the oaths of office and secrecy in alphabetical order. To my utter surprise, the Cabinet Secretary walked up to my seat and handed over the text of the Oath to me. I felt a ripple of joy in my heart, but, perhaps, few could have read it on my face. I had learnt it long ago to exercise control over my emotions. Adversity could not distract me easily, nor could happy tidings make me feel exultant. So sudden was the gesture of giving me the text of the oath that momentarily I suspected it to be a mistake. Probing rapidly the deep recesses of my mind, I could sense the germination of a vague ambition to be a Minister in the Central Cabinet. I guessed that I would probably be assigned the portfolio of Defence or Agriculture, and never could I entertain the hope of being invested with the responsibility of Home Affairs. The chair of Home Minister had been so illustriously occupied by stalwarts like Sardar Vallabh Bhai Patel and Pandit Govind Vallabh Pant. It was only after the swearing-in ceremony, that I came to know of my name having been included in the list after long and careful consideration, but it has always remained a mystery to me, why Mrs. Gandhi did not consider it necessary to inform me of this fact expressly and seriously. I recollected a casual remark by Yash Pal Kapur, a former member of Mrs. Gandhi's personal staff, that I was the future Home Minister of India, though I had taken it only as having been said in a lighter vein. I would have been more credulous, if it had come from R.K. Dhawan, whose loyalty to Mrs. Gandhi was synonymous with his astuteness. His allegiance was another name of his adoration for her. His attitude towards me was helpful, but he would not hesitate to be good to my detractors as well. I never resented anyone having friendly relations with my adversaries, unless I perceived a deliberate effort to harm my vital interests.

After the swearing-in-ceremony, the Prime Minister escorted senior members of her cabinet to their respective offices in the Secretariat. She graciously accompanied me to my room. As Minister of Home Affairs, I became a member of the Political Affairs Committee of the cabinet, as also of the Appointments Committee and some other committees.

I told Mrs. Gandhi that before taking up any new assignment or taking any momentous step, I used to pay my obeisance at the Curdwara at Anandpur Sahib, the city of Bliss, made sacrosanct by the tenth Guru. She asked me to follow this practice without any delay. I travelled by train incognito and, from the Railway station, made straight for Gurdwara Takht Sri Kesgarh Sahib, where I wanted to say my prayers Remembrance of God every moment has been a part of my existence, and to say prayers has been my constant creed. But never have I tried to seek any particular favour of fulfilment of a desire from the Almighty. Eternal beneficence of the Lord has been my book of faith. I have been fascinated by the holy ambience of Anandpur Sahib. When I was once locked in any election contest with Jathedar Shivdev Singh from the Anandpur Sahib constituency, reaching the holy temple I found my adversary coming out of the complex along with the priest, who had said prayers on his behalf. In solicitous expression of warmth, the priest offered to say prayers for me too, but I respectfully declined the overture. I vowed then that I would never ask anyone to pray for me. The omniscient and omnipresent God knows every one's needs, ambitions and aspirations and there is hardly any need to enlighten Him of one's expectations. His will shall always prevail and He knows what is in one's interest. I won the election. The second time I was to fight election from the same constituency, I went to pay my obeisance and was successful again. After having been elected leader of the Assembly Congress Party and being sworn in as Chief Minister, I had gone straight to Gurdwara Kesgarh Sahib and then to the Secretariat in Chandigarh to begin my work. A report on this itinerary was welcomed both by Sikhs and Hindus. When I stood for election to Parliament, I made pilgrimage to Gurdwara Kesgarh Sahib, and though I had a strong wish to succeed at the hustings, I did not articulate this desire. Having attained victory, I visited the holy spot once again for thanksgiving. After being inducted in the Central Cabinet, I had a strong urge to visit the temple to express my gratitude to the Almighty. Later, when I was chosen to be the President of the Republic, I went to Gurdwara Kesgarh Sahib once again to acknowledge the Lord's grace.

On assuming office, I called a meeting of all Heads of Department under the Home Ministry and for three or four days thoroughly studied its working. My predecessor, Chaudhary Charan Singh, had ensured that the Ministry of Home Affairs should encompass all that had once been under the charge of the first Home Minister of free India, Sardar Vallabh Bhai Patel. I inherited a sprawling Ministry including subjects like Personnel, Police, Internal Security, Justice, Intelligence services, Administrative Reforms, Regional Councils, Scheduled Castes and Scheduled Tribes and Union Territories etc. I suggested to the Prime Minister that in case she wanted to trim the Home Ministry of its feathers, this was the right time to do so, because such an exercise a little while later might cause embarrassment to me. The Prime Minister declared she did not intend to slice any part of the Ministry and assigned two Ministers of State to me, authorising me to allocate work to them. They were Yogendra Makwana and Venkatasubbiah, who was later appointed Governor of Bihar and later of Karnataka. The Secretary to the Ministry, though very competent, was the one who was responsible for stern measures against Mrs. Gandhi during the Janata rule. After three months or so, he was eased out.

One of the first tasks I focussed my attention on was enhancing the pensions of freedom fighters and speedily processing the applications of those who had not been covered under the scheme earlier. They were allowed medical facilities and orders were issued to accord them a place of honour in the celebrations of the Independence Day and the Republic Day. Freedom fighters should be next only to the Ministers on such occasions.

Scheduled Castes, Scheduled Tribes and Minorities needed special attention and my Ministry took several measures for their welfare.

Communal riots in various parts of the country came as a great challenge. Law and order is a State subject, but whenever there was a communal outrage or large scale killings, crimes against Scheduled Castes, Scheduled Tribes or the Minorities, arson or loot, it caused serious concern to us at the Centre and we thought of some long-range remedies to prevent such ugly situations from developing in secular India. Our two pronged policy was to strengthen the forces of harmony, amity and goodwill and to adopt a strategy that would restore a sense of security in the minorities. The separatist tendencies had to be curbed and the feelings of fraternity and national integrity had to be fostered. Disruptive and fissiparous elements seemed to be eager to strike at the very foundations of free, socialist, secular India. They were fanning casteism, communalism, regionalism and parochialism of every kind. On 25 February 1980, in the Pipra village of Bihar, hardly 30 km away from Patna, an armed mob mowed down a number of Harijans, economically very poor and injured many more. Women were molested, the huts were set ablaze and a large scale looting was done. I was moved to tears seeing the plight of those deprived, hapless people, whose only fault was that they were destitutes and demanded justice. I directed the authorities to seize all arms in the area, as the Harijans and other weaker sections were being intimidated. Properties of some families of land-owners were also attached.

On 9 May 1980, clashes between Harijans and caste Hindus took place in the Kafalta village in the Almora District of Uttar Pradesh, which sent shock waves in the area. Some fifteen persons were massacred. I visited the place of the violence and asked the State administration to appoint a special judge to try the culprits.

On 13 August 1980, major communal riots were triggered in the prosperous city of Moradabad in Uttar Pradesh. It seemed to be a sinister attempt on the part of those who did not relish communal amity and national unity. Stories full of anguish carne to light, which would put any man of conscience to shame. On 18 November 1981, in a small village of Deoli in the Mainpuri district of Uttar Pradesh, twentyfour Harijans were done to death including women and children by some well-to-do Thakurs. Visiting the place I was reinforced in my conviction that the backward classes in the country were being victimised with vengeance for the only reason that they were poor, socially backward or belonged to the so-called low castes. On 30 December 1981, in the Sadhupur village about 40 km from Deoli, ten Harijans were killed including five women with the help of sophisticated weapons. I visited the scene of the carnage. These incidents saddened my heart and more so because of complaints of communal bias on the part of the police, which was supposed to be the major instrument of keeping law and order. We raised half a dozen new battalions of Central Reserve Police and issued special instructions for giving weightage to the Harijans and the Muslims in the recruitment. We also issued instructions for reorientation of training to the police and para-military forces aimed at more effective control of the mobs with the least casualties.

I was firmly of the view that the intelligence machinery had to be strengthened and made more efficient for curbing the activities of the disruptive elements. I was in favour of offering more incentives to officials working in the Intelligence Bureau as they had to pay the price in anonymity away from the razzle dazzle of the executive branch. In fact I wanted to separate the Intelligence Bureau from the Police, as it would be unrealistic to expect unbiased and unadulterated intelligence from the officials belonging to the Police department, who were also responsible for maintaining law and order. The Central Intelligence officials worked in collaboration with the State Intelligence departments, which are influenced by the State Ministers. I was also in favour of setting up a Banks Security force on the lines of the Central Industrial Security Force. I ordered intensive training for the latter organization.

Chapter 24

THE CONGRESS (I) AND THE NON-CONGRESS (I) STATES

When Congress (I) came back into power, the question of the non-Congress (I) ruled States loomed large over the horizon. So momentous and massive was the Congress (I) victory, that it gave rise to a natural impression that the Opposition parties no longer represented the will of the electorate. There were demands to dismiss the non-Congress (I) governments and to order fresh elections in those States. Congress (I) wanted to implement its poll pledges and to make certain amendments in the Constitution. I told Mrs. Gandhi that personally I was not in favour of dissolving the non-Congress (I) State Assemblies. It appeared, however, that those governments had themselves lost self-confidence to a great extent. In an emergency meeting of the Central Cabinet on 17 February 1980, it was decided to recommend the dissolution of nine State Assemblies. The action of the Janata Government in dissolving nine Congress (I) ruled State Assemblies in 1977 after their landslide victory was repeated by Congress (I). The Secretary in the Home Ministry, T.CA. Srinivasa Raghvan, used almost the same wording in the note, as was done at the time of the [anata regime taking similar action.

The Assemblies now dissolved were those of Bihar, Gujarat Maharashtra, Madhya Pradesh, Orissa, Punjab, Rajasthan, Tamil Nadu and Uttar Pradesh. The same day these nine States were placed under the President's rule under Article 356 of the Constitution. As for Haryana, thirtyeight members of the State Assembly led by Bhajan Lal had crossed over to Congress (I) on 22 January 1980, from the Janata Party, thus averting the need for its dissolution.

One of the most important and urgent tasks, before the new Government was to extend the reservation of seats in the Lower House of Parliament and State Assemblies for the Scheduled Castes and Scheduled Tribes. The reservation was due to lapse on 27 January 1980. I piloted a Bill on 24 January for the 45th amendment of the Constitution with the purpose of extending reservation for these less-privileged people for ten years. The failure of the Janata Government to extend the period of reservation had to be tackled in this manner. The constitutional amendment was later ratified by the State Assemblies.

Chapter 25

PUBLIC ISSUES

On 18 June 1980, an incident at Baghpat near Meerut hit the headlines in newspapers. It was alleged that a lady Maya Tyagi was molested and manhandled publicly and some persons were shot dead. This in fact created a furore in Parliament and outside. On June 30 a call-attention motion was tabled, on which a number of important Opposition leaders vehemently spoke criticising the role of the police, the members of which were alleged to have been involved in the outrage. I visited Bhagpat alongwith ten women Members of Parliament and studied the situation. Later, in a lengthy trial, those found guilty of murder were handed severe sentences.

When I assumed charge as Home Minister, the most complicated issue faced by the Government was that of Assam. The crisis developed with the Assamese students launching an agitation against the 'foreigners' who had infiltrated into Assam causing widespread resentment on ethnic and economic grounds. Though the problem existed earlier, it manifested itself forcefully in 1978, when the All-Assam Students Union backed by politicians launched a consistent campaign for the ouster of the "foreigners". Though the basic stand of the students was genuine and there was some veracity in their arguments, it was obvious from the beginning that their demands were not fully justified, and, if conceded, would open the doors for other problems of unmanageable proportions.

Their anger at the entry of the Bangladeshi nationals into Assam without any intention of returning to their country was understandable, but those who had gone and settled there from West Bengal were also their target. The All-Assam Students Union and the All-Assam Gana Sangram Parishad spearheading the movement for the deportation of the "foreigners" based their claim on the National Register of Citizens of 1951 and the electoral rolls of 1952.

The topography of the area with long borders criss-crossed with innumerable rivers and streams was responsible for virtually unchecked entry of people into the promising land of Assam.

The President's rule was extended in Assam for six months from 12 June 1980. I assured Parliament that the Government would try to find the best possible solution. There could be no hesitation in detecting and deporting the foreign nationals, but the Government could not agree to consider such persons as "foreign nationals" who were recognized as Indian citizens under the Nehru-Liaquat Agreement and the Indira-Mujeeb Agreement.

The Assam agitation became so vigorous that no political party could summon courage to speak against it, except for the Communist Party, which, of course, suffered in the elections later in the State. The students had adopted seemingly an apolitical posture taking a plea that they were only struggling for the legitimate rights of the Assamese people. The all-pervasive agitation was snowballing into nerve-rattling tension, which made it impractical to hold Assembly or Parliamentary elections or for that matter even the census, which took place in the whole country except for Assam and Jammu and Kashmir.

I reached an unfortunate conclusion that Governor L.P. Singh, though a highly intelligent person and experienced civil servant of long standing, could have done better to tackle the situation. He could have at least worked for holding the elections, which would have kept the kettle from boiling over. In the initial two rounds of talks held between the Prime Minister and the Assamese delegation, I was present.

In the first meeting, the students proposed to pay condolences for those, who had lost their lives in the movement, and for this purpose they wanted everyone in the meeting to observe a two-minute silence. They were persuaded not to insist on the Prime Minister standing up to join in such a tribute, though she would express her sorrow over the loss of precious lives. They were also told that it was not necessary for them to speak in the Assamese language and to conduct the discussions with the help of an interpreter.

I had also come across some pamphlets with inscriptions "Printed in U.S.A." which stood for the "United States of Assam." These pamphlets disowned any affinity with the Indian people and called upon them, besides, the Bengalis, to quit Assam. When confronted with this printed material, the students emphatically denied having any connection with such literature. They also claimed that their movement was non-violent and non-secessionist, but they could not, they asserted, tolerate the continued existence of Bengalis and other non-Assamese on their soil, irrespective of the fact that they had become well-versed in the Assamese language.

Inspite of a large delegation fielded by the Assamese, they often asserted that they would go back and put the matter before their Executive for a decision. I was constrained to point out that though they were being prompted by their elderly advisors to keep up the intensity of their agitation at all costs, they were not being given the potentiality to arrive at a settlement.

The Assamese delegation initially insisted on treating 1951 as the cut-off year, but gradually they came down to 1961, whereas the official position was to settle on the basis of 1971. When history took a sharp turn bringing into existence Bangladesh as a sovereign state, an agreement reached between the President of the nascent nation and the Indian Prime Minister stipulated the return of the Bangladeshi refugees from Assam to their own country, but out of millions of such emigrants of the Pakistani terror, a large number of them had quietly decided to stay back in Assam or West Bengal. A majority of them were Hindus, but the economic implications weighed more with them than the religious affinities.

The Bharatiya Janata Party and the militant Rashtrya Swayam Sevak Sangh displayed their sympathies with the movement in the belief that mainly the ouster of Muslims was being demanded. The Assamese approach was economic and empirical and the movement had the support of almost everyone including the civil servants. At the drop of a hat they could endorse a general strike and to show their strength, as it were. They killed two senior central officials in cold blood.

The agitators suggested the venue of talks to be shifted from Delhi to Guwahati. To keep the negotiations going and to pre-empt further pretexts for announcing the strikes, I agreed to go to Assam. There I told the delegation that steps would be taken for Bangladeshi migrants to be sent back to their country, reacting to which the Governor of Assam and the Union Home Secretary said that it was not so simple a question, but was fraught with several complications. On my assurance, the students offered to withdraw their agitation. I intended ringing up Mrs. Gandhi to apprise her of the changed attitude of the students, but I was advised by the Governor not to do so. In retrospect, I think it was a mistake on my part to accept the Governor's line, as at that stage the modalities of detection and deportation of foreign nationals could have been very easily worked out. Had an agreement been finalised then and the agitation withdrawn, it could not have assumed the dimensions, it did later.

I assured the Assamese delegation that in principle we agreed on the deportation of the intruders and infiltrators, which prompted them to declare that they would continue the dialogue with the Centre. I was keen on maintaining the prestige of the Central Government and at the same time giving due consideration to the Assamese negotiators. The next meeting was fixed for Delhi after about two months.

On my return to the capital, I briefed the Political Affairs Committee of the cabinet, as also the Prime Minister personally.

I was feeling deeply about the disruption in the flow of oil from Assam being caused directly by the agitation, which was not only resulting in a huge financial loss, but also a serious irritant to the nation. The work in almost all Departments of the Government in Assam was frequently coming to a halt under the stress and duress caused by the agitators. I made up my mind, therefore, to effect a break in service of the Government employees taking part in strikes. I called servicemen to resume production of oil and arranged for protection of the pipelines. With initiative in the hands of servicemen, a major portion of the civilian workers went back to their duty.

I persuaded the All-Assam Gana Sangram Parishad (AAGSP) and the All Assam Students Union (AASU) to come to the negotiations table. They pleaded for the break in service of the civilians to be condoned, without which they would not agree to the resumption of talks. I advised them not to leak the reports of our negotiations to the Press, about which they made the promise, but hardly kept it. Regarding condonation of break in service, we promised to examine each case individually on merit, which did not satisfy them and they went back.

On resumption of talks, AAGSP and AASU insisted on 1961 being treated as the cut-off year. I suggested this to be treated as Reference year, and in case of a claim by any individual of older residence in Assam, he could be asked to prove his contention with the' help of a bank passbook or the wages register with an evidence of the venue of work. In the meantime the Bangladesh Government disowned their responsibility to accept any person claiming. that none of their citizens had migrated to Assam. I told the Home Secretary that we should concentrate on detecting the foreign nationals, thereafter deleting their names from the voters' lists. If any legal hurdle came up, we would have to find a way to tackle it.

On the Prime Minister's visit to Assam, when I accompanied her, we were shown black flags. The agitators were putting in a huge effort at intimidation, but Mrs. Gandhi was not impressed. She would not waver from her stand on 1971 as the cut-off year. On 22 May 1981, the Action Committee of the self-styled Bengali Hindu refugees in the northeastern region of India and the Citizens' Forum of Assam pleaded with me not to fix any cut-off date for members of the minority communities, who had to flee Bangladesh and to cross over to Assam for personal security. The Government was committed to preserving the cultural and linguistic identity of the Assamese and to dispersing all unauthorised foreigners or inflitrators. We agreed to strengthen the border to check further inflitration and took several measures to reduce dissatisfaction.

Chapter 26

TO RASHTRAPATI BHAVAN

In the beginning of May 1982, speculation about the new President of the Republic became rife in the newspapers. Several names were being mentioned and my name also figured among the probables. Quite a few friends and well-wishers advised me not to accept the candidature for the Presidency on the plea that though the office was invested with a good amount of pomp and grandeur, in actual fact it was devoid of any real power. If the President had any political clout, they argued, why would not Mrs. Indira Gandhi herself have assumed that office?

They emphasized that the post of the Home Minister was much more important, as at that time the Departments of Personnel, Administrative Reforms, Justice, Industrial security etc., formed part of the Ministry of Home Affairs. In addition, the Home Minister held the charge of paramilitary forces like the Border Security Force, Central Reserve Police Force, Assam Rifles, besides the investigating agencies like I the Intelligence Bureau and Central Bureau of Investigation, as also the work relating to Scheduled Castes, Scheduled Tribes and other Backward classes. My friends took pains to explain that such power, as, I was wielding as Home Minister, would never come my way, once I was lodged in Rashtrapati Bhavan.

On the other hand, some friends expressed their happiness over the prospect of my achieving the highest position in the country. They were of the view that the President commanded higher respect then even the Prime Minister, and if the nation was inclined to bestow this honour on me, I should not vacillate a moment and should accept it readily. I reflected on these divergent views and finding myself in a dilemma, I did not make any specific effort to secure the nomination for contest to the office of the President.

It goes to the credit of some of my friends in the Congress Party, that they tried for my nomination. What influenced me to some extent not to oppose this move was the realization that I was over-burdened with work in the Home Ministry. I persuaded myself to let things take their own course. If the choice ultimately fell on me, I should not decline it. Without much surprise I found myoid political opponents busy working overtime for getting the move in my favour scotched.

I had some supporters among those who were close to Mrs. Gandhi. To forestall the efforts of my adversaries, they spread the word that a decision had been taken to make P.V. Narasimha Rao the Congress party's candidate. This was in spite of rh . fact that Mrs. Gandhi had completed the round of consultations with important members of the Government and the Party and had almost settled for my candidature. But her decision was known only to the very few who were enjoying her close confidence.

One of them tried to give the impression that the new President would be from the South and that could be P.V. Narasimha Rao or R. Venkataraman or even B.D. Jatti. A cabinet colleague came and confided in me that Narasimha Rao was the dark horse, but his candidature was being opposed by another important personality from his own State, Andhra Pradesh. Rajiv Gandhi, who had very warm relations and a close rapport with me, once accosted me with the inquiry, if I had any doubts about his sincerity in supporting me. I assured him that I had no such misgivings and had full faith in him.

Ultimately, when the matter was discussed in the meeting of the Congress Parliamentary Board, my name was favoured and it was decided that Mrs. Gandhi would make the announcement. Gundu Rao of Karnataka, who was a member of the Congress Parliamentary Board, on being confronted by pressmen, disclosed to them about the decision, adding that a formal announcement was expected to be made by Mrs. Gandhi. It was published in the newspapers the following morning, which made Mrs. Gandhi change her mind about making a formal announcement. She sent me a word to file my nomination papers. She had taken the precaution some days earlier of conveying to me that I should ascertain my particulars in the voters' list.

After I filed my nomination papers, Mrs. Gandhi advised me to tour all the States in the country to personally meet the legislators, who along with members of the Parliament constituted the electoral college. She was certain to muster votes of all the members of the ruling party as also of some other parties which had pledged their support. In her view, it would have salutary effect, if the ruling party candidate for Presidency would meet members of State Assemblies to win their goodwill Mrs. Gandhi wanted Rajiv Gandhi to accompany me on the countrywide tour, to which he agreed. But later she decided that a senior Minister and Congress leader, N.K.P. Salve should undertake this job. Accordingly he and my daughter, Dr. Gurdip Kaur, went with me to the capitals of various States, where I met a large number of State legislators of different parties. During the tour Salve remarked more than once that they would miss me in the Parliament.

When the polling took place in Parliament House and various State assemblies, it transpired that, besides Congress, many members belonging to other political parties cast their votes in my favour. These included Dravida Munnetra Kazhagam and AIDMK of Tamil Nadu, National Conference of Jammu & Kashmir and the Muslim League. Akali party was the last to decide in my favour. They had a divided house on this issue. Ultimately, they took a decision to support me. Apart from them, some members of the Lok Dal and a few other smaller parties voted for me.

On being elected, I was sworn in as President on 25 July 1982, in a ceremony in the Darbar Hall of Rashtrapati Bhavan by Y.V. Chandrachud, Chief Justice of the Supreme Court, in the

The young Giani Zail Singh presenting freedom fighters, savagely beaten and injured by the forces of the Raja of Faridkot, to Sheikh Mohd. Abdullah and Pandit Nehru.

The narrow cell in Faridkot jail, where Giani Zail Singh spent five years of incarceration during the freedom struggle.

The first lady, Mrs. Pradhan Kaur.

As Chief Minister, Punjab Gianiji honouring the mother of Martyr Bhagat Singh as 'Punjab Mata'.

Receiving Saropa from the Head Priest of Gurdwara Janm Asthan, Sri Patna Sahib.

With Heads of States of six-nation initiative on Disarmament.

With King Birendra and Queen Aishwarya Devi of Nepal.

With former Prime Minister, Morarji Desai.

With President Jayawardane of Sri Lanka.

With President Mitterand of France. On the President's left are Mrs. Indira Gandhi and Dr. Gurdip Kaur.

With foreign dignitaries. In the centre is Margaret Thatcher, Prime Minister of U.K.

With Queen Elizabeth and the Duke of Edinburgh on their State visit to New Delhi.

With daughter Gurdip Kaur, son-in-law S.S. Virdi and grandchildren.

With his Officer on Special Duty and the writer of these memoirs, Manohar Singh Batra.

With the J&K Governor, Jagmohan and Chief Minister, Dr. Farooq Abdullah.

With Yasser Arafat, the PLO Leader.

Giani Zail Singh, on the right, after release from the Raja of Faridkot's prison, with his eldest brother and father.

With Pandit Jawaharlal Nehru and Sardar Pratap Singh Kairon.

With Akali Leaders G.S. Tohra, Balwant Singh and Prakash Singh Badal.

With former Prime Minister, Chandra Sekhar.

With President and Begum Zia ul Huq of Pakistan.

With P.V. Narasimha Rao.

With the Award winning journalists, Pritish Nandy, N. Ram, Khushwant Singh and Arun Shourie. On the right is the retired Chief Justice of the Punjab and Haryana High Court, R.S. Narula.

Sharing a joke with the Vice President, Prime Minister and others at Rashtrapati Bhawan.

presence of the Prime Minister, her cabinet colleagues and a galaxy of public men and bureaucrats. When I addressed this distinguished gathering after exchanging seats with my predecessor, Neelam Sanjiva Reddy, I was quite full of trepidation. I made the following speech on the occasion:

> "I am deeply moved by the great honour my people have done to me by electing me as the seventh President of our great Republic.
>
> "The duties of the President are solemn, delicate, onerous and crucial to the nation. I am conscious that the presidential obligations demand not only the highest virtues of the heart and the mind but can be fairly comprehended and discharged only, if I receive grace of God and the goodwill of the nation, On my behalf, I solemnly pledge not to spare any effort to live up to the highest and noble traditions of my distinguished predecessors.
>
> "The imperative need of the hour is to visualise the grave dangers not only to our cherished political and social system, but to the very foundation of our values, if there is not greater discipline in national life.
>
> "We have to resolutely and devoutly rededicate ourselves to create a climate, as would be salubrious to social and economic emancipation of the weak, the undernourished and the downtrodden. We must strive to achieve unity of minds and heart-s amongst people of different states, religions, castes and speaking different languages. For the spirit of. the Indian culture, the very foundation of India's life is unity in its diversity. Each one of us should bear his responsibility to the nation and to the community with utmost devotion irrespective of the trials and tribulations that we may be confronted with.
>
> "Undoubtedly, the nation has registered progress, especially during the last two or three years, but we must accelerate the pace and increase the momentum. We need vigour and the will to rekindle the moral timbre to channelise our energies for constructive. purposes. We have to eschew communal frenzy, caste distinctions, fissiparous tendencies and the cult of violence. The ten-

dency to terrorism can only enervate us, take a toll of the legacy left behind for us by our leaders, statesmen, saints and seers. Our culture is so rich and aesthetically so pure. Our literature is endowed with precious content. Our traditions enrich our lives in the midst of modern technology. The situation demands from us assiduous work and utmost devotion to duty. Our nation is blessed with a stable democratic set up, a hard working and versatile people, highly talented scientists and technicians, Courageous men of our armed forces, workers and peasants are engaged in the service of the nation. Progress, prosperity and advancement will attend our efforts, if we have determination. We must skilfully harness our human and natural resources.

"Around us, we see strife, violence, terrorism and wanton destruction of property. We also witness loss of precious human lives. For the survival of the human race, we must create more rational and human conditions. We must cultivate freedom from fear, distrust and want.

"Dependence on force, violence and piling up of nuclear armaments have the potential of extermination of the human race from the face of this earth. In a nuclear war there will be no victor or vanquished. It will spell total . destruction. We need peace and harmony in the world. We are particularly anxious about our neighbourhood. We would like to be friends with one and all and live in a spirit of camaraderie and friendship with our neighbours. In international arena, India has always stood for peaceful means of settlement of all disputes and has strived for a just and viable economic order.

"I shall discharge the duties enjoined upon me by the Constitution and maintain the dignity, prestige and honour of the highest office created by the founding fathers of our Constitution, as a servant of the nation, without-fear and favour. In all humility, I appeal to all friends, comrades in public and political life, and to the nation to extend to me, in the days ahead, their generous co-operation."

When the ceremonies were over, I went to the Delhi airport to see off Mr. Reddy, where Mrs. Gandhi and a number of dignitaries were already present. The next day Mrs. Indira Gandhi and Rajiv Gandhi called on me at Rashtrapati Bhavan. Rajiv presented me with a wrist watch. The atmosphere was full of warmth and cordiality. When I stepped out of my study to see off my distinguished guests, Mrs. Gandhi politely asked me not to take the trouble.

In the days that followed, Mrs. Gandhi often used to ring me up to find out my convenience to call on me. She would also make use of the telephone to inform or consult me on various matters. On substantial issues, it was invariably her endeavour to come to see me personally. She would never fail to call on me before proceeding on a foreign tour and would always give a report on her return.

She made it a point to discuss with me major events and issues facing the country, but I realized that she developed some hesitation to discuss the Punjab problem, which she had entertained even during my tenure as Home Minister. The then Chief Minister of Punjab, Darbara Singh, had tried to persuade the Prime Minister to let his government have a free hand in dealing with the Akali agitation without interference from the Union Home Ministry. Mrs. Gandhi had conceded this request, after which I had stopped tendering advice on the Punjab affairs. This had happened towards the end of 1981.

Under my directions, the Home Secretary was to submit files direct to the Prime Minister for orders. This was an understanding between me and the Prime Minister and except the Prime Minister and myself, very few persons were aware of this arrangement. I was dealing with all other issues coming in the purview of the Home Ministry. I was totally dissatisfied with the handling of the Punjab problem by the State Government. The Prime Minister, Mrs. Indira Gandhi, did not show much inclination to advise them to mend their ways. I did not press the issue, but did point out to her that all was not well with the functioning of the Government of Punjab. The picture was quite unsavoury.

During my Presidency, Amarinder Singh, a scion of the erstwhile ruling family of the Patiala State, made efforts to bring about an understanding between the Government and the agitating Akali Party. These efforts did not bear any fruit.

In December 1983, when I was about to leave on a tour of Czechoslovakia, Qatar and Bahrain, Mrs. Gandhi told me that the Punjab tangle had become more complicated and it would be helpful to utilize the services of someone who could bring about a rapproachement. I suggested to her to find somebody who enjoyed the confidence of the Government as well as of the Akalis. When the name of Swaran Singh, a veteran leader from Punjab and former Union Minister came up, I supported it strongly, as he was obviously the best person to assist in this ticklish matter. I noticed with interest that Rajiv Gandhi was also keenly involved in the matter, as in many other matters of national character. He tried to discuss important issues without inhibition. The Punjab problem occupied his mind, which he broached frequently.

I told Mrs. Gandhi that the Punjab affairs were being mishandled for quite some time resulting in an impasse and it was unfortunate that she had not shown much understanding of this diagnosis. Mrs. Gandhi admitted that this had been my consistent opinion, the non-acceptance of which had made the matters more serious and intractable. But now she wanted my advice how best to untangle this problem, which was becoming more and more complicated. Both of us agreed to make use of the persuasive abilities of Swaran Singh, who was the right man to hold negotiations with the Akalis.

On my return from tour of the three foreign countries, I was met by Swaran Singh, who gave me the tidings that an understanding had been reached between the Government and the Akalis. It was agreed upon by the two sides that the Anandpur Sahib Resolution would be referred to a 'Parliamentary Committee, the contentious city of Chandigarh would be transferred to Punjab and the question of compensation to the Haryana State would be referred to a judicial body. Sikhs would be allowed to wear small *kirpan* (which was their religious symbol) even during their aeroplane flights.

I was told by Swaran Singh that the Central Government had accepted these propositions and was about to make an announcement to this effect. It was also decided that a committee would be set up to look into the question of Punjabi speaking areas left out of Punjab, to include them in the State. The Akali Party had also accepted the arrangement.

But the Government changed its stance and sprang a surprise. An altogether different statement was made by the Home Minister, P.C. Sethi in Parliament. Swaran Singh felt aggrieved and thought that he was let down by the government by its somersault. He seemed shocked beyond words, but it went to his credit that he abstained from making any sour comment publicly at the turn of events caused by the Central Government for inexplicable reasons.

Though I admired Swaran Singh's forbearance and stoicism, I was struck by a feeling that he should have at least let the nation know of the debacle for which the Government alone was responsible. I came to know later that it was due to the intransigent attitude of Darbara Singh, the Chief Minister of Punjab, who took the oft-repeated line, that if these solutions were accepted, things would go out of his control. He also thought that if Swaran Singh got the credit for solving the tangle, it would lower the prestige of the State Government. Obviously, the Punjab State leaders were more interested in their prestige than in finding an acceptable solution to the long-standing problem.

Chapter 27

SIKHS—A SEPARATE NATION?

As a result of the dithering on the part of the Punjab Government to get out of the impasse, the Akalis went on merrily with their agitation. I asked Mrs. Gandhi what was the real hurdle, to which her answer was that it was necessary to carry both the Punjab and the Haryana Governments along and any solution to the imbroglio should have the acceptance of both. But when the Akalis realized the futility of their efforts to forge a negotiated settlement, they hardened their attitude. Though the Anandpur Sahib Resolution, by which the Akalis swore, was basically a document asking for greater autonomy for the States within a federal framework, yet it had ramblings of separatism, because it envisaged a special status for the Sikhs *(Khalsa Ji Ka Bol-bala)* in the region.

Now the Akalis introduced a dangerous element in their misadventures by announcing their opposition to the Constitution and asserting that Sikhs were a separate nation. This was the manifestation of extreme alienation of the Sikhs from the mainstream, and in ample measure it was the outcome of a sort of megalomania on the part of the Punjab governmental leaders, who were throughout averse to finding any tangible solution to 'the misfortunes of the State, which would not bear the imprint of their own supreme importance.

The Chief Minister, Darbara Singh, was keen on using strong-arm methods against the Akalis following the example of Pratap Singh Kairon. His role in setting at naught the efforts of the likes of Swaran Singh was of a piece with earlier miscarriages of similar endeavours. When the Punjab government had come to know of the possibility of a solution owing to the efforts of Amarinder Singh of Patiala, they had leaked out the outlines of the proposals to the Press. It had created a strong reaction in the States of Haryana and Rajasthan, which had nullified the conciliatory efforts and had perpetuated the stalemate.

The stand taken by the Akalis over Article 25 of the Constitution was highly untenable. Their action in tearing and burning of this Article caused widespread aversion in the country. It is ironical that these very leaders, who had sworn by the Constitution at the time of assuming high offices in the Government, decided to desecrate this momentous document. If at the time they received all-round denunciation of this unfortunate action, they could not lay the blame on the doorstep of anyone but their own.

Explanation II of Article 25 specifies that the reference to the Hindus in clause (2) of the Article shall be construed as including a reference to persons professing the Sikh, Jaina or Buddhist religion and the reference to Hindu religious institutions shall be construed accordingly. Explanation I states that the wearing and carrying of *kirpans* (swords) shall be deemed to be included in the profession of the Sikh religion.

Constitutional lawyers, retired Chief Justices of High Courts and others were unanimous in their opinion that Article 25 gave certain advantages to the Sikhs, Buddhists and Jains. In no way was it to the detriment of these communities.

Some Akalis pleaded with their leader, Sant Harchand Singh Longowal, to refrain from committing the indiscretion of burning a part of the Constitution, as it would lead to unpleasant consequences. It would be more pragmatic te canvass support for moving an amendment to the Constitution instead of desecrating the document, which no-segment of, the people would tolerate, much less support it. Had the Akalis shown a measure of maturity they could have highlighted their viewpoint in Parliament. Instead of using such an effective forum, they chose the sanctity of the *gurdwaras* to burn a portion of the Constitution.

Those Akalis who had approached Sant Longowal in favour of sanity conveyed to me that the Sant had expressed his helplessness, as he had already cleared the move to resort to the burning of the "offending" article of the Constitution. The Akalis did not see reason and went on with their, negative. and unproductive approach. It gave rise to a widespread disapproval of their step by even those political parties which had professed sympathy for the Sikhs. It created an unfortunate impression that the Akalis had little respect for the Constitution which symbolised the sovereignty of the nation.

I had no desire to say or do anything that might be construed as overt or covert interference in the Punjab affairs. But I could not help expressing my opinion that mishandling of the matters by the Punjab government led to the worsening of the situation. Taking out processions, holding rallies, staging demonstrations and calling for strikes in certain spheres excepting essential civil services etc. however unpalatable, were allowed as legitimate methods of protest, to the Opposition, in a democracy. There was no justification in silencing dissent by bullets.

I reminded Mrs. Gandhi of the strategy adopted by me in handling such situations during my Chief Ministership of Punjab.

The agitation launched by the Akalis had lasted nineteen months, during which they had sent about forty two thousand volunteers to court arrest. I had issued verbal instructions to the police that as soon as the agitators emerged from the gurdwaras, they should be taken in vehicles upto the gates of a jail. The protesters neither asked for being shown the warrants of arrest, nor did they question the verbal orders of being set at liberty. I, therefore, advised my officers to keep the vehicles, in which the agitators had been taken to the gates of the jail, standing right there with the detainees sitting in them. As the evening approached, they should be told that orders to set them free had been received. Most of them demanded to know where they should go at that inconvenient hour. Some of the protesters, of course, insisted on being taken in and locked up, but a large number would accept the situation and agree to go back to their homesteads by the same vehicles in which they had been detained. Since they came in groups from a cluster of villages, the same vehicles, which they had boarded to proceed to the jails, would carry them back.

Some of my officers were of the view that it was an infructuous expenditure on petrol, as the agitators were set at liberty after arrest without being lodged in the prisons. But I overruled them, as I thought that the arrest of the agitators would give them some psychological satisfaction and at the same time their return without proper detention in jail would save the government of the obvious strains. I had told the police that I would not like the detainees to use jails as study circles at the expense of the Government and it was best that they, after enjoying the satisfaction of having courted arrest, should return to their homes. I had never allowed more than five thousand agitators at a time to be lodged in the Punjab jails. I had never found any need to transfer prisoners to jails in other parts of the country. Since most agitators had not even entered jails, there was hardly any necessity even to record their arrests. During my tenure as Chief Minister, only twelve thousand persons had been taken under actual arrest. I had cautioned the Chief Secretary, Inspector General of Police, Inspector General of Prisons, Home Secretary and Inspector General, CID that arresting the Akalis would not curb their spirits as they had ample potential for offering more and more volunteers for arrest.

All the jails in the State were not spacious enough to accommodate the Satyagrahis. They had no compunction in rushing into prisons.

It was also not politic to coerce them to seek apology. In case the Akalis resorted to other methods like obstructing traffic, I told Mrs. Gandhi, I would tell the public as to who was guilty of causing them inconvenience. But now the Punjab government had resorted to the arm-twisting measures, and instead of tact, were using unnecessary force. The agitators blocking the Sangrur-Ludhiana road were mowed down by bullets. The police was reported to have set fire to two jeeps and a police station to give an impression that the agitators had become violent and it had become expeditent to open fire. I told Mrs. Gandhi that this was surely not the right way of dealing with political agitations. Mrs. Gandhi pondered over the situation and, seeing logic, intervened with the Punjab government to free the detained volunteers.

Chapter 28

THE METHODS OF THE AKALIS

The Akalis had avowed a peaceful agitation. But when Sant Jarnail Singh Bhindranwale was shifted from the suburb of Chowk Mehta to Guru Nanak Niwas in the Golden Temple complex by the Akali leaders of the Shiromini Gurdwara Prabhandak Committee, headed by Jathedar Gurcharan Singh Tohra, the spectre of violence appeared on the scene and repeated incidents of unprovoked killings of hapless people started taking place. Lala Jagat Narain, a veteran journalist and freedom fighter, was shot dead by the extremists. When the militants stopped a state-owned bus and murdered some persons in cold blood, Mrs. Gandhi called on me and suggested the imposition of President's rule in Punjab. She asked for my suggestion about a new Governor to be appointed.

My view was that. the Government should reconsider its decision about the President's rule in the troubled State as the step would embroil the Central government directly in the imbroglio. But Mrs. Gandhi said that the Governor's rule for a little while seemed necessary. It would do some good, she asserted. We should better steer clear of the situation, I suggested. But she seemed to have made up her mind already on this issue and asked me to suggest the name of a possible incumbent, who could handle the ticklish situation with firmness and tact. Our choice fell on B.D. Pande, who was then Governor of West Bengal and was considered an able administrator. His earlier tenure as Cabinet Secretary had provided him with a good opportunity to demonstrate his decision-making ability and acumen.

Then Mrs. Gandhi discussed about the persons to be appointed as Advisors to the Governor. I suggested four Advisors, so that they could act as sounding boards to the people, who were so accustomed to lodging complaints and expressing grievances to Ministers and high officials. Accordingly, Messrs S.s. Sidhu, Harbans Singh, Subramaniam and Gavai were appointed Advisors to the Governor of Punjab, after promulgation of the President's rule. Subsequently Sidhu and Gavai were withdrawn. Sidhu was too astute and straightforward a person to be able to survive in such an atmosphere.

The situation went on deteriorating with the result that the Union Government had to face the criticism for the rot. At the time President's rule was promulgated in the State, the Central government had sent up two Ordinances to me for signatures, without any previous consultation. With hindsight I feel that, perhaps, this was a blunder on the part of the Government. One of the ordinances aimed at conferring powers on the Governor to declare any part of the State a disturbed area. This would automatically authorise the Governor to call in the army for help in restoring law and order, without any reference to the Central government. I signed one of the ordinances and detained the other. I wanted to give a chance to the agitators to realise that since popular government had been shown the door, they should think of some common solution acceptable to them and the government.

Some leaders of the Akali Party (Longowal) met me and I advised them to postpone their agitation for at least one month to enable negotiations to be held in a healthy atmosphere. But, unfortunately, neither the Akalis nor the Government rose to the occasion. I had some positive suggestions to offer to end the deadlock, but I realized that the Prime Minister was in no mood to receive any advice. I told her that this ordinance would be construed as a measure of repression and would cause deeper cynicism. And this is what actually happened. The attitude of the Akalis hardened and they called for greater sacrifices from their followers proclaiming that the struggle would be a long-drawn affair. The Akali leaders led their trusting adherents downhill towards lower levels of pessimism and to uncertainty of a solution and prompting them for greater sufferings in the name of religion.

The Akali supremo, Sant Harchand Singh Longowal convened a meeting of Sikh intellectuals to discuss the 'crisis' facing the community. It was followed by a meeting of the Sikh ex-officers and men of the armed forces. It was a misguided step on the part of the Akali leadership, as involving Sikh ex-servicemen in agitational moves would reflect on the loyalty and integrity of those actively engaged in the service of the Armed forces.

I wondered why the Akalis were fighting shy of using the Assembly and Parliamentary fora for airing their political grievances. As elected representatives of people, they had a right as well as a duty to raise political matters on the floor of the House, which would create public awareness of their case, and if their demands were just, they could win people's sympathy and support by initiating debates in Parliament and State legislatures.

I questioned them about their obsession with resignations, and in fact advised them to withdraw their resignations from the State Assembly. They approached me with a suggestion that I should resign from the Presidency. I told them that I was not inclined to do so, as I was not elected by the Akalis alone, but by a vast electoral college consisting of Members of Parliament and all State Assemblies. People professing all religions belonging to all castes and coming from all parts of the country had voted me into office.

Chapter 29

THE ASIAD AND THE TRAVAILS

The Ninth Asian Games were to be held in New Delhi in 1982. The Akalis, who seemed to be on the lookout for any opportunity to embarrass the Government, decided to hold demonstrations at the inaugural ceremony of the games and, if possible, during the games themselves. Mrs. Indira Gandhi was obviously annoyed at this ill-advised move of the agitating Akalis. She expressed her anguish that the Akalis were bent upon creating a scene, which would give an adverse impression of her Government internationally.

The agitators, who had threatened to spoil the atmosphere of the Asiad, had to pass through Haryana for coming to Delhi. The Haryana Government resorted to frisking the Sikhs and searching their baggage in the cars and buses, which caused inconvenience and harassment even to those Sikhs, who had absolutely no sympathy or link with the agitators. In their over-enthusiasm or pique, the police in Haryana did not spare even the womenfolk from their rough treatment. Anyone with a beard and turban and a woman accompanying him came in for such rude behaviour, that caused deep resentment among the Sikhs, who had not entertained any thought of creating an adverse condition by shouting slogans or by any other method causing the country embarrassment in the eyes of the international community.

There were reports that the Sikhs coming to Delhi on their normal visits were jostled about by the Haryana police and were not allowed to proceed towards the capital. Some members of the intelligentsia in the Sikh community including lawyers, judges and even members of the Armed forces were subjected to humiliation and were singled out from the hordes of passengers for discriminatory treatment. This created bitterness among the Sikhs. But I had to say that though it was very wrong and improper on the part of the Haryana authorities to indiscriminately harass and humiliate members of the Sikh community passing through the State territory, the Akalis could not absolve themselves of the blame, as they had announced their intention to disrupt the Games by ill-considered and ill-advised demonstrations in the presence of foreign athletes and foreign media men.

Ironically those Sikhs who had no sympathy with the Akalis' agitational tactics, were drawn towards the manhandled and the aggrieved, so much was the hurt caused to the Sikh psyche. Those who felt the pinch of the high handedness of the Haryana police, started lending their sympathy to the hard-boiled elements, who were the primary cause of this debacle.

It is also paradoxical that on the one hand the Akalis were complaining of the Sikhs being treated as second class citizens in the country, but on the other, all the five important dignitaries leading the inaugural ceremonies in the Jawaharlal Nehru Stadium were Sikhs viz., myself, the President of India, Buta Singh, the Cabinet Minister, Raja Bhalindra Singh, President of the Indian Olympics Committee, Umrao Singh, a Punjab politician and K.S. Bains, an official. Rajiv Gandhi called them *Panj Pyaras* (Five beloved ones created by the Tenth Guru, at the time of baptising them and metamorphosing the Sikhs into a martial community).

The calling of conventions of Sikh intellectuals and 'Sikh ex-servicemen by the Akali leaders added fuel to the fire of discrimination against the community at the hands of the intolerant and petty people. I reminded the government that during my Chief Ministership of Punjab, we used to hold rallies of ex-servicemen at the district and State levels and give them opportunities to express their grievances. I suggested that a convention of ex-servicemen should be called now asking them to condemn the Akalis' move, asserting that they never had spoken the language of communalism. The Punjab government kept sitting like a sphinx without taking any step. They were, perhaps, conjuring up visions of crushing the movement with batons and bullets.

The Punjab government had spent huge sums to cope with the Akali morcha. I told Mrs. Indira Gandhi that not even a fraction of that amount had been spent on publicity to mould public opinion against the communal activities. Sikhs were considered to be an extraordinarily enterprising community, whose members had migrated to over 50 countries of the world over the past two or three decades. Most of them were poor and unskilled, but by the dint of their hard work and consistent endeavours, they had done exceedingly well and had managed to impart higher education to their children in various fields.

The agitators and militants had adopted the strategy of publicity offensive among this class of people and had been substantially successful in inciting their communal passions, feeding them on exaggerated accounts of atrocities on and discrimination against the Sikhs. But the Government had not taken sufficient notice of this propaganda blitzkrieg. The Akalis were stirring communal sentiments of the Sikhs settled in foreign countries, because they were well-to-do and could be liberal with their money in the name of religion.

Chapter 30

OPERATION BLUE STAR

As I have mentioned earlier, I detained the Ordinance authorising the Punjab authorities to declare Disturbed Areas in the State, for a number of days before signing it. The Governor declared the whole of the State as disturbed area. It conferred on District Officers the power to call in the Army for assistance in the maintenance of law and order. It needed no orders from the President to call in the army.

Towards the end of May 1984, Mrs. Indira Gandhi mentioned nonchalantly that some people had suggested to her to send the police into the Golden Temple complex to flush out the militants entrenched therein, but she was not exactly convinced of this course, as it was likely to have an unfavourable fall out. But at the same time, she said, she could not see any alternative.

I seriously pondered over Mrs. Gandhi's thinking. I told her that this course would not be proper, as it could have serious repurcussions. The entry of police into the Complex was bound to inflame the public mind. Plausible alternatives could definitely be considered. She positively gave me, an impression that she agreed to what I said. I tried my best to persuade her not to take any provocative step, but to adopt subtle methods to dislodge the armed men from religious places. Reflecting over this suggestion, she said that she would certainly apply her mind to other means, but did not disclose how her mind was actually working.

Seven days elapsed and I did not hear a word from her on the subject. Nor did she send me a report on the situation. On 5 June 1984, the Government launched *Operation Bluestar* in the complex of the *Golden Temple,* Amritsar, for which I was not given even an inkling beforehand. This coincided with the celebrations of the anniversary of Martyrdom of Guru Arjun Dev, the fifth Guru, for which hundreds of folks from rural areas had converged on the complex. They were those devout people, who on such religious occasions come from their villages to spend three, four or even more days in the lodgings within the complex, or in the 'parikarma' the compound surrounding the huge holy tank, listening to devotional hymns and discourses, suffused with a leisurely feeling of divinity. I got, information on the morning following the action, when I demanded confirmation from the Government, which was readily given.

I asked the Government whether they had issued a warning on the loudspeakers to the people inside the complex to come out, to which they replied in the affirmative. Later, I came to know that no such warning had been issued by the authorities and the Operation had been suddenly launched. A curfew had been imposed on the city of Amritsar and the movement of people in the streets had been totally banned. I queried the Government whether they had exhausted all other methods to flush out and arrest the extremists, who had ensconced themselves in the complex, before taking armed action. The Government took the stand that the extremists had collected a large number of arms and ammunition and the situation had assumed serious proportions. They had done fortifications in several parts of the complex and there was no way out for the Government except to launch armed action trying to force them into surrender.

I told the Government that they could have had a word with me before taking such a drastic step, to which they had no explanation, except suggesting that it was the plea of the State administration, to which the Central government had given their approval. The Government further said that the situation had almost slipped out of their hands, as the extremists had planned to declare the establishment of Khalistan (Sikh state) and to seek recognition from a foreign power, after forming an interim government. .

Notwithstanding these arguments, I told Mrs. Indira Gandhi that it would have been more appropriate, if I had been given prior information of such a significant and far-reaching decision. Parrying this observation, Mrs. Gandhi said that special instructions had been issued to the armed forces not to damage Darbar Sahib (the sanctum sanctorum, where incessant recitations from the Holy Book and devotional music are performed). She did not talk about the Akal Takht situated opposite Darbar Sahib, which is also a very sacred place, established by the sixth Guru, Guru Hargobind Sahib.

In anguish, I asked Mrs. Gandhi what were our intelligence agencies doing all those months, when arms build-up was going on in this religious place. And why action had not been taken to apprehend Sant Jamail Singh Bhindranwale, the leader of the extremists, when he had lodged himself in Guru Nanak Niwas before shifting his headquarters to the Akal Takht building. I asked Mrs. Gandhi to tell me, if any police officer had been taken to task for negligence of duty in allowing terrorists to smuggle arms into the building for almost two years. It was ironical, I supposed, that innocent people had to pay with their lives for the dereliction of duty by the security forces and the intelligence organs of the Government. Mrs. Gandhi had obviously no plausible answer. With a distant look in her eyes, she replied feebly that it was the duty of the Punjab Government to take care of these aspects.

She got into a reflective mood. She said that if the Government had issued a prior warning, there was a distinct possibility of a larger number of people gathering into the Temple Complex, which could have led to greater bloodshed. I told Mrs. Gandhi that I could not disagree with her more. The Government could have imposed curfew even in villages, curbing the movement of the people, and at the same time made use of the electronic media like Radio and Television informing people about the nature and extent of stockpiling of arms and ammunition in the complex of the Golden Temple and told the people about the probable number of desperadoes hiding inside, bent upon subversive and disruptive activities. And this could have influenced the opinion among the Sikhs against the anti-national forces.

In fact, I suggested that the names of extremists and the crimes committed by them should have been announced, which would naturally have created revulsion in public mind about the anti-social elements. Why could not the Government have enlisted the help of prominent Sikhs, including religious and spiritual leaders in making an appeal for the need to preserve the sanctity of this holiest of the holy shriness of the Sikh community? A consistent publicity campaign could have been mounted for three days and nights, at the end of which a warning could have been issued to the extremists to come out and surrender and save the temple from avoidable desecration, which, in fact, was a symbol of tolerance and amity among the Hindu, Muslim and Sikh population.

When I pointed out to her that military action was taken on a day, when the Temple complex was full of pilgrims—men, women and children-assembled to observe the Martyrdom anniversary of Guru Arjun Dev, most of whom perished in cross-firing between the security forces and the militants, she seemed full of remorse. I told her that if notice had been given to those pilgrims over Radio, Television, and loudspeakers, a majority of them would have come out, including some extremists, to surrender.

On the other hand, till the last day, official media had gone on proclaiming that the Government had no intention of entering the Golden Temple. The Prime Minister agreed that some lacunae had been left, but now that the action was over, there was need to salvage the situation. She said that she could direct the Home Minister to see me for further explanations, if I so.desired, but I told her that there was no need for doing so.

Two days later, Arun Singh and some others paid a visit to the battle-scarred Golden Temple. On their return, Rajiv Gandhi brought Arun Singh to me to give an account of the situation. According to Arun Singh, no damage had been done to Darbar Sahib and only one balcony of the Akal Takht had fallen. He reported hundreds of casualties including about one hundred officers and men of the Armed forces. I told Rajiv Gandhi and Arun Singh that though I accepted what they said, the unofficial reports suggested damage at a much larger scale. They left Rashtrapati Bhavan with a well-deserved impression that I was unhappy at the way things had been handled.

Mrs. Indira Gandhi rang up and suggested that I should visit Amritsar and see things for myself. She said that she was deputing her Special Assistant R.K. Dhawan to accompany me. As chance would have it, a special plane of the Indian Air Force, usually made use of by the President, was not available that day, and, due to this, I could not, perhaps, have proceeded. But on learning of the position, Mrs. Gandhi sent a word that a chartered Indian Airlines flight should be arranged, so that I could go that very day. Accordingly I left for Amritsar in the company of R.K. Dhawan and Arun Singh. The weather was extremely hot and sultry. I entered the Golden Temple complex through the Deodhi (covered entrance) on the side of Ghantaghar (Clock tower). I could hear the kirtan (singing of holy hymns), which, later, I discovered was being performed by the Sikh army men. Though all efforts seemed to have been made to cleanse the area, through which I was to pass, yet stench of human flesh was hanging heavy in the air. No amount of cleansing could have wiped out the strong smell of so many decomposed bodies in that scorching summer heat, as obviously it would have taken time to remove the corpses from every corner of the basement, where the fighting had raged.

This was the place built by the fifth Guru, an apostle of peace, as a symbol of love and unity of mankind. This was the temple of God, the foundation stone of which had been laid by the Muslim Sufi saint, Hazrat Mian Mir. This was the shrine built on a lower level than the surrounding land in a spirit of humility. It has doors on all four sides proclaiminig its accessibility to people of all faiths and creeds.

It is most essential for everyone to put off his shoes before entering a Sikh religious place, and so did I. General A.N. Vaidya, Chief of the Army staff, Lt. General K. Sunderji, GOC-in-C, Western Command, Lt. General Ranjit Singh Dyal, Lt. General T.S. Oberoi and Major General Kuldip Singh Brar were present. The first look at the ravages caused to this holy place gave me a rude shock, I wondered at the fanaticism and destructive instinct of the militants, who had caused their most important religious spot to be brought to this state and at the lack of wisdom and discretion on the part of the Government, who took such ill-advised, drastic action without proper assessment of its ramifications.

I was assailed by currents of grief and anguish over the misplaced zeal of the extremist fringe among the Sikh community, who had tarnished the traditions of justice, fairplay, compassion and the spirit of sacrifice for protection of the weak and the downtrodden evolved through the annals of history and had brought the prestige of the Sikh brotherhood crashing down. I was equally sad over the lack of foresight and statesmanship on the part of the governmental leaders, who had not taken timely action to prevent the situation from taking such dreadful proportions, resulting in an unprecedented holocaust and tragic death of innocent pilgrims alongwith terrorists responsible for violation of the law and disturbing the public order.

Walking through the complex, I found Arun Singh and Dhawan following me like a shadow. They seemed to be straining every nerve to ascertain to whom I would talk and how I would react. Seeing them tense and taut, I asked them to relax. I sent for the head priest of the Golden Temple, Giani Sahib Singh, with whom I had a brief conversation.

Jathedar Kirpal Singh, Head priest of the Akal Takht was not available. The Governor of the State, Army officers, the District Magistrate and other officials were present. Giani Sahib Singh told me that the scarves for covering the Holy Book were missing.

With whomsoever I exchanged words, I noticed that Arun Singh and Dhawan were trying desperately to overhear the conversation. They were more attentive to watching over me than assessing the damage caused during the action. Arun Singh appeared to be more worried, because of the verbal report given by him earlier lacking in accuracy about the extent of damage caused to the holy buildings. A glance at his face would betray the anxiety pulsating in his mind.

As I was to enter the Parikarma—the wide promenade surrounding the holy tank and the Temple for circumambulation by the devotees, I heard the report of a gun. The bullet fell just a few feet away from where I was standing. It was followed by another shot, which hit one Col. M.P. Choudhary in his shoulder. He was one of the officers surrounding me for security. The bullets were obviously aimed at me, but they missed their target. I was told that the remnants of extremists had still been active from the towers of the 'Ramgarhia Bunga' firing away their weapons in desperation. The only access to the tower was through a narrow staircase. Attempts to send up security men had been in vain, because of the showers of bullets raining from the above.

The officers requested me to move to a verandah as the sun was too hot. Giani Sahib Singh informed me that three or four days earlier, in the firing exchanged between the two sides, the building of the Golden Temple had been hit by bullets. The goldsheet covering the walls got pock-marked and those portions had just to be replaced, as repairs to them were not possible.

At the site of the Akal Takht, I advised the repairs to be undertaken with great dispatch. A couple of days later, I was told, immediate repairs were not possible. Even pieces of goldsheet covering the dome had fallen off.

On my return to Delhi, I sent a letter to Mrs. Indira Gandhi telling her about the great dimensions of the damage that had occurred to the Akal Takht and the Golden Temple. I also informed her that a bullet had struck the Holy Book. Such was the sacrilege, which must have hurt the minds of millions of people.

In the wake of the Operation Bluestar, a great deal of pressure started mounting on me to tender my resignation from the Presidency. A number of Sikh personalities and organisations from home and abroad started exerting their influence asking me to give up my office. They included among others some well-placed Sikh members of the ruling Congress Party. Letters and telegrams were pouring in torrents. I took pains to tell people who called on me, that it was most unwise to turn the holy places into fortresses. Gurdwaras were meant for worship and spiritual solace and not for building arsenals.

Had the Sikh community as a whole raised its voice against the sinister moves of a few short-sighted and misguided persons, all this humiliation and suffering could well have been avoided. Of course, the Government too could not be exonerated of the damage caused by its policy of drift, indifference to reality and the ultimate debacle, but, I did not think, my resignation would restore the lost glory to the Sikhs. It was quite likely that in the event of my resigning from the Presidency, I would earn the community's approbation and be lionised by some people, but had they given thought to the damage it might cause to the country as a whole, including the Sikhs?

In the first instance I had taken the oath as the President of all Indians and I was not the President of the Sikhs alone. Moreover, my resignation might bring more harm to the Sikhs than gain. Since I was the Supreme Commander of the Armed Forces, my resignation might generate a sense of guilt among the serving Sikh members of the forces, giving rise to a feeling of persecution and a desire to square up things with the authority.

There were over one hundred and sixty thousand Sikhs in the Army, over a hundred and fifty thousand in the Navy and Air Force, besides many more in para-military forces and civil services. Sikhs were holding positions in almost all ranks both in civil and military organs of the State, and my taking the step of resigning from the highest position in the country might set an example for others to follow, and it could result in incalculable harm to them and the country as a whole. Any confrontation between the Sikh army men and others would lead to unprecedented bloodshed and a mind-boggling disaster.

There were others who pleaded that I should not resign. They included a large number of enlightened Sikhs, intellectuals, sober and realistic persons. No doubt, I might be given adulation by a major part of the community, but it might prove injurious to the nation. Resignation by me as President would have put the defence of the country in grave peril. It could have triggered a revolt in the armed forces providing an easy opportunity for a lightning attack from across the border. In the prevailing situation, the people of Punjab would not have co-operated with our forces to resist the attack. They would have remained indifferent.

The weak flank of Punjab could easily have resulted in a most undesirable situation, as the state could have been run over by foreign forces. This would have started a chain reaction and the Sikhs in other parts of India could have been massacred in large numbers for their lack of will to stem the foreign aggression. As President, it was my duty to defend and not to endanger the integrity of the nation. I had to look after the interests of the whole country. I could not be sentimental while taking a momentous decision to resign or to stay in office to perform my duty.

Chapter 31

THE AFTERMATH

Consequent on the *Operation Bluestar,* the entry of devotees into the Golden Temple was restricted, which created a wave of resentment among them. The extent of damage to the places of worship over which the Sikhs had taken pride throughout their history, the loss of life and the sense of injury were exacerbated by the ban on their entry to offer prayers. The water in the holy tank which the devotees used to savour as nectar and in which they used to take a dip was mixed with human blood. All this caused a great deal of sullenness and a mortal sense of resentment among the people. The Government wanted time to put things in 'shape before allowing access to the complex. They removed the rubble, but the repairs naturally needed time.

The Governor and the army personnel in control were of the view that the extensive repairs necessary to restore the buildings to their previous status would be a prolonged affair. The Government was keen to carry out repairs in such a way that no tell-tale signs of damage should be visible. They arranged the matching stone and other building material from other parts of the country and pressed into service those workers and artisans from different states, who were traditionally in the trade and whose forefathers had contributed their skills at the time of erecting the original structures.

The extremists took a different stand. They did not want the Government to carry out the repairs, and, obviously, in an attempt to exploit the unfortunate situation, they declared that anyone who would cooperate with the authorities would face their retribution. According to the Sikh tradition, the cleansing of the holy tank and any repair to Hari Mandir (the main hall of assembly and prayer), the Akal Takht and other important holy places has to be done by *Kar Sewa* (voluntary labour), to be undertaken by a large number of devotees without considerations of the rich and the poor, the high and the low, men and women. Anyone can join in this sacred task, which lends a feeling of service, humility and surender and is supposed to earn virtue and blessings of the guru.

The government approached a saintly Sikh, Baba Kharak Singh, who had managed the construction work at various shrines earlier, to lead the *Kar Sewa.* He, after initial hesitation, agreed and called upon the other devout to lend their helping hand. Unfortunately, the tempers were so frayed and the matter was so freakishly handled that the holy man retraced his steps. Thereafter the Government contacted the Nihang Chief, Baba Santa Singh to undertake the task. He readily accepted the proposition. After offering customary prayers, he took his band of traditionally armed followers to the site and started *Kar Sewa* alongwith others. Of course, a vast contingent of skilled and unskilled workers drafted by the Government were at hand to help.

The Akalis and the militants did not take the gesture of Baba Santa Singh kindly and publicly condemned him for being a lackey of the Central Government. While his band of followers lent their services in the repair of the buildings, their chief had to be given heavy police protection in the face of dire threats from militants. The high priests 'of Akal Takht, Darbar Sahib, Damdama Sahib, Kesgarh Sahib declared Baba Santa Singh a *Tankhahya* (Guilty in religious parlance).

These high priests declared me *Tankhahya* and gave the following reasons for this edict: That I had entered the Parikarma with my shoes on. I had walked around with an umbrella over my head and I had sanctioned as the Supreme Commander of the Armed Forces an attack on the Golden Temple complex. The English version of the Hukamnama issued by them is given below:

SRI AKAL TAKHAT SAHIB, AMRITSAR

No. 3/5/84 Sri Amritsar 2.9.1984

"On 4,5 and 6 June 1984, Indian Army in accordance with the order of Zail Singh attacked 38 Sikh Gurdwaras all over Punjab including Sri Darbar Sahib and also fired at Sri Harmandir Sahib. Darshni Deodi was damaged by tank cannons and Sri Guru Granth Sahib within Shri Harmandir Sahib also received bullet injury. 2500 copies of Sri Guru Granth Sahib and hand written manuscripts of Dasham Granth were incinerated. The holy weapons of great Sikh Gurus and Sikh martyrs, invaluable chandni in Toshakhana and symbols of great cultural heritage deposited in Sikh Reference Library were also destroyed by fire. Guru Ram Dass Sarai, Teja Singh Samundri hall and Sri Guru Nanak Niwas were intentionally damaged. Thousands of pilgrims who had gathered for prayers in different Gurdwaras were put to death and such atrocities on Sikhs are still persisting in Punjab. This most barbarous and murderous attack has wringed the heart of the entire Sikh community.

"In spite of the fact that Zail Singh had visited on 8 June 1984, the scene of extreme cruelty at Amritsar, he, in his speech on AIR and Doordarshan did not even refer to the blood-curdling cruelties committed against the Sikh community nor did he express remorse. Zail Singh, as the Supreme Commander of the Indian Army, is responsible for continuing atrocities being committed by the Indian Government on Sikhs. On 8 June 1984, Zail Singh had insultingly transgressed the great Sikh traditions and precepts by having an open umbrella carried and wearing shoes on the Parikarma of Harmandir Sahib.

"On account of the above mentioned actions, Sri Akal Takhat Sahib in accordance with Khalsa traditions declares him Tankhaiya. We appeal to the Sikh community all over the world that unless and until Zail Singh by presenting himself at Sri Akal Takhat Sahib repents for his actions and accepts the traditional punishment, Sikhs should not have social dealings with him and, if any Sikh violates this order, proceedings would also be initiated against him in accordance with Gurmat traditions."

Sd/-	SEAL	Sd/-
Jathedar Kripal Singh		Sahib Singh Head Granthi
Sri Akal Takhat Sahib		Sri Darbar Sahib
Sri Amritsar		Sri Amritsar
Sd/-		Sd/
Jathedar Harcharn Singh Mahalon		Pritam Singh Head Granthi
Takhat Sri Kesgarh Sahib		Sri Akal Takhat Sahib
Sri Anandpur Sahib		Sri Amritsar

Sd/-
Jathedar Lakha Singh,
Takhat Sri Damdama Sahib
Talwandi Sabo.

I examined this edict carefully, consulted legal experts and jurists in the Law Department. I also saw earlier 'Hukumnamas' issued by the Akal Takht to ensure, if there was any justification in the action of the high priests. I reached the conclusion that their action was quite unfair. None of the counts on which I was declared guilty was correct.

The high priests and others who had probably watched my visit to Amritsar on television saw me with shoes on, and this must have been the cause of misunderstanding. But actually the TV footage was not that of my visit to the Golden Temple complex. I had gone around the Gobindgarh Fort, where the arms and ammunition captured from the extremists had been on display by the military authorities, while I was wearing shoes. Since it was high noon in June and the sun was very hot at the spot, I was under the shade of an umbrella. When the high priests saw me on the television, they confused it with my visit to the Temple complex. It is correct that when I had just stepped into the 'Parikarrna' my attendant had tried to open an umbrella to protect me from the blazing sun, but I had stopped him from doing so. As regards my role as the Supreme Commander of the armed forces, there was, in fact, no need to seek my approval to enlist the services of the army to assist the civil authorities in the maintenance of peace, as the State administration had already been armed with such powers under the Ordinance issued earlier. Moreover, all orders are issued in the President's name, which gives the impression that the President's approval has been obtained before taking any action. It was the State Government which had called in the Army under the powers conferred on them by the Ordinance.

I was advised that there was a cogent case for proceeding against the high priests on the grounds of misrepresentation and also the fact that the Shiromani Gurdwara Prabhandak Committee was the product of an Act passed by the legislature, and no institution established under an Act can proceed against the President of the country. It was suggested by legal experts that I could seek heavy damages for defamation. The first meeting for electing the Executive of the Shiromani Gurdwara Prabhandak Committee is presided over by the District Magistrate, in the Town Hall. The elected Executive then appoints the Jathedars (high Priests). Though they are the appointees of the executive body of a Committee, the existence of which is due to a piece of legislation, they become ex-officio members of the Committee without voting rights. As such, according to legal opinion, they have no authority to indict the President of the Republic.

Rawail Singh, an ex-Minister of the State came and told me that all concerned had got a clear appreciation of the matter and there was no need to bring action against anyone. Atma Singh, another ex-Minister and the acting President of the Shiromani Gurdwara Prabhandak Committee also felt that declaring the President *Tankhaiya* (guilty on religious grounds) was incorrect. He suggested to me to address a letter to the high priests and the matter would become clear.

Rawail Singh met the Prime Minister, Mrs. Indira Gandhi, and the Central Minister, Buta Singh, a couple of times. The latter had also been declared *Tankhaiya* by the high priests.

I sent a letter to the high priests clarifying that I had not gone into the *Parikarma* with my shoes on, nor had I walked under an open umbrella, and there could not be any doubt that being a Sikh, I had the greatest respect for the holy places like Darbar Sahib and Akal Takht. An English translation of my letter addressed to the Head Priest, Sri Akal Takht, Amritsar is as follows:

New Delhi
25 September 1984

"1 have received a copy of the Hukamnama issued under your signature. In this regard, I have been in consultation with a number of Puran Gursikhs. Among them are some who are very close to you, who might have apprised you of the reality supported by papers and other facts.

"Even then I would like to clarify through this letter that I have never been in Parikarma with my shoes on. It is also wrong to say that an open umbrella was over my head. One of the members of my staff, Shekhawat Khan had brought the open umbrella for me and I had asked him to take it away immediately.

"So far as army action is concerned, it relates to, as you are also aware, the Constitution and law of the country. But the speech which I delivered on 17 June 1984, which you might have heard and read was the painful expression of my feelings.

I, as per the sermons of our great Gurus and the holy scripture, respect all religious places and I have tremendous reverence for Darbar Saheb and Sri Akal Takht Saheb which are the holiest of religious institutions."

Sd/-
(ZAIL SINGH)

Consequently, the high priests issued another edict on 26

September 1984, to the effect that since the picture was now clear, they would like their earlier verdict to be considered infructuous. I was thus absolved of the charges of religious indiscretion. Their letter in English translation is reproduced below:

SRI AKAL TAKHAT SAHIB, AMRITSAR

Sri Amritsar
26-9-1984

"Special Emissary of Giani Zail Singh, Shri Rawail Singh, Advocate met Singh Saheban on 25 September 1984, regarding the Hukamnama which was issued by Sri Akal Takhat Saheb against Giani Zail Singh. He presented the written clarification of Giani Zail Singh. Singh Saheban considered the explanatory letter and asked for more information. In this connection Shri Rawail Singh, Advocate and Shri Kulwant Singh (Private Secretary to the President) gave the required information to Singh Saheban. The photographs taken during the visit of Giani Zail Singh to Harmandir Saheb and other record were also shown.

"After considering the received clarification and hearing the representatives, we have reached the conclusion that the information received is satisfactory and no further action whatsoever is needed."

Sd/-
(Singh Saheb: Giani Kirpal Singh)
Jathedar, Sri Akal Takhat Saheb
Sri Amritsar
Sd/-
(Singh Saheb: Giani Saheb Singh)
Head Granthi
Sri Darbar Saheb,
Sri Amritsar
Sd/ - (Singh Saheb Giani Harcharan Singh
Mahalon), Jathedar Takhat Sri Kesgarh Saheb
Anandpur Saheb

Sd/-
(Singh Saheb Sant Lakha Singh)
Jathedar Takhat Sri Damdama Saheb
Talwandi Sabo
Sd/- (Giani Pritam Singh)
Head Granthi, Sri Akal Takhat Saheb
Sri Amritsar
ATTESTED
Singh Saheb Giani Kirpal Singh
Jathedar, Sri Akal Takhat Saheb
Sri Amritsar
SEAL
Dt. 26-9-1984

Mrs. Gandhi made a suggestion that I should again go to the Golden Temple. The matter came up in the Political Affairs Committee of the Central Cabinet, when some members suggested that Buta Singh should accompany me and I should also get him exonerated of the verdict of *Tankhaiya*. It was said in the meeting that since the President had been absolved by the priests, he would be going on a pilgrimage. I told Mrs. Gandhi that I would be in no position to take the responsibility of getting Buta Singh exonerated, and it was also not fair to equate a Minister with the President. I could not be sure of the attitude of the clergy towards Buta Singh.

So I visited Amritsar, when the Governor, the Army Commander, Inspector General of Police, several other senior officers including the District Magistrate and the Superintendent of Police accompanied me. The high priests expressed their desire that I should have a brief conversation with them in the Darshni Deodhi (the covered entrance passage), as Baba Santa singh, the Buddha Dal Nihang Chief had organised an Akhand Path (incessant reading of the holy scripture) at the Akal Takht. I had told the Prime Minister that I would not be making any announcement at the Golden Temple. The Prime Minister had agreed to this and confided that she would also like to pay a visit to the Golden Temple.

During my talks with the high priests in the *Darshani Deodhi,* the Advisor to the Punjab Governor, Subramaniam and a few other officers were present. The priests were somewhat reluctant to have them there, but I suggested that if they wanted to be present during the conversation, they should be allowed to do so.

The high priests wanted the possession of the Akal Takht. I suggested that they should cooperate and join in the Bhog of Akhand Path (completion of the incessant reading of the Holy scripture) organised by the Nihang Chief, Baba Santa Singh; otherwise the building could be transferred to them after the exit of Baba Santa Singh's followers on the completion of the ceremony.

When I went to Akal Takht, the high priests had organized a congregation. I had to make a brief speech on the occasion, which was reported accurately by the Press except the daily *Tribune.*

In my speech I expressed anguish over the chain of events that had led to the storming of the Golden Temple complex by the armed forces. Had the militants not turned the holy place into an embattled fortress with so many arms and ammunition, the community and the country could have been saved from this agony. Now that the damage had been done, the services offered by the Government for repairs should be accepted without rancour.

The Sikhs, I said, had never tried whole-heartedly to explain the history, ideology and principles of their great religion to non-Sikhs. It is a tragedy that a majority of Hindus in India had scant understanding of what the Sikh faith stood for. The Sikh leaders and organisations in general and the Shiromani Gurdwara Prabhandak Committee in particular had made no serious efforts to make others understand the noble principles on which the foundations of this modern faith had been laid. All that they had been able to accomplish was to give the Sikhs a political identity and to establish distinctions of flags, banners and slogans.

The teachings of the great gurus were being equated with the expressions of politicians and priests but the human love and the spirit of sacrifice for which the Sikh Gurus had always stood for was not being propagated. A premier Sikh organisation like SGPC had not taken the initiative even to reach the intelligentsia including academicians, jurists, social workers, scientists and opinion leaders with basic literature on the tenets of Sikhism. People at large took *Panth* (the community) as a political party. In a democracy everyone' had a right to support or oppose a political party, and when people opposed the Sikhs, they believed they were opposing a political party.

To use religion for political purposes was grossly incorrect. To mix politics with religion was quite inappropriate. It was extremely wrong to equate those who lost their lives in political agitations and armed conflicts with the Sikh martyrs, who had made supreme sacrifices serving the cause of the Gurus in defence of the weak, the poor and the victims of tyranny and injustice.

After my speech the High Priest of Akal Takht, Jathedar Kirpal Singh stood up to read a pungently worded Memorandum, which created a piquant situation. I told him that he could have handed over the Memorandum to me earlier, or could have read it out prior to my address, so that I could have dealt properly with the points raised by him.

Rajiv Gandhi, as General Secretary of All India Congress Committee, made a statement that the withdrawal of the army would be possible only, if the Akalis accepted certain conditions in writing. An impression was intended to be created that he was unhappy at my visit to Amritsar. Though in our frequent meetings, I had been acquainting Rajiv Gandhi with the Sikh traditions, of which, I thought, he had a fair appreciation, yet at the instance of his advisors, he issued this statement. The frequency of Rajiv Gandhi's visits to me also decreased,

On 17 June 1984, I broadcast to the Nation on AIR and Doordarshan. I expressed anguish over the chain of events that had led to the storming of the Golden Temple complex by the armed forces. Had the militants not turned the holy place into an embattled fortress with so many lethal arms, everyone could have been saved of this agony. In the recent past, the situation inside the Gurdwaras of Punjab, especially the holiest of the Sikh religious places—The *Golden Temple* and the Akal Takht had so developed that even the elected Management Committees of the Gurdwaras could exercise no control. Under these circumstances, despite repeated appeals, all that was against the teachings of the Gurus took place in these holy places with impunity. Even the appeals of the Gurdwara Management were ignored, with the result, that the Gurdwaras, which are for our spiritual upliftment, for inculcating the teachings of Guru Nanak as enshrined in his supreme spiritual poetry, and as ordained by Guru Gobind Singh, for imbibing the message contained in Guru Granth Sahib, and were also for the devotees to visit, passed into the hands of a few terrorists. All types of dangerous weapons and other articles contrary to religious traditions, were piled up at these places, and even used, ultimately making it difficult for the devotees to visit Gurdwaras.

In this context, I said that I could not absolve those in control of the Punjab Administration of their responsibility in the matter. The situation continued to deteriorate because of their laxity and carelessness. The responsibility was also of the terrorists, as of those who encouraged the terrorists while harbouring hostile intentions towards the country. The situation in Punjab provided them with the opportunity to seek to divide our nation and break our age-old bonds by violating the sanctity of our holy places. Getting inspiration from these powers, some young men and women and even some elderly persons took to the wrong path.

And the path led to the unconscionable murder of many Hindus and Sikh businessmen, farmers, journalists, politicians and religious leaders. Even the former venerable Jathedar of Akal Takht, Giani Pratap Singh, was not spared. As is widely known, he was a great personage, a renowned scholar, a writer of repute, a preacher and a selfless person. His only fault lay in his not sharing the views of those who had occupied the Gurdwaras through improper means. He was mercilessly murdered, although he was 85, while resting at his place.

Such heart-rending incidents became the order of the day. Many appeals had been made to stem the tide of terror and vandalism.

I had been trying, at times even going out of my way, to put an end to such acts, while maintaining the dignity of the President's office, but these happenings had gone on unabated. Two religious and political leaders, Sant Harchand Singh Longowal and Jathedar Gurcharan Singh Tohra, allowed themselves to be arrested from the Golden Temple. Similarly, the militants should have come out of the Gurdwaras to save their sanctity from being spoiled. It would have been more understandable, if they had offered themselves for arrest and to be put on trial.

It was not proper to pave way for an armed conflict by taking shelter in Gurdwaras and the holy Akal Takht. This had pained every right-thinking person, especially those who had faith in the Gurus and those Sikhs who knew their traditions well.

I further said that during the days of the country's subjugation, many had to lay down their lives to rid the Gurdwaras of the Mahants and their misdeeds. At that time, the Government of the day had been supporting the malcontents. Then the Sikhs were compelled to make huge sacrifices. The Shiromani Gurdwara Prabhandak Committee was formed with a view to preserving the sanctity of the Gurdwaras, to make certain that Gurbani was preached and the Gurdwaras were managed in keeping with the pious teachings of the Gurus. In the *Guru Granth* is written:

"At the Guru's door one hears the Lord's Praise:
Yes, meeting with the True Guru, one utters the Lord's
Praise with the tongue,
And one is rid of one's woes and afflictions, and the
Lord blesses one with glory in His court;
All that seems is Thou, O God
And, All that we hear is Thy speech.
Yes, there is no place where Thou art not, and
It is thou who upholdest all.

and Gurdwaras are those places:

> Kabir, seek Thou the door that is ever open
> Unto thee, And, leave not that door ever;
> Yes, cling to it tenaciously."

The *Golden Temple* had materialized as conceived by the Fifth Guru. Its foundation stone had been laid by a Sufi saint, Hazrat Mian Mir, at the behest of Guru Arjun Dev. Later on, the beautification of its structure had continued. It became *Swarna Mandir*. The *Akal Takht* was founded by the Sixth Guru, who kept his residence at the Chehharta Sahib, about seven miles away, to establish the Supreme tradition of the Takht. But those traditions were shattered and the condition became such that:

> "Such intense is our suffering, a Lord, and
> Thou feelest no pain.
> In the powerful duel with the powerful I grieve not.
> But if the ravenous lion falls upon a flock of sheep, then
> the Master must answer."

Guru Nanak Dev had so said in his pious works. I did not want to repeat the account of the damage caused to the holy spots, but, as claimed by the Government, serious damage to the *sanctum sanctorum* was avoided, even at the cost of the lives of men of the Security Forces and many others. But the tragedy of human loss had left an indelible mark on my heart. These events could have been avoided, but this became rather impossible as the extremists had taken over the premises. It was also being investigated, as averred by our Generals as to how these terrorists had acquired such dangerous weapons of foreign make and what part had the foreign powers played in this game. All this testified to there being a deep-rooted conspiracy.

Now, the question was how to heal these wounds and how to face the facts. This was the duty of the Government and the society as a whole. We should recall the martyrdom of Guru

Tegh Bahadur and his pledge to protect those who had come to seek his help for the protection of religion: Guru Teg Bahadur who protected the frontal marks and sacred threads of the Hindus.

And displayed great bravery in the Kali age.

When he set out, all his devotees, in particular Saifuddin, did not allow him to move on for more than a month. They said. "You are going to Delhi. If you reach there, you will be beheaded." Guru Tegh Bahadur replied, "No, I would like to be beheaded. I would go to my killers; but I would not hide in a holy place. I would also not seek refuge in the house of a friend. I would not deceive anybody" because:

"To whomsoever we give our hand,
May we lose our life, but we must not leave his hand."

I felt very sorry that some people had appealed that the Sikhs in Government positions, especially in the Army, should give up their offices. Did religion sanction this? Religion, in other words, meant duty. Once a person took an oath of duty in the name of the Guru, but did not abide by it, it was nothing short of cowardice and going astray. I thanked those who performed their duties honestly and loyally.

The Government had not acted with the intention of vanquishing anyone, while adopting its course of action. The Government was above the issues of victory or defeat.

The real issue was how to heal the wounds. It had been quite some time since these wounds had occurred. Who was responsible for this? Only history would tell. The Punjab which once smiled, played, danced and sang, which was vibrant and prosperous because of its traditions of hard work, was now closeted in houses. Why did this happen? It was necessary to examine this in depth.

The Hindus and Sikhs had common ancestry. They were products of the same environment and the same milieu. They had wept and smiled together, But the time came, when one community wept and the other smiled. This had never happened before. I wanted that they should once again share their joys and sorrows. We should all join hands to serve our motherland.

We, the inhabitants of this country, are the progeny of this soil. It was our duty to ensure that our mother was not beset with any trouble. All our religions had been nurtured in the lap of Mother India. Our country had holy places. Saints and seers, heroes and patriots, scientists and servicemen, workers and farmers all received nourishment from this common mother. It was our bounden duty to share the concerns of all sections of the society. We should foster unity, not only talk but work for peace. We should constitute committees, which should help improve the atmosphere. This way, we could forge close bonds once again. There was no harm in seeking pardon for mistakes one might have committed.

There was need for us to pay attention to rendering voluntary service in the holy places. And, I hoped that, not only the Sikhs but other devotees having faith in their own religions and respect for other religions would volunteer for *Kar Sewa.* It was my desire that we undertook the Kar Sewa of the holy tank also, and shared the religious fervour by carrying baskets on our heads. This way the spirit of love and affection, once generated by Guru Arjun Dev in the city of Guru Ram Das, would be revived. We should restore the glory of that place. I told my countrymen that our great Guru taught us the unity of mankind, notwithstanding the faith one professed and the way one offered his prayers.

There was need for us to remember the sayings of the Tenth Guru. He had said:

> Some are accepted as Sanyasis, some are shaven heads,
> Others are Yogis or Brahmacharis, and Jatia,
> Some are Hindus and others Muslims; among the latter
> are Rafzis, Imams and Shafis.
> Know that all human beings are one.
> Karta (the Creator) and Karim (the beneficient) are the
> same; Razak (the Provider) and Rahim (the Merciful) are
> the same;
> Let no man, even by mistake, suppose there is a
> difference.

> Worship the only God, who is one divine Guru for all;
> Know that His Form is one, and that He is the one light diffused in all.

I expected especially from the Sikh religious leaders that they drew inspiration from the works of the Guru as our tenth Guru had said that: "the Guru of the Sikhs after me will be Guru Granth Sahib". In the Holy Granth are enshrined the sayings of saints like Sheikh Farid, Kabir, Ravidas, Namdev, Ramanand and others. I could name all of them. There was need for us to exercise caution, so that we did not go astray. We should recall the pious saying in *Guru Granth Sahib:*

> "Listen all, the truth I hereby proclaim;
> Only those practising loving devotion shall attain God."

Chapter 32

LAST MEETING WITH MRS. INDIRA GANDHI & THE APPOINTMENT OF A NEW PRIME MINISTER

On the eve of my departure on visit to Mauritius, People's Democratic Republic of Yemen and the Yemen Arab Republic, I received a telephone call from Mrs. Indira Gandhi that she very much wanted to see me before I left, but, owing to indisposition, she would not be able to visit the Rashtrapati Bhavan. I had been given complete briefing about our relations with these three countries, she said, and, therefore, she would meet me only at the Delhi airport to see me off. She was there before I reached. Almost immediately on my arrival, she took me aside, and said that there were many things to talk about, which we might do after my return from the foreign tour. Some problems needed serious attention, she added, and it would be possible to give thought to them, when I came back. Turning to my visit to Mauritius, Mrs. Gandhi said that there were lots of people of Indian origin in that country, and I should try to have a heart-to-heart talk with them over matters of common cultural interest.

When Mrs. Indira Gandhi waved to me while I boarded the plane, I could hardly realize that it was the last time I was seeing her alive. From Mauritius, I proceeded to the People's Democratic Republic of Yemen and then to the Yemen Arab

Republic. On the morning of 31 October 1984, my Private Secretary received a telephone call from New Delhi informing me of a shoot-out at the residence of the Prime Minister, and her having been wounded. It caused me a great shock. I asked them to let me know her condition. In reply New Delhi sent me a word that I should immediately return to India.

I was about to have my breakfast, after which a meeting with the President of the host country was scheduled, but without waiting a moment, I asked my Military Secretary to arrange the flight back home. In the meantime, Foreign Secretary M.K. Rasgotra talked to me on telephone and told me that Mrs. Gandhi had been seriously injured and that it was necessary for me to return at the earliest possible. This caused me grave concern and anxiety. I informed the President of the Yemen Arab Republic of my inability to see him for the meeting, as I was leaving for home. The formal farewell ceremony at the airport was dispensed with, but the President came to see me off. He made inquiries about Mrs. Gandhi's health, but I could share with him only what limited information I had.

In the aeroplane, I reflected over the tone of the Foreign Secretary, which gave me a foreboding of something serious that might have happened. At about 3 p.m. the pilot of the aircraft informed that according to a BBC news broadcast, Mrs. Gandhi had breathed her last, though they' added that the report had not been confirmed. I got hold of a copy of the Constitution and consulted it afresh. I also discussed the matter with my senior officers about the appointment of a new Prime Minister. Section (1) of Article 75 of the Constitution specifies that "the Prime Minister shall be appointed by the President and the other Ministers shall be appointed by the President on the advice of the Prime Minister." It is left to the discretion of the President to appoint a Prime Minister, who should be able to seek the confidence of the members of Lok Sabha (Lower House of Parliament) within six months.

My first thought about Mrs. Gandhi's successor was rivetted

on Rajiv Gandhi. Apart from the fact that I had great respect for Pandit Jawaharlal Nehru and affectionate feelings for Mrs. Gandhi, I wanted to appoint someone, who would be acceptable to the majority party in the Lok Sabha. One who could give proper lead to the country at that particular juncture. Wellbeing of the nation was my greatest concern. I wanted a Prime Minister who should be connected with the largest political party, who should be honest and clean. I felt Rajiv Gandhi possessed these qualities, as he was considered to be simple, straight-forward and spotless. He had an attractive personality without conceit or cunning.

Rajiv belonged to the Congress Party, which was the largest political party in India, while other parties were in disarray. The negative side to Rajiv was that he had never been tried in any official position and was inexperienced. But, I thought, he would have the advantage of the experience and sagacity of senior members of his Party and the Council of Ministers. Thus my choice fell only on Rajiv Gandhi, though one way open to me was to appoint the senior-most member in Mrs. Gandhi's cabinet. I ruled out that option and firmly made up my mind to appoint Rajiv Gandhi as the new Prime Minister.

In my cabin in the aeroplane, I asked my Secretary, Bandopadhyay to try to find out the whereabouts of Rajiv, and wherever he might be, he should be asked to reach New Delhi. A journalist accompanying me on the tour came and stood in the door way of the cabin and overheard my communication with my Secretary. There were more than half a dozen senior press people in my entourage and they got the inkling of my mind about the appointment of the new Prime Minister.

On arrival at the Delhi airport, I found R.K Dhawan, Special Assistant to Mrs. Indira Gandhi, and Arun Nehru waiting for me along with some other Ministers and a few senior officials. I asked both of them to get into my car. I was in a state of unspeakable grief at the loss the nation had suffered. My heart knew no bounds of anguish at my own personal loss. Dhawan and Arun Nehru suggested that we should proceed to my official residence, *Rashtrapati Bhavan*.

On inquiry, they told me that the mortal remains of Mrs. Gandhi were still lying in the All-India Institute of Medical Sciences. I directed them to take me to the hospital. On the way, I noticed some persons trying to commit arson. Burly people with menacing faces were carrying burning torches at the ends of their long bamboo poles. At a little distance, I saw a car ablaze. Black smoke was billowing from many buildings. Arsonists had set about their job already. Misgivings arose in my mind that innocent people might be made the target of fury, yet by no stretch of imagination could I foresee the death dance that was looming large on the horizon.

On reaching the All-India Institute of Medical Sciences, I was taken to the floor where the body of Mrs. Indira Gandhi was kept. I was met by Rajiv, to whom I expressed my deep sorrow and offered condolences. I wanted to have a look at the body or Mrs. Gandhi, but Rajiv told me that the doctors were stitching the wounds and We could not go in. As I was about to move, I asked Rajiv to accompany me to the Rashtrapati Bhawan for taking the oath as the Prime Minister. He accompanied me down the lift and before I got into the car, he said, he wanted to go home for change of clothes.

As I reached my study, I found the Vice-President, R. Venktaraman, waiting there. I informed him of my intention to swear in Rajiv Gandhi as PM, to which he replied: 'As you like.' Pranab Mukherjee and P.V. Narasimha Rao, Union Ministers, and a Secretary of the Congress Party came in. When Rajiv Gandhi arrived, I sent him up to the *Ashoka Hall* to wait for a while. I told the two Union Ministers about my decision to place the mantle of Prime Ministership on Rajiv Gandhi. Both of them gladly agreed that my decision was correct. They, however, suggested that the death of Mrs. Gandhi should be announced before the swearing in of Rajiv.

I asked the Vice-President to go and make the announcement over All India Radio. On his return from the studios of AIR in the Parliament Street, after making the official announcement of Mrs. Gandhi's demise, we went up to the *Ashoka Hall,* where Rajiv Gandhi was waiting. In that sombre atmosphere, I administered the oaths of office and secrecy to Rajiv Gandhi, who stepped into the shoes of his illustrious mother, who had become a legend in more ways than one in her life-time. On the advice of the Prime Minister, four Ministers were sworn in the following day.

In the evening, after the swearing-in of Rajiv Gandhi, I broadcast the following message to the Nation:

> "On this the saddest day of my life, I speak to you when I am totally overtaken by the dark clouds of cruel fate. Our beloved Mrs. Indira Gandhi is no more. I have lost my dearest friend. We have all lost one of the greatest leaders our country has ever produced; and the world has lost an ardent champion of peace, who was undoubtedly the greatest woman leader mankind has ever seen.
>
> "My association with her family spans over four decades. Panditji's passing away was my first personal bereavement. To me the loss of Mrs. Gandhi is unbearable. Inspite of her preoccupation with her official duties, we often met. For me each such meeting was a memorable experience. She was gentle, soft spoken and brilliant. She was an epitome of culture. She was a daughter Panditji would have been proud of.
>
> "Now all that has ended. The dastardly act of assassins, has put the nation to test at an extremely critical juncture of our history. The unity and integrity of the nation is being challenged. Let our grief not cloud our good sense and maturity both as individuals and as a nation. God shall grant us the strength to meet the new challenges. Let us rally round the ideals we have inherited from our forefathers. Let us demonstrate to the world that India's stability cannot be jeopardized by a handful of crude assassins."

Chapter 33

THE HOLOCAUST

Shortly afterwards, I started receiving telephone calls about the attacks on Sikhs by others, hurting, maiming, looting and killing them. There were reports of burning of houses and the Sikh places of worship, apart from molestation of women. There was clamour that the police were not helping the victims and were watching the mayhem as silent spectators. I telephoned Rajiv Gandhi to say that these disturbances were not a good augury for his regime, as innocent people were being made the targets of retribution by the hoodlums. Inertia or collusion by the authorities in the breakdown of law and order would paint the new government in unfavourable colours. I asked the Prime Minister to intervene and caution the police to do its duty conscientiously and not let any law-abiding, innocent person suffer. The Prime Minister told me that he was aware of the eruption of violence in some parts of the city and had ordered the Reserve Police to control the riots. But there was no let-up in telephone calls to Rashtrapati Bhawan from the beleaguered Sikhs, who frantically tried to convey that the police were acting in tandem with rioters and murderers, who had let loose a reign of terror on the hapless people. Some Sikhs having licensed guns or revolvers, could have used them in self-defence. But as the police had information about such people, they were reported to have confiscated their weapons in a large number of cases and then signalled to the hoodlums to pounce upon the holed-up, defenceless, men, women and children and to vent their wrath on them. The same night I suggested to Rajiv Gandhi to call in the Army to control the situation. He reacted in a lukewarm manner saying that he was reviewing the position, and, if he found the police incapable of grappling with the matter, he would send for the army to assist. I had faith in Rajiv Gandhi that he would not allow riots and wanton killings.

Lawlessness and vandalism went on throughout the night. It was reported that the police transported rioters and killers from suburbs to stage a death-dance in various parts of the capital. In most cases the Hindu neighbours helped their Sikh brethren by giving them shelter or even by taking a bold stand against the marauding mobs. There were touching instances of Hindus saving the lives and honour of their Sikh friends at grave personal peril. Even the Rashtriya Swayam Sevak cadres were not a party to the carnage. But killings by rapidly cruel and unscrupulous people went on unabated. I could hardly believe this ruthlessness and vengeful retribution. Everyone was claiming the police hand in the massacre. I again rang up Rajiv Gandhi to say that I wanted to visit the riot-affected colonies. Rajiv said that according to reports received by him, the police was ineffective, but since the people were incited, it would not be prudent for me to visit those places. He himself, he said, was going to tour the affected areas. If necessary, he would depute other leaders also to visit the trouble spots.

Ultimately, the Army was called in, but they were told not to fire. They were used for flag-marches only. This did not dampen the spirit of the hordes, who were quenching their blood-thirst and simultaneously looting the belongings of their victims. This went on during the day on 1 November 1984, and the following night. I again telephoned Rajiv Gandhi to tell him that though the Army had been asked to put up their appearance, they had not been authorised to open fire upon the hooligans. On 2 November, Rajiv rang up to say that the situation had been controlled and attacks on the Sikhs had abated. It is strange that after the evening of 1 November, I did not receive any call from the victims, nor could I contact anyone. The telephone lines had been doctored by the authorities.

I came to know later that there was a spate of calls from persons under attack, but they could not reach me. Their desperate cries for help were falling in wilderness. All that could be done on my part was to ask the Prime Minister of the . country not to allow the blood of the innocents to be spilled for the crime committed by two misguided security men on the staff of Mrs. Gandhi, who were employed to protect her, but, instead,' had committed the heinous crime of killing her. I had known the temperament of Mrs. Gandhi for long. It was a tribute to her credulity and affectionate nature that it did not occur to her that after Operation Bluestar, there could have been a change in the mental outlook of some people, who could mow her down in rage. But if Mrs. Gandhi were alive, she would never have allowed the massacre of the innocents, who were in no way responsible for a cruel deed done by someone else. I thought the assassins could not claim themselves to be true Sikhs. Being members of the Sikh community, they really did not understand the true tenets of Sikhism.

I was surprised when a large number of Hindus called me up to express their disapproval of the police inaction, rather their complicity. One Congress leader vehemently told me of the macabre drama deliberately staged to kill members of the Sikh community as a deterrent, as also to put them in their place. Those Hindus and others, who were noticed by the police trying to protect the Sikhs, were chided, belaboured and even threatened. Some buckled under, but most of them showed courage and camaraderie for their friends and neighbours. One diabolic aspect of these riots was that Sikhs had to become victims of this unprecedented wave of vengeance irrespective of their political creed or affiliation. Even those who had been staunch supporters of the ruling Congress, and in every election had voted for the candidates of this party, were not spared. There was no distinction on the basis of status, profession or sub-caste. A Sikh was a Sikh and, if he could be cornered by death-hounds, he must be bludgeoned to death· with iron rods or burnt alive. A Hindu lady telephoned my Secretary to say that she had witnessed Sikhs being given the "garland treatment," i.e., being done to death by placing blazing motor tyres around their necks.

To the utter dismay and sorrow of the just and fair-minded Indians, there were large scale killings of Sikhs in Kanpur and Bokaro. A large number of affluent Sikhs residing in Kanpur, the biggest city in Uttar Pradesh, who had been making enviable contributions to the prosperity of the State, were looted, molested or murdered. To ridicule them in some cases, their tormentors cut their long hair, which is a symbol of their faith, and set their shops and houses ablaze. In Bokaro, a number of faithful, devoted, experienced Sikh engineers employed in the State-owned steel plant fell victims to the frenzied mobs. A large number of Sikhs travelling in trains were taken out of their compartments at railway stations to be lynched. In some cases they were not even aware of the reason of the wrath that was visiting upon them, as the news of Mrs. Gandhi's death had not reached them. Some Sikh Officers in military uniforms were also done to death in trains. Children were not spared. It was a strange coincidence that the iron rods used to bludgeon the victims throughout were of the same size and shape. In some States, where the influence of the north Indian Congress ruling class was not pronounced, there were little disturbances. Some States remained totally free of this taint.

Chapter 34

THE MASSACRE OF INDEPENDENT OPINION

The persons at the helm of affairs in New Delhi expressed their regrets at the violence and the loss of life, and said that there were a few hundred casualties. They did not tell me the exact figures, which were much more. It was in addition to the killings in other parts of the country, the detailed reports of which came out after a few days. Two independent non-party organisations conducted their own inquiries about the massacres in Delhi in the aftermath of Mrs. Gandhi's assassination. One of them was People's Union for Civil Liberties (PUCL) and the other was People's Union for Democratic Rights. (PUDR). They described the role of police all through the period from 31 October to 4 November 1984, the height of the riots—as of (i) total absence from the scene; or (ii) a role of passive spectators; or (iii) direct participation in or abetment of the orgy of violence against the Sikhs. During their tours of the affected parts of Delhi, they found the police conspicuous by their absence, while the shops belonging to Sikhs were being set on fire and looted. Young people armed with swords, daggers, spears, steel tridents and iron-rods were ruling the roads,

In the resettlement colonies, according to the reports, the police came out from their passive role and directly participated in the violence against the Sikhs. The police reportedly accompanied the arsonists and provided them with diesel from their jeeps. A few individual police officials, who did try to intervene and stop the riots, found their efforts frustrated primarily through the lack of cooperation from the top. As per one particular instance, on 1 November 1984, when almost all of Delhi was aflame, an opposition Member of Parliament rang up' two Central Ministers to inform them about the situation in the city and the need for Army action. The Ministers were reported to have assured him that the Army was about to be called and curfew would be imposed. But till late at night there were no signs of either curfew or the Army, while miscreants were on the rampage in the presence of the police. In the heart of the city Connaught Circus, the Sikh-owned shops were being set on fire right under the nose of heavy para-millitary and police pickets.

Members of PUDR and PUCL were intrigued to find Doordarshan (official Television) allowing the relay of highly provocative slogans like *Khoon ka Badla Khoon* (blood for blood) by some members from the mourning crowd at Teen Murti House, where the dead body of the assassinated Prime Minister was lying in State.

Another study was conducted by yet another independent non-party organization "Citizens for Democracy" and published under the title *Truth about Delhi Violence!* The foreword was written by an eminent jurist, V.M. Tarkunde, in which he stated that although there was a communal element in the violence, which erupted in Delhi after the tragic death of Mrs. Indira Gandhi, it could hardly be described as a communal riot. It was, in the first place, an entirely one-sided affair. The Sikhs did not play any aggressive role in the Delhi riots. They were at the receiving end. It was on 1 November, and the two succeeding days that a massacre of hundreds of Sikhs and the burning and looting of their shops and houses took place. The rioting was organised by a number of unscrupulous politicians, who are habitually associated with anti-social elements and down-right criminals. That is the reason why looting' was so extensive and the killings of the Sikhs were attended with unparalleled brutality. Scores of Sikhs in Delhi were literally burnt alive. The report stated that the State had forgotten its role of the protector. Instead, it became the collaborator to violence against a minority.

Unmindful of any personal danger, a larger number of Sikhs had gone to Teen Murti House in the early hours of 1 November 1984, just like others, to pay their homage to their departed leader, Mrs. Indira Gandhi, but within an hour and a half the presence of the Sikhs from those queues was completely gone. By that time the plan (of wreaking vengeance on the Sikhs) had been put into operation. Systematic violence, as distinct from sporadic, had erupted in the capital on 1 November, between 9 and 11 o'clock in the morning. The initial target of attack were the Gurudwaras, followed by loot, arson and killing of the Sikhs, first the men, particularly youths and then members of their families.

A team of Supreme Court advocates visited some violence-affected localities of New Delhi, where the neighbours of the victims told the same story that they wanted to save and protect their Sikh brethren, but were helpless against the highly organised mobs having superiority in numbers. But thousands of Sikhs were saved by their Hindu friends at the risk of their being killed and their own houses being set on fire by the threatening mobs. Many survivors said that the violence was not communal, but that it was instigated.

A Citizens' Commission was formed with Justice S.M. Sikri former Chief Justice of the Supreme Court, Badr-ud-Din Tyabji former Commonwealth Secretary, Rajeshwar Dayal a former Secretary to the Government and T.C.A. Srinivasavardan, former Home Secretary. They published a report on the events in Delhi after visiting various relief camps and *Gurdwaras* housing the afflicted, several localities, particularly the worst affected during the violence and examining numerous victims and eye-witnesses. Dealing in depth with numerous cases of violence, the Commission found that according to the accounts furnished to them, there was the least indication of the presence or active concern shown by senior police officials or others in what was happening in the affected localities. The Commission did not find it possible to say how they occupied themselves during the situation of escalating violence. Members of the Commission found no evidence to suggest that any systematic steps were taken to restore a sense of security or confidence amongst the residents of the several localities, which were subjected to continuing outrages during the four days. They also could not find any information of the perpetrators of mayhem, arson, murder, rape, abduction etc. having been prosecuted. On the contrary, they came across accusations that those who were initially arrested, were soon freed on police bail, the quantum of bail being ridiculously low. Even those arrested for brutal killings were released by the police either on bailor, in several instances, reportedly at the intercession of some political leaders. The Commission was told that in some areas the police, instead of searching for and retrieving looted property, appealed to the looters to hand it over voluntarily, in return for which the police would grant them immunity from prosecution.

Many who came forward to relate their experience and provide eye-witness accounts to the Commission, specifically and repeatedly named certain political leaders belonging to the ruling party. They were accused of having instigated the violence, making arrangements for the supply of kerosene and other inflammable materials and of identifying the houses of the Sikhs. Some of them were accused of interceding with the authorities to obtain the release of their followers, who had been arrested for various crimes. The apathy and ambivalence of other political parties was equally disturbing. Few of them played any significant role in providing either protection or shelter, relief or succour, in any of the affected localities.

Commenting on the role of the information media, the Citizens' Commission observed that apparently the coverage of the crisis by the official radio and visual media, beginning with news of the assassination had not been formulated with adequate care and foresight in relation to the psychological impact of their transmission. It was necessary at that critical juncture that the greatest care and prudence should have been exercised in selecting the material for transmission. It was equally pertinent in the case of live coverage. Efforts were made by responsible and well-meaning citizens, from the very day of the outrage, towards minimising the effects of the expectedly sharp reactions to it, but unfortunately, every attempt to seek the intervention of authorities at the highest possible levels failed. Even more deplorable was the almost universal complaint of the apathy, indifference and complicity of many members of the police force, especially at the junior level.

As regards the extent of the damage, over two thousand were murdered, leaving behind over a thousand widows and numerous orphans. Sikh educational institutions, several large and many small houses were burnt. Trucks, taxi-cabs, three-wheelers, cars, motor-cycles and scooters were burnt in their hundreds. Movable property, cash and jewellery were stolen or destroyed. Factories and business premises, together with their machinery and stock-in-trade, were looted, damaged or destroyed. A disturbing feature of this occasion was that for the first time in the history of mob violence in India, a systematic attack was made on places of worship. Of about 450 gurdwaras in Delhi, some three-quarters were reported to have been damaged or destroyed. The loss to the nation was phenomenal.

The Commission accepted the fact that large numbers of Sikhs also shared in the sentiment of grief and revulsion over the tragic death of Mrs. Indira Gandhi, but instead of this national calamity being the occasion for the exercise of the utmost caution and restraint, certain elements exploited the situation as a pretext for rousing public feelings and channeling them into the dangerous direction of seeking revenge against a particular community for partisan advantage. The outrages and crimes committed were instigated and directed to a large extent by political elements abetted by the indifference, if not active complicity, of the custodians of the law. The Commission urged the government to identify all the culprits, regardless of their social, political or economic standing, and to deal with them in strict accordance with the law of the land. Those who had been named or identified on several occasions should be brought to trial without any delay.

Justice S.M. Sikri, former Chief Justice of the Supreme Court, addressed several letters to the Prime Minister and the Home Minister to seek appointments for explaining specific aspects of this great human tragedy. Copies of these were sent to me.

When I met Rajiv Gandhi and P.V. Narasimha Rao, then Home Minister, at a function, I suggested to them to arrange a judicial inquiry into the disturbances to enable the truth to come out before the people to remove any misunderstanding about the extent of the damage. Rajiv said that the reports of PUCL and PUDR and of Citizens' Commission were biased and one-sided. My reaction was that a judicial inquiry could set the speculation at rest. The Home Minister did not say anything. Rajiv Gandhi, however, said that he would give it a serious thought.

Chapter 35

DIFFERENCES WITH RAJIV GANDHI

After three or four days, it was a Sunday when I sent for Rajiv Gandhi, but my Secretary was informed by the Prime Minister's Secretary that Rajiv Gandhi would call on me in a couple of days time and that he wanted me to take rest on a Sunday. I was surprised at this suggestion. But he never came, and in the following days and weeks I realized that he had started avoiding me. Those days Arun Singh used to call on me and talk things over on behalf of the Prime Minister. At a function, I told Rajiv Gandhi that there were some very important matters to be discussed, to which he said that he would definitely send Arun Singh or Arun Nehru to meet me. I said, it was a matter for him to decide. Arun Singh continued to call on me. I noticed that whenever something of substance came up for discussion, and I expressed certain views, he promised to pursue the matter, but nothing tangible came out of it. Perhaps, he had instructions from PM just to listen to me and then forget everything.

The Government ordered a judicial inquiry into the November 1984 riots at the instance of Sant Harchand Singh Longowal, then President of the Akali Dal, but the findings of Justice Ranganath Misra of the Supreme Court left a wave of sullenness and disappointment among the public, especially the witnesses and victims of the holocaust.

I still had a feeling that Rajiv Gandhi would not disagree with me on many issues, and once again I told him at an official function that there should not be a communication gap between us, as it could cause unnecessary and avoidable misunderstandings. Rajiv's line was that there was actually no misunderstanding and there was no question of any misunderstanding occurring either. I again believed him.

The Prime Minister suggested that a hot line could be installed for our emergent discussions. I told him that already there were Rax telephones. But, Rajiv Gandhi said, the Rax telephones were not entirely a safe channel of communication, as eavesdropping on them was possible. I thought, if a hotline was established between us two, then Rajiv would never consider it necessary to call on me at Rashtrapati Bhavan for briefings or consultations. I was not quite thrilled at the prospect of the Prime Minister talking on telephone with the President on important State subjects ignoring the convention of personal meetings. In fact when I meet a person, I make it a point to read his face and also watch the reaction in his eyes. I did not, therefore, encourage PM's proposal for setting up a hot-line.

After elections to the Parliament, Rajiv Gandhi brought a list of names for his Council of Ministers. He had promised to come half an hour before the time fixed for the swearing-in ceremony. As was customary with Mrs. Indira Gandhi to have prior discussions with me about the constitution of the cabinet, I was under the impression that Rajiv Gandhi also wanted consultations. But when he came and was closeted with me, a couple of Advisors stationed in my ADCs' room sent in an ADC suggesting that the oath-taking ceremony was getting late. After a few minutes, this was repeated. It caused me annoyance and I asked the ADC to tell PM's advisors to take it easy as the delay was none of their concern. Obviously, they were itching to know what was going on between the President and the Prime Minister. I asked PM if he had kept some scope for further expansion of the Council of Ministers. He said that this proposition had an advantage as well as a disadvantage. On the one hand, it gave PM freedom to induct fresh talent when spotted and deserved encouragement, and on the other it induced hope and expectation among Members of Parliament, who sometimes vied with one another to get a berth in the Cabinet. I particularly inquired if he had any intention of inducting a particular M.P. in the Council of Ministers later, but, Rajiv Gandhi said, he doubted his loyalty. After due discussions, I administered the oath of office arid secrecy to the members recommended.

Rajiv Gandhi often stated that he assessed the merit of his Ministers after monitoring their performance. Some of the members of the Union Council of Ministers were those, who had already served as Chief Ministers of States and some had served in Mrs. Indira Gandhi's team. It was a matter of speculation if their ability had decreased and their efficiency dropped. But hardly had anyone of them shown pique or lodged protest. They had shown tremendous adaptability.

One day, when Rajiv Gandhi came to *Rashtrapati Bhavan* to attend a formal dinner, I asked him if he had assessed the performance of his Ministers, to which he said that some of them had been evaluated, but some were still under scrutiny. I told Rajiv that he was still very young and there were persons available with long experience. It would be to his advantage, if he would seek their advice and gain by their wisdom. He should not forget, I told him, that some others had made great sacrifices in the national struggle and had seen many ups and downs. They had considerable administrative experience and with the good of the country at heart, they wanted to strengthen his hands. He must set greater store by the concern and affection for him rather than their loyalty to new-fangled ideas. Love and genuine concern were more valuable than mere fawning. Objectivity was more important than obsequiousness. Rajiv then asked who were the people he should consult for advice. In general terms, I said there were some Chief Ministers of States, members of the Parliamentary Board, Presidents of the State Units of his political party and others, who would be only too glad to render him sincere advice without any expectations. I specifically mentioned Professor N.G. Ranga, who was the most seasoned Parliamentarian, who could be of use. The Prime Minister seemed to have taken it conscientiously and affirmed to try this.

The Governors of States send their requests for leave of

absence to the President. B.K. Nehru, the Governor of Gujarat wanted to go abroad for about three weeks. He sent me a letter and then I received a file from the Government recommending that the Chief Justice of the State should be given the charge of Governor, for which he should take the oath. '1 made a query if this arrangement was necessary. The Government reiterated their stand, when I accorded my approval to their request. The next day B.K. Nehru called on me and questioned the propriety of the Central Government in deciding to swear in the Chief Justice as Governor, when he was going to be absent for hardly three weeks.

I had a chance meeting with Rajiv Gandhi that evening, when I asked him why the Government were insisting on swearing in of the Chief Justice as Governor, when the latter would be away only for a short while. Rajiv lamented that the Chief Justice of the Gujarat High Court was also not a very fit person. I then pointed out to him, that if B.K. Nehru went abroad as Governor of a State, he would receive greater attention and respect, rather than as a person who had vacated his office. Rajiv expressed his helplessness, as the oath to the Chief Justice had already been administered. B.K. Nehru took it with a pinch of salt and remarked that the Government's action had really created a piquant situation.

The Prime Minister stopped consulting me on many subjects. An undercurrent of hostility took the place of formal demonstrative courtesy. Overt and covert measures were taken to keep the persons once close to me, away from positions of influence. Some of them were made to pay for their connections with me. I would rather refrain from citing examples of discrimination and hostility to these people, as the narrative would be nauseating.

A programme had been made for my visit to three foreign countries. The visit was called off on the ground that the situation in India was not normal. It was only a subterfuge. The real .motive of the elements inimical to me was to stall my foreign tour. These elements were searching for a way to get me removed from the Presidency. Before the Punjab Accord was signed by the Akali leader, Sant Harchand Singh Longowal and the Prime Minister, Rajiv Gandhi, two

Congress leaders, Bhajan Lal (then Chief Minister of Haryana), and K.C. Pant (a Union Minister), had come to see me individually and then jointly to talk about the Punjab problem. They tried to sell the idea that this complicated problem could be solved only by me and that would be possible, if I took over as Chief Minister of the State. They postured that it would mean a great sacrifice on my part to step down from the Presidency to the Chief Ministership of a State, but the sacrifice would not be too great in the interest of the country. This reminded me of the halcyon days of Punjab, when I had been the Chief Minister for over five years and when this strategic state had registered all round progress free from any communal conflict. They emphasized that a leader like me, who knew the pulse of the State so well, was needed there at that critical juncture to control the situation and to arrest the downslide in communal relations. I asked both of them, if they had consulted the Prime Minister before coming to me or whether they had been sent by the Prime Minister himself. They did not admit or deny this, but said that it was their own thinking. I asked them if they had not come without the approval of the Prime Minister, how could they be so sure that he would accept this proposition. I frankly told them that I could not persuade myself to believe that they had made this suggestion on their own volition, but if they insisted, I had nothing more to say.

On their second visit, I asked them to make a clean breast of everything. If they had been directed by the Prime Minister to work on me about this suggestion, they should not beat about the bush. If the government was desirous of easing me out of the Presidency, they should say so and I would have no hesitation in quitting the office immediately, but this indirect method was not quite palatable. I had a hunch that their move was calculated, but I wanted to go to the bottom of it.

I came to know that the Prime Minister and his friends had also considered the possibility of impeaching me. Legal experts had told them that they were on a weak ground. They should not take a false step that might land them in an embarrassing situation. When the two luminaries broached the topic with me again, I could not help remarking that instead of trying to find a genuine solution to the real Punjab problem, they seemed to be more interested in making me the Chief Minister. And if it were so, would the Central Government guarantee its cooperation with me? I suggested to these gentlemen to ask the Prime Minister to discuss the proposal with me himself. But they repeated their earlier stand that they had thought of it themselves and the Prime Minister was not aware of it.

Chapter 36

DENIAL OF INFORMATION TO THE PRESIDENT

The daily reports filed by the Intelligence Bureau with the Government are always sent to the President for his information. These reports were being forwarded to me. The government also receives coded messages from our Embassies abroad, which, after decoding, are regularly put up to the Prime Minister and the President. These reports were being sent up to me also. But suddenly these stopped coming to me, which caused me great surprise. I did not know the reason or the intentions of the Government. Once, when the Prime Minister happened to see me, I asked him the reason behind this negative approach. I wondered if it was an indication of the President having lost the confidence of the Government or was it due to some other reason? If it was the loss of trust, then the President could be impeached. And even if the Prime Minister would take me into confidence, I would be ready to give up my office. The Prime Minister denied this and said that there was no question of the Government not having the fullest confidence in me, and the question of my quitting did not arise. I also mentioned to the Prime Minister that there were several invitations from the Heads of State of other countries for my visits abroad, and it was mystifying that the Government had not cleared the visits. I told the Prime Minister that I was receiving proposals for appointments of Ambassadors, Judges and Governors from the Government and I was clearing them with great dispatch, but the Government was taking inordinate time in deciding matters relating to me. "I asked PM to be frank. I had no love for office and power, I told him, and I could walk out any time, when I realized that my stay in *Rashtrapati Bhavan* was not to the liking of the Prime Minister. I was like a sojourner in an inn, and I would have no regret checking out any time. But the way the Government was dealing with me, it was not too appropriate or dignified. I wanted the Prime Minister to open his heart and express his real feelings.

Regarding invitations from the foreign States, the Prime Minister took pains to elaborate that the capital had been rocked by transistor bomb explosions, and the Government was of the view that the President's presence would be necessary here. And that is why the Government had refrained from making plans for my visits abroad. but now when the situation had been brought under control, a foreign tour of the President was on the cards. The Prime Minister suggested that I should not entertain any idea of the Government being indifferent to me or my dignity being ignored. Rajiv Gandhi went further and recalled the days when he was not the Prime Minister and I was not the President, when he used to show more respect to me than any other leader. Of course, as President, I was entitled to all respect and consideration from him and the Government, he said. Without mincing words, I told Rajiv Gandhi that I found it difficult to share his feeling as my impression was different. He reiterated that there should be no cause for my misgivings. As regards the Intelligence Bureau reports, the Prime Minister said that he would ask the Home Ministry to cooperate with me. He pointed out that as a result of the activities of a spy ring, which was responsible for passing on sensitive information to outsiders, the Government had become more wary. Photostat copies of one or two papers were supplied by a Stenographer in *Rashtrapati Bhavan* to a spy gang.

It was the same espionage scandal in which most papers involved were smuggled out of the Prime Minister's Secretariat, for which constructive responsibility was owned by

P.C. Alexander, Principal secretary to the Prime Minister, and he ultimately resigned from the post. The stenographer involved in the President's Secretariat was arrested by the police.

Though the Prime Minister promised to resume the supply of the daily Intelligence Bureau reports, it was not put into practice. I felt unhappy, but did not put it on record, as I did not want this inconsistency on the part of the Government to become a part of history. It was always my attempt to settle matters between the President and the Prime Minister in a spirit of mutual understanding and sincerity. One reason for my exercising the utmost patience and perserverance on this particular subject was to keep the problems between the President and the Prime Minister beyond the pail of public controversy.

After a little while, I received a proposal from the Government for appointment of P.C. Alexander as India's High Commissioner to the United Kingdom. I had nothing against Alexander, so I approved his appointment. But after some time there was occasion for me to ask the Government, how it was that a man, who had owned constructive responsibility for the espionage scandal, had been rewarded with a prize post. On the other hand, hardly one or two papers had been leaked out by a junior employee in the President's Secretariat, which had been magnified to a such a great extent, and was being quoted as the reason for withholding important reports from the President.

Obviously, the Government was obliged to give a second thought to the matter and the supply of the reports from Indian missions abroad was restored. But the Government could be choosy and withhold such information as they wanted to. A senior official of the Ministry of External Affairs came and showed me the notings precluding the President from receiving reports from the Ministry emanating from the Heads of Diplomatic missions. The flow of Intelligence Bureau reports, though resumed, was quite irregular. Instead of Daily reports, they would send me weekly summaries after a lapse of time. Whenever I mentioned these things to the Prime Minister, he never said the reports would not be sent. He always wanted a little more time to ponder over the matter. Very often I wondered if it was the right way for the Government to treat the Head of State, but I never wanted their indiscretions to become a matter of public controversy. I did not cherish the idea of entering into a confrontation. They seemed to be bent upon trying my patience, and I was determined to keep my poise. I wondered if the Government would treat the next President in the same manner, as they were trying to treat me.

As whispers started making the rounds about my visit to some foreign countries, my Secretariat made enquiries from the Ministry of External Affairs, if there was any concrete proposal in this regard. They were told that the programme was being finalised. After some days they were asked to earmark certain days in the following month for the President's foreign visit. Again, the Ministry of External Affairs conveyed that the proposal had been put up to the Prime Minister and the file was being awaited from him. When I was apprised of the position, I told my officers not to make any enquiry. If the Government were not interested in their President's visits to other countries, which necessarily afforded them an opportunity to strengthen their bonds with those nations and to derive advantage, then it was entirely their own outlook. Some heads of State like the King of Bhutan, and the Presidents of Sri Lanka, Pakistan and Bangladesh, who had visited India had been repeatedly extending invitations to me to pay return visits to their lands. During the Prime Minister's visit to Calcutta, a journalist inquiring of him about the President-Prime Minister's relations, asked why the President's foreign tours were not being cleared, to which PM said he was not aware of any hitch and the President could go whenever he liked.

After appearance of this report in the Press, there was a word from the External Affairs Ministry that a programme for my foreign" visit was being given final touches. It was for Nepal.

My visit to Nepal.in July 1986, was very useful. The King had free and frank talks with me without any aides on either side. The only other persons present at this meeting were Aishwarya Devi, the Queen of Nepal and my daughter, Dr. Manjit Kaur, who was accompanying me. On my return to New Delhi, the Prime Minister was leading a group of Ministers at the airport to receive me, When Rajiv Gandhi asked me about the trip, I told him that there were a number of important things for me to apprise him of. Apart from my impressions of the Nepal visit, there were some other matters needing urgent attention. Rajiv said, he would call on me very soon. I waited but he never came. It was not the first time he had made such an illusory promise. Whenever he made a commitment like this, he did not keep it. After a little while I sent him a resume of my impressions of my visit to Nepal and suggested once again that he should find time for a meeting to enable me to give him a detailed picture of the Indo-Nepalese relations as perceived by the King and other leaders of Nepal, especially of what .transpired between me and the Nepalese monarch during our discussion without any aides being present. All I got in return from Rajiv Gandhi was a one-line acknowledgement of my letter.

One day I had to tell him that, perhaps, he had become forgetful in spite of his youth. Some significant matters had been left to linger on only to die their natural death, because he had not found the time to discuss them. He denied forgetfulness, whereupon I had to express my misgiving for the third time that in that case possibly he had no faith in me. Such tension was detrimental to the interests of the country. Rajiv Gandhi then said that he would make it a point to call on me at least once a. fortnight. 'It would end the controversy in the public mind about the Prime Minister nor briefing the President on important matters of State. But Rajiv Gandhi did not translate these promises into practice. When a newsman asked him at a Press conference as to why he had not been observing the convention of meeting the President, he replied that he had broken hundreds of conventions.

Chapter 37

STATEHOOD TO UNION TERRITORIES

In June 1986, the daily newspapers carried reports of negotiations between the insurgent leader of the north-eastern Union territory of Mizoram, Laldenga, and the Central Government to arrive at a settlement to end dissidence and for the restoration of peace in that troubled region. While fully sharing concern over the disturbed conditions of life and the difficulties created by the terrorist elements in the territory and earnestly appreciating the Government's efforts to resolve the long standing problems through purposeful negotiations, I told Rajiv Gandhi that unfortunately I had not been kept informed of the stand of the Government on the Mizoram issue, especially when the newspapers were full of stories regarding the impending formation of a coalition government headed by Laldenga and the proposed grant of full-fledged statehood to Mizoram. Guided by my obligations explicitly laid down in the Constitution to advise, encourage and warn the Council of Ministers, I drew the Prime Minister's attention to the possibility of a charge of placing premium on insurgency and violence by making Laldenga the Head of government after displacing the elected Chief Minister, who then happened to be Lalthanhawala, and, who incidentally belonged to Rajiv Gandhi's own political party, Congress (I). I also advised Rajiv Gandhi that in case it was considered unavoidable in the national interest to grant full Statehood to the Union Territory of Mizoram, the Government should keep in mind the claims to statehood of two other Union Territories-Goa and Arunachal Pradesh, lest they felt that their peaceful demand over the years had not been of any avail. I expressed the hope that the likely repercussions would be assessed properly and the timing and the modalities of conferring statehood on these two Union Territories would be carefully worked out because of the larger implications of the issue.

At the time of communicating these thoughts to Rajiv Gandhi, I could not least expect the hasty and acerbic reaction it would evoke in the young Prime Minister. Trying desperately to clear his conscience of the guilt feeling of his Government going out of its way to bring to the centre-stage an insurgent leader responsible for considerable loss of life and property by adopting extra-constitutional means, he harked back to the negotiations carried on with Laldenga in 1976 and 1978 and then resumed in 1980-81, when the latter had meetings with the then Prime Minister, Mrs. Indira Gandhi, myself as Home Minister and the Home Secretary. Prior to these negotiations, cases against Laldenga had been withdrawn and in August 1980, it had been agreed to by the Central Government to suspend operations by the Security forces against insurgents. Rajiv Gandhi tried to remind me that I, as the Union Home Minister, had four meetings with the Mizoram National Front delegations during April-May 1981, and that I had indicated to them the Government's willingness to consider withdrawal of the pending cases against the personnel of the Mizoram National Front. Rajiv Gandhi also recalled the role of certain officials, who had been entrusted with the task of talking to the MNF leaders and the indication given by the former of the Government's willingness conferring statehood on Mizoram, when the MNF personnel came overground and surrendered· their arms. Rajiv Gandhi vehemently asserted that the decision to give statehood to Mizoram was taken presumably in my knowledge as Home Minister in August 1981. He also stated that he considered certain attitudes adopted in the past as detrimental to the larger interests of the country. For example, the Government in earlier stages had agreed to withdraw prosecutions against MNF activists without giving thought to the rights of Chakma minorities. Rajiv Gandhi expressed his disapproval to a constitutional provision with regard to non-operation of any law of the Union Government in respect of the land and its resources in the state of Nagaland, without the concurrence: of the State Assembly and the Government's willingness to extend such a provision to Mizoram.

It was amazing the way Rajiv Gandhi chose to interpret the manner in which negotiations to bring the Mizoram insurgents into the mainstream of national life had been conducted earlier. He conveniently forgot that it was the Government headed by his mother, Mrs. Indira Gandhi, which had initiated negotiations with the MNF leaders and the Horne Minister alone was not responsible for such important decisions. He also overlooked the import of my advice as President to consider the claims of Arunachal Pradesh and Goa for Statehood along with that of Mizoram. Since MNF activists had been adopting violent methods to press their demands as compared to the mild, peaceful and constitutional manner adopted by the other aspirants, it was my concern to avoid the impression gaining ground that violence and extremism alone could wrest decisions from the Centre. Rajiv Gandhi shrewdly evaded the issue regarding the method .of inducting Laldenga into the political structure, but promised to keep in view the relevant considerations.

I was dismayed at the tone of Rajiv Gandhi's response. It was obvious that he was being swayed more by pique than by reason. Perhaps, he could not perceive the existence and the role of constitutional institution as the President, whose bounden duty it was to ensure the welfare of the people of the country enjoined upon him by the oath of his office.

It is understandable that I had some information available with me as Horne Minister along with the then Prime Minister, Mrs. Indira Gandhi and it would have served the purpose of Rajiv Gandhi's Government better, had he shown willingness to discuss things with me. During my negotiations with Laldenga, my brief had been to offer general amnesty for all those who laid down arms and swore allegiance to the Indian Constitution. But this was not acceptable to Laldenga. In addition to wanting a dispensation somewhat similar to that of Nagaland under Article 371 (A) of the Constitution, he insisted on heading the Government and getting the traditional trade links with Burma safeguarded without interference from the Government of India. I had conveyed this position to Mrs. Indira Gandhi. I had strong reservations about the elements like the President's rule having been promulgated in Mizoram to pave the way for Laldenga to take over as Chief Minister. I held the same views now as Rajiv Gandhi's Government seemed to be capitulating to the forces adopting militant postures. I also strongly felt that legitimate and peaceful demands of political units like Arunachal Pradesh and Goa should be considered simultaneousiy with that of Mizoram. Though with the passage of time some adjustments might be necessary in approach, the Government should never give an impression of succumbing to militant advocacy and ignoring peaceful attitudes. Rajiv Gandhi tried to give a fallacious impression that whatever situation there had been, it was due to the handling of the issue by the Horne Ministry. It would have been only fair and honest on his part to attribute whatever faults he was trying to find now, to Mrs. Indira Gandhi's Government as a whole, and not to a particular individual. But obviously, either in his impetuosity or due to co loured advice, he was trying to throw discretion to the winds and to justify his own inconsistency with brave words and a show of bold postures. Mrs. Indira Gandhi was no more in this world, and I wondered what she would have thought if she were present today, of her son finding many acts of her Government as leading to a tempest of violence and disunity. Mrs. Gandhi had a much broader mind and a much wider vision. She generally shared her perceptions with her colleagues and took responsibility for collective decisions.

I told Rajiv cordially that it was unfortunate that my concern about important national issues failed to evoke the right responses in him and that his tone and tenor were a cause of deep anguish. I did not see any point in entering into a wordy duel with the Prime Minister, who lay much store by his youthfulness and, perhaps, took pride in deliberately showing lack of consideration for the people of older generation, even though the person on the other side might be the President of the country. I had also to tell him that much of what he had said was not based on facts. Once again I expressly suggested to him to come and discuss things.

In June 1986, I had just returned from a five-day visit to Jammu and Kashmir, where I had an occasion to meet a cross section of the people. It would be helpful, I told Rajiv Gandhi, if he were to come to *Rashtrapati Bhaoan,* so that I could share my impressions with him, but it failed to touch any responsive chord in his heart.

H was a matter of great surprise that Rajiv Gandhi was not only not following the convention of meeting the President to inform him on matters of State, he was ignoring wilfully all suggestions and overtures of the President for such periodic discussions, in national interest. That was not all. The Government chose to withhold the reports of the Commissions of Inquiry from the President. By about August 1986, the Parliament passed the Commissions of Inquiry (Amendment) Bill, 1986, seeking to empower the Government not to table the Reports of Commissions of Inquiry before Parliament. When it was sent to me for assent, I wanted a clarification whether in cases where the Government issued a Notification under the provisions of the Amendment, they would furnish the Report or any part thereof to the President. Rajiv Gandhi rang me up to emphasize the urgency of the matter and offered to send Buta Singh, Home Minister, to meet me. When the latter came, I gave him a sealed note for the Prime Minister. I drew the Prime Minister's attention to the fact that lately certain Reports of Commissions of Inquiry received by the Government had not been furnished to me even though my Secretariat had written to the Home Ministry on three occasions to convey my desire for persual of the Reports.

Buta Singh assured me that it was not the intention of the Government to withhold the Commissions of Inquiry Reports from the President, even in cases where the Reports were not placed before Parliament.

On getting this clarification from the Home Minister, I gave my assent to the Amendment Bill. Buta Singh solemnly promised to personally bring the various Reports asked for by me the next morning. But the promise was never fulfilled.

Rajiv Gandhi, while acknowledging my note five days later, stated that he was getting the matter examined. Several weeks passed and there was no word from the Prime Minister or the Home Minister about the substance of my note or the Reports I had asked them to send me. I was constrained to write to Rajiv Gandhi in October 1986, reminding him about the Home Minister's verbal assurance and his own written promise that the matter was being examined. I told the Prime Minister that I wanted these reports in the discharge of the obligations cast on me under the Constitution. Rajiv Gandhi once again replied by saying that he was asking the Home Minister to look into the matter immediately. But in actual fact nothing happened. No action was taken by anyone in the Government to send me the reports. Buta Singh was reminded personally on more than one occasion. He was apologetic every time and promised to make amends without delay, but it appeared that every time he left the courtyard of the Rashtrapati Bhavan, he forgot his promises. I often thought that if they could treat the President in such a manner, what would be the fate of a common citizen. It caused me hurt, when the Prime Minister said that my request was being examined. It needed quite an effort on my part to put up with such a posture. The Head of Sate was being told by the Head of Government that his request for papers was being considered. I made a note that the Prime Minister was not working in the framework of the Constitution. It became almost a routine with the Prime Minister and some of his colleagues to overlook the constitutional niceties they owed to the President. There were two options before me-either to react with similar indifference to force the persons concerned to realise the folly of their attitude or to show endurance by ignoring their faults and foibles. 1 tried to adopt the latter method, as I did not like their non-too-statesmanlike behaviour to attract public notice and wanted to see the wheels of the constitutional machinery to run smoothly.

In 1986, India transferred the mantle of leadership of the nonaligned movement to Zimbabwe. Earlier, in 1983 the responsibility of chairmanship had fallen on the shoulders of India and Mrs. Indira Gandhi had discharged the onerous duties of the chairperson admirably. In early September 1986, I wrote to Rajiv Gandhi greeting him over his contribution to the movement during a short span of two years and the prestige earned by India. Referring inevitably to the manifold and pressing challenges facing the developing countries in general, and India in particular, I reminded the Prime Minister about the increasing significance of our foreign policy priorities in the subcontinent. I expressed my hope that alongside the wider Indian role, the immediate security environment would receive closer attention in the coming months.

When I sent this brief note to Rajiv Gandhi, I was dictated solely by a desire to convey my appreciation for the role played by Mrs. Indira Gandhi and Rajiv Gandhi himself in strengthening the nonaligned movement and to express my concern about the threat posed to our security environment. But Rajiv Gandhi magnanimously thanking me for kind words about his role in NAM and acknowledging himself as the inheritor of a great tradition built by Pandit Jawaharlal Nehru and Mrs. Indira Gandhi, as if by reflex action, went on the defensive about safeguarding our national security. He termed my advice to devote close attention to our immediate security environment as a recapitulation of what was already being done by him in ample measure. From the very beginning of his term, he said, measures to enhance the defence capability and to safeguard national security had the highest priority on the agenda. Claiming that unceasing vigil had been kept, he emphasized that it had been done so in the past and would continue to be done not only in the coming months, but at all times!

I could not understand why Rajiv Gandhi had to go on the defensive every time I tried to make an observation albeit on a matter concerning the nation. It was not clear whether he had a feeling of insecurity, or he wanted to convince himself that he had all-pervasive power and every other institution in the country had to playa tributory role to him. One incident that occurred in the middle of September 1986, gave me an inkling of how his mind worked and how he could take umbrage on something blown up by him and hi's friends out of all proportion. It was when seven prominent citizens came to me at *Rashtrapati Bhavan* and gave me a Memorandum. They consisted of Pranab Mukherjee (Finance Minister in Mrs. Indira Gandhi's Cabinet), R. Gundu Rao (former Chief Minister of Karnataka), Prakash Mehrotra (former Governor of Assam), Sisir Kumar Bose (a well-known freedom fighter and nephew of the legendary hero of the freedom struggle, Netaji Subhash Chandra Bose), S.S. Mahapatra (former General Secretary of Congress (I) party), F.M. Khan (M.P.) and Ashok Bhattacharya. All these were public men and had held important positions in national life in one form or another. They wanted to express their deep concern over the developments affecting our national life. They sought an appointment with me, which was given to them by my Secretariat. They were of the view that the manner in which important and vital national issues were being handled by Rajiv Gandhi's Government was not in the best interests of the nation and since they could not remain "silent onlookers" to the fast deteriorating situation, they had come to communicate their views and concerns to the Head of State.

These gentlemen had stated that when after the assassination of Mrs. Indira Gandhi a grave national crisis had arisen, the political leadership of the country had manifested remarkable maturity in removing the political uncertainty and instability. In the general elections of December 1984, the people of the country had demonstrated their strong desire to preserve the unity and integrity of the nation. But unfortunately, the message conveyed through this election was not properly understood and, instead of strengthening the forces of unity and solidarity, measures were taken to encourage the divisive, disruptive and sectarian forces which posed a serious threa t to the country.

They had dwelt at length with the complacency of the Government at the intrusion of China into our land by construction of a helipad in Arunachal Pradesh and the casual way the Union Government had dealt with the situation. The Government had issued two contradictory statements in a short span of time and had not taken note of the information obtained and made public by the Chief Minister of the Union Territory. The Parliament and the people were misled. The

Government had failed in its primary responsibilities of protecting the national borders and territorial integrity.

The instrumentality of 'accords' offered by the Govemment had reached the point of ridicule. Since July 1986, three important 'accords' had been signed by the Government at the level of the Prime Minister. These had been publicised with great fanfare and efforts were being made to project them as symbols of the new Government's achievements in solving the long-standing complex problems of Punjab, Assam and Mizoram. As regards the Mizoram Accord, the Union Government had shown eagerness to settle an issue which, in fact, had ceased to exist. It also showed how the democratic institutions like an elected Government could be sacrificed for the convenience of the ruling party. Such agreements could only serve to encourage other separatist forces which could intensify their acts of violence for increasing their bargaining power. This phenomenon was already evident in Tripura and West Bengal, where the Tripura National Volunteers and the Gorkha National Liberation Front activists were indulging in murder and arson with impunity.

These gentlemen decried the way Laldenga had been chosen by the Congress Party to head its legislative wing—the man who had declared war against the country, sought political asylum in a foreign land, caused loss of life of hundreds of security personnel and civilians. This person had been chosen to head a Government without any sanction of the people. This Agreement would seriously jeopardise the position of the nationalist forces in the north-eastern region. The people of Mizoram were forced to accept as head of their State Government a person, who had never considered himself an Indian citizen owing allegiance to the Indian Constitution.

The delegation had also pointed out the pathetic state of the two other Accords. Peace in Punjab was elusive and terrorism was going on unabated. Implementation of some of the provisions of the Punjab Accord had yet to be seen. The whole exercise of Government in this regard was being looked upon as ridiculous.

In Assam, as a result of the Agreement, the problems of minorities, both linguistic and religious, had aggravated. It was surprising that even after one year of the signing of the Accord, no authoritative interpretation of the various provisions of the Accord was available.

The delegation had further said that the whole country was surcharged with communal tensions. Communal riots were breaking out in different areas. The sense of belonging to one nation and one country was vanishing fast. An unending series of political murders and other crimes was being committed in different parts of the country. This demonstrated the lack of political will on the part of the Government and a gross inefficiency on the part of the Administration.

These persons had complained that for petty partisan consideration, decisions of the Government were attempted to be projected as individual decisions. Character assassination of the political opponents by misuse of official position and government media had become the order of the day, though some chosen politicians, businessmen and bureaucrats etc., were considered to be above the law.

In the name of tax reforms Government revenues were being sacrificed, while Government's expenditure was being met by borrowings including heavy doses of deficit financing. The inevitable result was high prices. Prices of essential commodities like cooking oil, gas, petrol, kerosene, pulses, garlic, onion, and vegetables had increased sharply. Millions of rural and urban poor belonging to the unorganised sector had no relief from the oppressive price rise. The deficit in international trade had reached a staggering figure of about Rs. 8,000 crore. The export growth had been negligible. Soon the country was going to face acute balance of payments problem. Unsteady rupee value with reference to US Dollar was a matter of concern.

The poverty alleviation measures like National Rural Employment Programme, Integrated Rural Development Programme and Rural Landless Employment Guarantee Programme etc. were not implemented sincerely. Without adequate financial support, these programmes would render the objective of poverty eradication meaningless. The Government's failure to provide adequate purchasing machinery to purchase agricultural commodities directly from the growers had created a .situation where the growers got less, consumers paid more and the profit was being made by the middlemen. Sickness of industries in the private sector was increasing. The hi-tech machinery imported with valuable foreign exchange was lying unused. The categorical assertion by the Prime Minister that there would be no further nationalisation had put the Government in a very rigid situation. Closures and lockouts in a number of industrial units throwing people out of jobs were matters of grave concern. Indiscriminate computerisation programme was bound to have adverse impact on the employment scenario.

On foreign relations, the delegation had expressed their distress over the deterioration in our ties with Pakistan. Bangladesh was in no mood to accept India's proposals to fence the Indo-Bangladesh border. The Government of India were unable to impress the Sri Lankan Government to find a human solution to the problem of Sri-Lankan Tamils. The Prime Minister's efforts to defuse the tension between Iran and Iraq had been fruitless. His position in regard to aggression on Libya had been ambivalent. As a founding member of the Nonaligned Movement and the immediate past Chairman, a dynamic positive role of India was expected in the Non-Aligned Summit at Harare.

The Government had been taking arbitrary decisions in regard to the appointment of Judges in the High Courts and the Supreme Court. Its intentions of subverting the independence of the judiciary had been obvious. The decision of the Government not to make public the findings of any Inquiry Commission was an evidence of high-handedness. The very essence of public enquiry was that people should know full facts of a subject under enquiry. By amending the relevant provisions, assuming the powers to keep such findings secret on the plea of public interest was highly questionable and objectionable. People's confidence in public enquiry would be totally shaken as a result of this Act. People were interested in knowing the findings of the Thakkar Commission, but the Government's attitude had created doubts and suspicious in the minds of the common people.

The delegation had pleaded that since the President was custodian of the Constitution and the Constitution entrusted him with the responsibility of preserving the unity and integrity of the nation, he had the right to advise and warn the Government and to be informed and consulted by them, In view of the grave situation being faced by the country, the President might respond to these submissions in the manner he considered appropriate,

It was widely known that I was accessible not to a selected few, but people from all walks of life, Having been a public man myself for a few decades, my instinct naturally was to let the people meet me to express their views and to convey their sentiments.

The same day I passed on the Memorandum to the Prime Minister without any comment of my own. Quickly reacting to such an innocuous move, Rajiv Gandhi went to town with harsh comments and described these gentlemen as loyal not to political principles or ideology or even to a leader, but to their own little niche of power. Without stating his stand on the points made by these persons, Rajiv Gandhi described it an exercise in evasion of political and socio-economic realities. He said that these gentlemen had completely disregarded the high traditions and dignity of the exalted office of the President by submitting what he described as a "political chargesheet" against the Government. He thought that they had overlooked the rule of fighting political battles in a political arena and had sought to involve the Presidency. Rajiv Gandhi took this opportunity to state that his basic policies, domestic as well as foreign, reflected an underlying continuity. These also reflected sensitivity to changing circumstances, he said, because to avoid stagnation, forces of change had to be accommodated within the structure of policy. He claimed to be following the principles laid down by Pandit Nehru and Mrs. Indira Gandhi.

Rajiv Gandhi took pains to remind that the policies of his Government had been extensively discussed in Parliament and vital issues such as Punjab and the need to actively combat communalism had been anxiously debated in the National Integration Council. The broad issues of economic and social strategy are the subject matter of annual Parliamentary debate arising out of the President's address. After claiming that his basic policies had received wide support because of their being in tune with the fundamental urges of the people, Rajiv Gandhi conceded that there was scope for debate and discussion on these fundamental issues, provided there were concrete and specific frames of policy, which needed to be articulated in a reasoned manner rather than being presented on a partisan and propagandist line.

I told Rajiv Gandhi that forwarding this paper to him by me was not an isolated instance. Hardly ten days earlier I had forwarded another paper to him personally, an acknowledgment to which had been received. It was in the best interest of the Government that all such representations received by the President were forwarded to PM or other Ministers for appropriate action. This was a channel of communication, which the Government should appreciate and welcome rather than entertain doubts or feel embarrassed.

I asked Rajiv Gandhi about the justification of other two dozen Congress (I) members of Parliament adopting a militant posture on this issue and criticizing the President in a statement. I had no ill-will for or any dispute with the Government. I would have no ill-will even after my retirement. But I would never allow the institution of the President to be denigrated. The dignity of the office of the President should not be allowed to be lowered in any case.

Chapter 38

A FOREIGN VISIT

In November 1986, I went on a State visit to Yugoslavia, Greece and Poland. I should have expected the Prime Minister to meet me personally before the visit for a general briefing, but he did not think it necessary to do so. The knowledge of perceptions of the Prime Minister of the countries to be visited by the President would have been helpful, but obviously Rajiv Gandhi had his own ideas.

I had two rounds of talks with President Sinan Hasani of Yugoslavia. There was a discussion on Africa Fund, disarmament and the role of Non-aligned movement. The Yugoslav President lauded the role of non-aligned nations and added that the nine non-aligned or neutral nations of Europe, induding Yugoslavia, had been functioning as an effective lobby for detente and disarmament.

The Iceland summit between President Reagan of USA and the Soviet leader Gorbachev and the situation in West Asia also figured in the talks. The Yugoslav Head of State rued the division among the Arab nations and the tangled nature of the problem which defied any solution. He was at pains to explain his country's relations with its neighbours, especially on the issue of national minorities in the Balkan states. I outlined our efforts to improve relations with our neighbours, especially Pakistan and China and their paradoxical conduct. I was struck by President Hasani's keenness to strengthen relations further with India, especially in the economic field.

In Greece, President Christos Sartzetalkis and I shared our

foreign policy perceptions with each other. Disarmament was considered as an issue of principal concern to mankind. He deeply appreciated India's role in the six-nation initiative on disairnament and welcomed the Harare resolution of the non-aligned countries. President Sartzetalkis stressed the need for extending assistance to the frontline States. He seemed to be very much concerned with the Cyprus issue and was bothered about what his country perceived was the rethinking by India on the whole issue of Cyprus. I felt that a recent visit to India by the Turkish Prime Minister, T. Ozal, had caused some irritation to the Greek leaders. Prime Minister, Andress G. Papandreau, spent most of his time, while paying a courtesy call on me, on the Cyprus issue and his country's disappointment over Turkey's role, though he did mention the almost neutral line being adopted by Greece within the Atlantic alliance. This was in conformity with our world view.

In Poland, the President, General W. Jaruzelski, spared no efforts in underscoring warm and friendly relations with India. He seemed to be in total agreement with our viewpoint on global issues and there was vast similarity on other global matters. President Jaruzelski showed keen interest in cultural relations between our two countries, the increased scientific and technological cooperation and greater exchange of academicians. He also suggested exchange of visits by Parliamentarians between our two countries. The Polish leader talked about the gradually improving internal situation in his country. Church, he said, was now recognised as a social force in Poland. Giving a comparative analysis of Poland's relations with super-powers, President Jaruzelski talked of the sanctions imposed by USA on Poland for having taken certain emergency measures to tide over its internal difficulties, whereas the Soviet Union, despite anti-soviet propaganda in Poland, had provided it succour.

He wished the Sino-Indian relations would improve. He had just visited China, where he had extensive parleys with the Chinese leaders. He advocated a "just" and "correct" settlement of the boundary question between India and China. He described India as the natural leader of the Non-aligned movement and extended support to Africa Fund. Poland, he said, had assisted the frontline states in Africa in the communications field.

On disarmament, President Jaruzelski was of the view that USA was propelled in its arms race by the pressure of its own arms lobby and the political desire to keep Warsaw countries economically under pressure by necessitating heavy defence budgets. Some other matters of mutual interest also figured in our discussions.

A radical change in the thinking of the Polish people was evident. People were moving away from the communist and leaning towards democratic ideals. I was taken to a church, where I exchanged views with some Polish citizens. They talked with effervescence about the co-existent role of religion with communism. There was a new development. People were saying prayers in the Church. I gathered a firm impression that the grip of communism was loosening and the people were heaving themselves up to enter a free society.

On my foreign visits, I used to convey a suggestion that if the hosts deemed it proper, they could show more places than included in their original programme. In most cases such a suggestion was accepted. Here, I was taken to some Polish homes. The standard of living differed from one to the other.

On my return from this tour, I informed the Prime Minister about my discussions with the leaders of the three countries and the variegated scenario their perceptions presented. I also conveyed to Rajiv Gandhi felicitations on his taking over chairmanship of SAARC. I can recall that I received no reaction from the Prime Minister to the impressions conveyed by me on my State visit to the three countries—one a founder member of the Non-aligned movement, another a conscientious objector of the Atlantic alliance and the third a Warsaw Pact adherent cooperating with the Church. That, I came to realise, was in keeping with his penchant for breaking the conventions.

Chapter 39

THE CONSTITUTIONAL RELATIONSHIP

Ever since the Government of Rajiv Gandhi came into power by the end of 1984, one trend was strongly visible that the President be sidelined and his office denigrated. They clearly wished to use the President as a mere rubber stamp. Some of the Ministers would not let any opportunity slip out of their fingers to let down the President even by innuendos and concoctions. One such incident occurred in August 1986, when the Government sent up amendments, proposed by three members of Parliament, to the High Court and Supreme Court Judges (Conditions of Service) Amendment Bill 1986, for recommendations of the President for their consideration by the House. The Minister of State for Law, H.R. Bharadwaj, made the following statement in the Lok Sabha:

> "We wrote to President's Secretariat twice, thrice every day and just now two have been sent, Shantaram Naik's and Shahabuddin's, third one is still not received."

This was entirely incorrect and baseless. I drew the Prime Minister's attention to this factually incorrect statement and told him that apart from the files containing these amendments, there was no other letter received from the Department of Justice. The files received by the President's Secretariat were dealt with promptly. A member of the Council of Ministers had no justification in misleading the Parliament by making a false statement, especially by involving the President in an unfair manner. I asked the Prime Minister to look into the matter and take suitable action. But, as far as my knowledge goes, he did not take any action. At least he did not care to inform me.

Since adoption of the Constitution in January 1950, a convention had come to be established that the Prime Minister called on the President periodically and informed him of important decisions of the Government and discussed essential matters concerning the Union. This was practised assiduously by the first Prime Minister, Pandit Jawahar Lal Nehru, who, inspite of differences in certain momentous matters with the President, Dr. Rajendra Prasad, frequently called on him at Rashtrapati Bhavan. Other Prime Ministers, like Morarji Desai and Mrs. Indira Gandhi adhered to this convention, which impinged on the constitutional relationship between the Head of State and the Head of Government. But, when Rajiv Gandhi was nominated as Prime Minister, he chose to deviate from this practice. He, perhaps, wanted to prove that the office of the President did not have much practical weight and that it was the Prime Minister, who enjoyed the maximum power and influence. Some people thought Rajiv Gandhi's approach was not in keeping with the requirements of the office of PM and was, perhaps, cavalier in nature. This was widely noticed by the media and the public. There were frequent write-ups in the newspapers and magazines and it became a hot topic of discussion in gatherings and meetings. Even members of Parliament sensed the inclinations of the Prime Minister and some of them referred to the relations between the Prime Minister and the President during the discussion in the two Houses on the motion of thanks on my Presidential address. Some members pointed out that the Prime Minister was not doing his duty of briefing the President on important issues of national interest. The Prime Minister denied this allegation and asserted that he had been duly briefing me and there was no such omission on his part. When the proceedings of the two Houses were brought to my notice, I sent a letter to the Prime Minister stating that though I appreciated the spirit behind his observations, which understandably were to put the issue of the relations between the

Head of State and the Head of Government beyond controversy, the factual position was at variance with what had been stated by him. The relationship between the President and the Prime Minister in this country was governed by certain well-established practices and conventions, besides express provisions of the Constitution. I was constrained to point out that certain well-established conventions had not been followed. After his visit to USA and his stopover at Moscow, where he had parleys with the top leaders of these super-powers, I had personally asked PM to let me know his impressions and, though he promised to do so, he conveniently forgot about it. The PM had also slipped up on briefing me after the SAARC meeting at Bangalore. That was not all, I was kept in the dark about important foreign policy matters relating to such of India's immediate neighbours in South Asia, with which there were outstanding problems.

I was quite amused at the Prime Minister's statement in his reply to the debate in Parliament on the President's address that the opposition was politicising the office of the President. I had to remind the Prime Minister that in fact the politicisation had been started by a member of the ruling party in April 1985, when I had to tell the PM that there was an emerging trend to drag in the President's office into political controversy. That very member, K.K. Tewary, had subsequently been included in the Council of Ministers. Had he by implication been rewarded for his labours?

I told the PM simply and clearly that if the relations between the Prime Minister and the President were maintained in accordance with the letter and spirit of the Constitution with national interests kept paramount, there would be no room for comment or speculation from any quarter. This delicate relationship had to be nurtured by mutual trust, concern for conventions and an empathetic and free exchange of views. I expressed the hope that, in future, ideal relations would exist between the Head of State and the Head of Government, and as the Prime Minister had already expressed his views to Parliament, I thought he should know the factual position.

Somehow my communication found its way to the Press. A

Gujarati daily *Sandesh* was the first to publish the text of my letter, in translation. A day later, the *Indian Express* published the English version on its front page. It created a furore throughout the country as the Prime Minister's stand in Parliament about the relationship between the Prime Minister and the President stood contradicted.

After a week of my sending the letter to the Prime Minister, he replied to me first expressing his anguish at the publication of the letter in the Press. He thought that a matter which should have been the subject of a dialogue under constitutional auspices had taken the turn of a public controversy. Rajiv Gandhi denied that there had been any deviation from the obligations imposed by the Constitution. He claimed it as his constant endeavour to uphold the dignity of the office of the President and that he would not depart from this sacred principle. He categorically stated that nothing he had said in Parliament was at variance with facts.

Rajiv Gandhi claimed that he would be serving the nation best by not making the Constitutional relationship between the President and the Prime Minister a subject of public controversy. He would persevere in his endeavour to keep the office of the President, and the relationship between the President and the Prime Minister above the play of partisan politics. He would not allow himself to be provoked by any extraneous considerations. He thought that those who had the welfare of the nation at heart should resist the temptation of making the Presidency a plaything of politics.

I was amazed at Rajiv Gandhi's words, which, I believe, were meant for record and at his tendency to sidetrack the real issue, which was his indifference to the duties he owed under the Constitution and his disregard for the healthy conventions evolved over the years. He tried to divert the attention from the subject matter and pointed out that India's consistent and bold stand for peace, disarmament, development and justice had antagonised internal and external vested interests and we were being subjected to serious pressures to change our independent policies. The nation was facing a serious threat to its unity and integrity from within and without. All political parties were working together to combat the pernicious trend of the forces of communalism and religious fundamentalism. The publication of my letter in the press at that juncture appeared to Rajiv Gandhi to have the potential of deflecting the attention and energy from a common task of the highest national importance. Rajiv Gandhi was afraid that we would have to reckon with the consequences. Dilating on his theme, Rajiv Gandhi said that political stability of India and the wellbeing, security and integrity of the nation transcended everything else. What happened to me and him was not important. The cause must not suffer, but it should triumph.

It caused me a great deal of astonishment to get this type of response from the young Prime Minister. I mused over the continuous neglect of duty to keep the President informed in the matters of State and the public reaction to this neglect. Instead of realising the omissions and commissions and taking steps to redress the situation in the future. Rajiv Gandhi resorted to bringing in extraneous issues and talking of the "cause," rather than his own role in the scenario. There could be only two reasons. for this. Either he was whistling in the dark or whispering his apologies at the altar of history.

Chapter 40

A VISIT AFTER ALL

Rajiv Gandhi called on me at *Rashtrapati Bhavan* on 28 March 1987, after a lapse of over two years. He had returned after a hectic election tour of the States of West Bengal, Kerala and Jammu & Kashmir and after preliminary niceties, I asked him to set the ball rolling. Rajiv Gandhi began with the assertion that the controversy about the relationship between the President and the Prime Minister was rather unfortunate. Referring to my letter of 9 March 1987, regarding the violation by the Prime Minister of constitutional provisions and well-established conventions to brief the President on all important national matters and providing the President with information on matters of State, Rajiv Gandhi denied these violations and expressed satisfaction at the role played by him. I asked him about the reports of the Intelligence Bureau, which had suddenly stopped being sent to me. Though the supply of weekly reports had been resumed after I had insisted on it, the daily reports were still a casualty. Rajiv Gandhi remained non-committal on the daily reports. He himself was not receiving these reports, he said, but he would try to see, if these could be sent to *Rashtrapati Bhavan.*

I drew his attention to the reports received from our ambassadors in other countries which used to be made available to the President for his persual, the flow of which had also been stopped. The Prime Minister said that these were 'secret' reports, which could not be sent. By way of explanation, he hinted that two such reports had been leaked out from

Rashtrapati Bhavan. I reminded Rajiv Gandhi that twenty reports had been leaked out from the Prime Minister's office and it was paradoxical that after that incident, P.e. Alexander, Secretary to the Prime Minister, had been given the important assignment of High Commissioner to the United Kingdom. Rajiv Gandhi complained that the President's Secretariat did not take action against the official concerned inspite of a communication addressed on the subject. Since I was certain of no such communication having been received I told him so and informed him that in the meantime, my Secretary, Bandhopadhayay, had retired from service. I clearly told PM that in spite of the fact that important information had been denied to me, I was trying to discharge my functions without a 'crisis' situation and the wheels of the Constitution were moving.

Rajiv Gandhi's observations about the Thakkar Commission's Report were quite upsetting. Even the Cabinet had not seen the report of Justice Thakkar, he claimed, and thus it was not necessary to show it to the President. I told PM that I differed with this perception. When the Prime Minister had seen the Report and discussed it with some of his Cabinet colleagues, there was hardly any justification of its being withheld from the President. It implied lack of trust in the Head of State and this position was not acceptable. PM asserted that Justice Thakkar had himself recommended that his Report should not be made public, as it would be detrimental to the national interest. It also had bearing on international relations, the Prime Minister said. I pointed out about the write-up in the Blitz Weekly, which was a leak from the Thakkar Commission's Report. PM used some epithets about this particular journal, which amused me. It was a popular belief that the Government had been using this publication for its ends. This journal had specialised in sensational writings. Its news reporting was based on fantasy than facts. I asked PM why a contradiction could not be issued by the Government to a most objectionable reporting done by the *Blitz*. His response was confined to his emphatic view that the Blitz write-up was a figment of its own imagination and there was no truth in its statement. I asked PM, if it was so, then what was the need to distribute copies of this particular issue of the journal among members of the Parliament? PM evaded this by urging that no credence should be placed on such unreliable writings and journalists did not spare anyone including the Prime Minister from their shafts.

I reminded Rajiv Gandhi, some members of the ruling Party were guilty of misdemeanour where President was concerned. K.K. Tewary's statement in Parliament came up for discussion, in which he had talked of the so-called links of Punjab extremists with the President and that two such extremists had been permitted to stay in *Rashtrapati Bhavan.* In fact, nothing could be more unfortunate for a Member of Parliament than to indulge in such baseless utterances by throwing discretion to the winds. I could not understand the purpose behind such actions. The Prime Minister's reaction was marked by a little remorse, and with a remote look in his eyes, he said that a contradiction should have been issued by Rashtrapati Bhavan. In fact a contradiction had been issued by the Secretary to the President.

When I had asked the Prime Minister for some Intelligence Reports for my persual and information, he had minuted on my communication that the matter would be examined. I asked PM if he thought the President was an applicant or a petitioner that his requests needed such minuting. It did not mean a personal dealing. It was a question hinging on the relationship between the two top functionaries of the Republic. Inspite of such a cavalier treatment, I had acted with patience and restraint.

As regards the leakage of my letter of 9 March 1987, I pointed out that on its receipt by PM, it was shown by him to some of his Cabinet colleagues and certain legal experts and when its zerox copies were prepared, some resourceful journalist got a scoop. In fact, according to a correspondent of a Gujarati newspaper, Minister of State for Law and Justice had got seven zerox copies made of this letter for distribution for seeking expert opinion. This daily was the first to publish the contents of the letter in Gujarati translation. Rajiv Gandhi chose to remain silent on this disclosure.

At a repeated mention of the Thakkar Commission Report, I

told PM that if it was true that I had links with Punjab extremists, then, perhaps, there was no need to provide me with any security. It should be taken for granted that these elements would visit me, and if they noticed the security guards, there could be a shoot-out and I could be killed either way. There would be no chance of my getting away alive from the *Rashtrapati Bhavan* in such an eventuality.

Rajiv Gandhi admitted that he had issued directions that the President should not be brought into picture about the Punjab Accord signed between him and the Akali Leader, Sant Harchand Singh Longowal, as well as other matters relating to Punjab. I had information about such directions having been given by the Prime Minister, but his own admission caused me quite a bit of surprise. He hinted that I did not like Darbara Singh to function successfully as the Chief Minister of Punjab. This reminded me of the perfidious moods and guileful times, when efforts were made to utilise the entire governmental machinery in Punjab to distort my image in the print media. I told PM that on my taking charge of the Home Ministry at the Centre, I myself had told Mrs. Indira Gandhi, the then Prime Minister, to get the files on Punjab direct from my Secretary, if she so desired. The Akali leaders had stated that they were opposed to the demand for Khalistan. I, as Home Minister, had suggested that a meeting of leaders of all political parties be convened for discussions. The Akali leaders had stated that they would not like such a meeting to be held under the chairmanship of the Chief Minister. Mrs. Indira Gandhi had advised that the Governor of the State could chair the meeting. When representatives of the political parties had gone away and only Mrs. Gandhi, Darbara Singh and I had been left, I had suggested that public meetings should be organised, in which the only matter to be emphasized should be the demand for a so-called Khalistan. Darbara Singh had opposed all these suggestions. Mrs. Indira Gandhi had been aware of the attempts made by my adversaries to see that I no longer remained the Home Minister.

It had been publicised in the Press that the President was unhappy over the Punjab Accord, and though he had cut short his tour of Hyderabad and had returned to New Delhi to keep himself abreast of the developments, he was not being taken into confidence. What was the need for such negative publicity, I inquired of the Prime Minister and how it was assumed that I was interested in the process or trend of the discussions between the governmental leaders and the Akali Party representatives. A Correspondent of the Hindustan Times had done this reporting. The Prime Minister's response to this was that some journalists had a propensity to weave stories with the flimsy yarn of their own imagination and these were the hazards public men had to face in a democratic society.

Consequent on this meeting with PM, I wrote to him thanking him for the discussions, but I told him that the basic issues regarding the observance of constitutional provisions and conventions governing the relations between the President and the Prime Minister had still to be resolved. I emphasized on Rajiv Gandhi that further early discussions on these important issues were called for.

I made a pointed reference to the report published in the *Blitz* weekly of Bombay regarding the so-called recommendations of the Thakkar Commission to investigate the role of the President, after he has demited his office, into the circumstances leading to the assassination of Mrs. Indira Gandhi. Though during our discussions, Rajiv Gandhi had urged me not to take notice of such baseless reports, I was intrigued at receiving information that copies of the magazine had been distributed among the members of Parliament and others presumably at the cost of the Ruling party. Some other magazines had also carried the item, as reported in the *Blitz.* I asked the Prime Minister why a contradiction could not be issued by the Government.

The Government did issue a routine, rather lame, contradiction to that bizarre write-up in the *Blitz.* The Director of Public Relations in the Ministry of Horne Affairs, instead of issuing a general Press release, addressed a terse letter to that very journal saying that the report, as printed, was factually incorrect. This is how the Government was safeguarding the reputation and dignity of the Head of state! Anyone could have thought that notwithstanding the freedom of the Press and our democratic set-up, when repeatedly such a virulent allegation was being made in its columns by a well-circulated weekly, the Government could have taken a serious note of such irresponsible and unfounded reporting and a conspicuous and forceful contradiction could have been issued, but the Prime Minister contented himself by forwarding a copy of the brief letter issued by the Home Ministry DPR, to me.

Chapter 41

EVASION OF RESPONSIBILITY

On 15 April 1987, speaking in Lok Sabha during the discussion on the No-confidence motion against the Speaker, P. Chidambaram, Minister of State of Home Affairs stated *inter-alia,* that when the President by virtue of powers vested in him under Article 78 (B) of the Constitution called for information, the Prime Minister was entitled to advise about the nature of the information, about the consequence of the information and about what information should be made available at what time and it was, therefore, subject to the advice of the Prime Minister.

It was a strange interpretation of the powers of the President as enshrined in the Constitution, by the Minister of State for Home Affairs, especially at a time when scribes and jurists alike were burning midnight oil, pouring again and again over the articles of the Constitution relating to the Powers of the President and the relationship between him and the Prime Minister. During Rajiv Gandhi's two meetings with me there were extensive discussions on these issues and there were differences in our respective perceptions, particularly regarding Article 78. In these discussions it was agreed upon by me that my Secretary and the Cabinet Secretary would discuss the issues involved.

I expressed surprise to the Prime Minister that the Minister of State should have made such a categorical statement in Parliament, which gave the impression of the Government having a closed mind on the subject. I had to exercise the option of telling the PM that in the circumstances, I stood by my own interpretation of Article 78, as I had explained to him during our discussion. I gave PM an offer to discuss the subject further with me, if he so desired.

Rajiv Gandhi attributed the Minister of State's intervention in Lok Sabha to an urgent need to provide a clarification on Article 78, which, in his view, became the central issue during the debate on the motion for the removal of the Speaker. Chidambaram, according to the Prime Minister, had adopted the line of interpretation on which Government had been acting. However, the Prime Minister averred that he did not have a closed mind on this question and noted with some sort of satisfaction that the issue was being discussed between the Cabinet Secretary and Secretary to the President. To conclude, Rajiv Gandhi asked, if for the sake of clarity and dispassionate examination of issues, I could convey what I considered to be the right interpretation.

It appeared that Rajiv Gandhi's government was confusing the supply of information under Article 78 to the aid and advice under Article 74 of the Constitution. The Prime Minister was conveniently overlooking the fact that if the President's right to seek information was to be governed by the discretion of the Government, then the founding fathers would not have felt the need for incorporating Article 78 in the Constitution. In case the President sought a clarification or asked for a Report on any matter of State, it would not restrict the advice of the Government. PM did not seem to realise that Articles 74 and 78 were not mutually restrictive or contradictory. If the President chose to exercise his right to call for any information, the Government could not deny such information. How could the Government assume that for exercise of his right under article 78 (D) of the Constitution, the President was expected to act on the advice of the Council of Ministers? The .Government were obviously turning their face away from the fact that failure on their part to comply with the President's request under Article 78 (B) would constitute a violation of the constitutional provisions and also a breach of the oath taken by every member of the Council of Ministers at the time of occupying office that he would bear the faith and allegiance to the Constitution and act in accordance with the Constitution.

Following this meeting with me, the . Prime Minister said that it was essential to clarify the basic position as quickly as possible and to place the matter beyond doubt. Since my perception was quite clear on the subject, I lost no time in sending a reply to the effect that the President had a right to be informed of the facts and issues relating to administration and legislation. He also had a right to exert his influence on the Council of Ministers to ensure that national interests were safeguarded. Without being properly informed, as envisaged in Article 78, the President could not fulfil his constitutional obligations.

Chapter 42

FAIRFAX AND BOFORS

I thanked the Prime Minister for briefing me in person on the issues relating to the Fairfax inquiry and also the procurement of the 155 mm howitzers from the Bofors Company of Sweden. But I told him that apart from the broad features mentioned to me briefly, I had followed very carefully the proceedings in Parliament and the press reports on these two matters. In the absence of detailed factual information on a number of aspects, I was not in a position to comprehend the total picture and to satisfy myself that policies had not been violated and national interest had not been put in jeopardy. In addition to finding out if middlemen had been employed in the Bofors deal and how large payments had been received by them, it was necessary for us to look into technical aspects in the interest of national security. I requested the Prime Minister to send me the Evaluation Reports on the merits and usefulness of these howitzers, the findings of the field trials, the progress review of the supplies made by the Bofors under the contract entered into with them and the progress of technology transfer to India in terms of the contract. I also requested for copies of telegrams exchanged between the Government and our missions abroad concerning the deal and the Fairfax affair. I conveyed urgency of the need in public interest to conduct a comprehensive inquiry into all aspects of the Bofors deal to allay effectively the doubts in public mind and the Defence services about this affair.

Rajiv Gandhi paid his next visit to *Rashtrapati Bhavan* on 8 April

1987. He took this opportunity to inform me that the terms of reference of the Commission of Enquiry to investigate the circumstances under which the services of the Fairfax Company of USA had been engaged by the Finance Ministry headed by V.P. Singh, had been made more comprehensive. The Government had asked the Chief Justice of the Supreme Court to nominate one Judge to constitute a Commission of Enquiry, but the latter had nominated two Judges, viz. Justice M.P. Thakkar and Justice Natarajan for the purpose. The Prime Minister said that even earlier, the Government had been enlisting the help of foreign agencies to ferret out information on important matters. But in this particular case, it was not clear to the Prime Minister on what grounds the Finance Ministry had sought the assistance of Fairfax without any reference to the Union Cabinet.

It became quite clear to me from PM's remarks that the objective of constituting a Commission of Enquiry was to establish that V.P. Singh as Finance Minister had overstepped his brief and that he must be cut to his size.

Rajiv Gandhi took pains to touch on the President—Prime Minister relations and pleaded that whatever omissions had taken place in the past must be overlooked and that he would take special care in the future to observe the formality of maintaining contacts and briefing the President on all important matters. In the same breath he added, that he did not realise that this constitutional obligation had not been fulfilled, as he was under the impression that there had been no default in this regard. This stance of the Prime Minister was quite baffling. I suggested to him to go through the various Articles of the Constitution and then to decide if he had been observing them in letter and spirit. Rajiv Gandhi thought that it would be cumbersome for him to do so and it would be time-consuming too, and since neither he nor I was a constitutional expert, why not depute two senior officials to ponder over the Constitutional provisions, as already agreed upon, and to draw certain conclusions. I had no objections to this proposal, I maintained, but ultimately the matter had to be hammered out by two of us ourselves. The Prime Minister, it appeared, had sought the advice of his aides on this issue and now he suggested that three officials viz., the Cabinet Secretary, the Attorney General and Secretary to the President should discuss the constitutional provisions with regard to the President-Prime Minister relations. I thought three would be a crowd and therefore, insisted that only the Cabinet Secretary and Secretary to the President should be deputed to go through this exercise.

I pointed out to Rajiv Gandhi that the Oath of Office of the President as per Article 60 of the Constitution lays down that he will faithfully execute the office of President and will to the best of his ability preserve, protect and defend the Constitution and the law and that he will devote himself to the service and wellbeing of the people of India. How could the President, I asked PM, discharge his functions without being fully informed of important affairs of the State? I also reminded Rajiv Gandhi that Article 78 enjoins upon the Prime Minister the duty to communicate to the President all decisions of the Council of Ministers relating to the administration of the affairs of the Union and proposals for legislation and to forward such information relating to the administration of the affairs of the Union and proposals for legislation as the President may call for.

The question of providing me with a copy of the Report of the Thakkar Commission again figured in our conversation. PM only responded by saying that this would be looked into. I told Rajiv Gandhi emphatically that there was no justification in withholding the Report from me.

To refresh the Prime Minister's memory about some other related Constitutional provisions, I pointed out that the President can use his discretion in appointing a Prime Minister. The Council of Ministers is formed on the advice of the Prime Minister. The Council of Ministers headed by the Prime Minister aids and advises the President, who should in the exercise of his functions, act in accordance with such advice. But if the President desires, he may require the Council of Ministers to reconsider such advice, either generally or otherwise, and the President shall act in accordance with the advice tendered after such consideration. I cited the example of the Governor of a State, who had withdrawn his pleasure and dismissed a Minister. The Prime Minister said that, perhaps, the Governors have greater powers within their States in certain matters.

The Prime Minister followed it up with a lengthy note of 5 May 1987, reiterating that he did not have a closed mind on the question. Nevertheless, it would have helped matters, if the Government could have had my views in regard to what I had described as "the President's right to be informed of the facts and issues relating to administration and legislation" which would enable me to fulfil my constitutional obligations. It was abundantly clear, the Prime Minister stated, that such obligations could only be discharged on the aid and advice of the Council of Ministers.

The Prime Minister's note had a whiff of history in it. He referred to the fact of some constitutional issues having been raised by President Dr. Rajendra Prasad concerning the powers of the President under the Constitution and quoted from a note recorded by the first Prime Minister, Pandit Jawahar Lal Nehru that he had consulted the then Attorney-General and Alladi Krishnaswamy Aiyar and they both had expressed the opinion that the President must act with the aid and advice of the Council of his Ministers and he could not act independently of that advice. The position of the President was weaker as compared to that of the British monarch. The President under our Constitution had no personal or other prerogatives, which the British King had. The fact that the President, unlike the King, was elected to his office for a term made no difference to his position. The election was merely intended for the choice of the Constitutional and executive head.

Rajiv Gandhi painstakingly quoted from the Constituent Assembly Debates Volumes 7 and 9 that every power conferred on the President had to be exercised according to the advice of the Ministers. He also referred to the Supreme Court judgement in Samsher Singh Vs. State of Punjab quoting Justice Krishna Iyer on the authority of Dr. Ambedkar's view to the effect that a President who refused to accept ministerial advice would be committing violation of the Constitution.

Rajiv Gandhi went on to expostulate what he called the fundamental logic of our Constitution, by reference to which all issues had to be tested and decided. If one did not do that and contrived a logic of his own, it would violate the basis of the Constitution. Since we had adopted the system of Parliamentary democracy, the lower House of Parliament, which was directly elected by the people, was supreme. The Council of Ministers was responsible to this elected House of Parliament alone. In this scheme of things, the President being the dignified part of the Constitution may exercise moral influence. If he so chooses, he may persuade, encourage or warn, but the Cabinet functions solely with reference to Parliament.

Rajiv Gandhi questioned my interpretation of the Articles of the Constitution pertaining to the President. While quoting his grandfather, Pandit Jawahar Lal Nehru as suggesting that such an exercise was inconsistent with our Constitution and was indeed foreign to the entire scheme of our Constitution, as depicted in his letter of 21 September 1951, R.ajiv Gandhi admitted that it was said in a different context. At the same time he insisted that it was valid for the matter under discussion. He persisted in his request that I, for the benefit of his Council of Ministers, furnish my interpretation of the role of the President in relation to matters which had been raised.

As regards the information I had demanded from him about the Bofors gun deal, Rajiv Gandhi informed me that the Cabinet in its meeting on 4 May 1987, had come to the conclusion that all relevant information necessary for the discharge of my constitutional obligations had already been furnished to me by the Defence, Commerce and Home Ministers and no question had remained unanswered. Moreover, according to Rajiv Gandhi, the matter had been discussed threadbare in Parliament. As no evidence had so far been produced of any wrongdoing in regard to the Bofors contract, there was no justification for any inquiry, as suggested by me. Rajiv Gandhi forwarded to me a copy of the minutes of the Cabinet meeting and expressed his belief that these decisions of the Cabinet represented faithful compliance with the provisions of Article 78 of the Constitution.

Rajiv Gandhi claimed that the morale in the defence forees

was high. The Government's decision to equip the armed forces with 155 mm Howitzers had been taken on the technical advice of the Army Headquarters, after most extensive trials and rigorous evaluation. There was no doubt in his mind that an inquiry on the basis of unfounded allegations could only have a demoralising effect on the defence forces. It was his sacred duty, the Prime Minister stated, to protect the defence forces from motivated criticism. Rajiv Gandhi claimed emphatically that the people had no doubt of the rightness of Government's actions. The doubt might be lurking in the minds of those, who wanted to weaken the country. From me he expected a befitting reply to such elements.

Naturally, I could not accept these arguments advanced by the Prime Minister. I was feeling concerned over the open allegations of kickbacks in the Swedish gun deal and I wanted additional information from the Government. The Prime Minister was denying me the requisite information on a matter of great public importance. In my view, the PM was obviously committing a violation of the Constitution. I wondered why a Resolution had to be passed by the Cabinet denying information to the President, in whose name the entire administration was being run. It also caused me a little measure of unhappiness that the deliberations of the Cabinet Committee on Political Affairs and the full cabinet on the subject had been leaked. At one stage PM was complaining that the leakages in certain matters were occurring at the end of officials in Rashtrapati Bhavan, but in this case leakage to the Press had been engineered by the PM's own aides. So much public interest had been roused by the Bofors and HDW deals that it created well-founded fear that the Government had something to hide, which, if made public, would damage its reputation. Some members of the Parliament did try to raise the issue in both Houses, but they were refused the permission. Some of them referred to the suppression of information to Parliament and refusal to provide details to the President about the Defence deals by the Government. One member in a statement called it a campaign of calumny against the President and called for its stoppage forthwith. Some people thought that the Government's refusal to place the cards on the table and its reluctance to provide full information to the President was a fraud on the interpretation of the Constitution and it was untenable. The President represented the nation and was Head of the State. Article 78(A) of the Constitution cast a duty on the Prime Minister to communicate to the President all decisions of the Council of Ministers. Article 78(B) conferred a right on the President to call for such information as related to the administration of the affairs of the Union. In case the President chose to exercise his right, there was no option left for the Government but to furnish information to the President. Some political leaders were of the view that it was unwise to deny the Constitutional right of the President to know what was going on in the Government.

On the question of Bofors gun, Swedish Radio had consistently maintained that there were massive kickbacks in the deal. The matter had attracted the attention of Parliament as well as of the public. They were all waiting to know the truth. The President had called for information on this important matter of great public interest, which the Government were not only denying, but also questioning the right of the President to ask for it. Some one from the ruling party claimed that since the President was not administered the oath of secrecy, the information given to the President might reach the ears of those for whom it was not meant. But such elements forgot that the President was administered a far more important oath - to protect and defend the Constitution and the unity and integrity of the country. This oath is taken by the President only and not by the Council of Ministers and though ordinarily the President is to act on the advice of his Council of Ministers, like the sovereign of the United Kingdom, the President must have certain residual powers to be exercised without the advice of the Council of Ministers. As the Prime Minister would have it, if the President needed information on an important subject, he would first have to seek the concurrence of the Council of Ministers to call for such information! The President could not be a functional cipher. Nor could he be a mere figurehead. In the Shamsher Singh case the Supreme Court had ruled that

"Like the King in England, he (the President) will still have the right to be consulted, to encourage and to warn. Acting on ministerial advice does not necessarily mean immediate acceptance of the Ministry's first thoughts. The President can state all his objections to any proposed course of action and ask his Ministers in Council, if necessary, to reconsider the matter. It is only in the last resort that he must accept their final advice. As has been well said, the voice of reason is more readily heard, when it can persuade but no longer coerce".

The Supreme Court judgement further clarified :

"The President in India is not at all a glorified cipher. He represents the majesty of the State, is at the apex, though only symbolically, and has rapport with the people and parties, being above politics. His vigilant presence makes for good government, if only he has what Bagehot described as the right to be consulted, to warn and encourage. Indeed, Article 78 wisely used, keeps the President in close touch with the Prime Minister on matters of national importance and policy significance and there is no doubt that the imprint of his personality may chasten and correct the political government, although the actual exercise of the functions entrusted to him by law is in effect and in law carried on by his duly appointed mentors, i.e. the Prime Minister and his colleagues. In short, the President, like the King, has not merely been constitutionally romanticised but actually vested with a pervasive and persuasive role. Political theorists are quite conversant with the dynamic role of the Crown which keeps away from politics and power and yet influences both".

It is the Prime Minister's duty to communicate the decisions of the Government to the President to enable him to know and to bring his influence to bear on the working of his Government. It is also the Prime Minister's duty to furnish such information relating to the administration of the affairs of the Union and proposals for legislation as the President may call for. If the President feels that a decision taken by a Minister requires reconsideration by the Council of Ministers, he may require the Prime Minister to place it before the Council of Ministers.

The President must receive the correct and authentic information, which can be supplied only by the Prime Minister. The President has to perform a wide range of functions and discharge prerogatives, which he can do only with the help of unsullied information supplied by his Ministers. He can seek essential information from the Cabinet relating to the exercise of his Constitutional powers. The President is the respository of the entire Executive power of the Union. He has to be aware of what is happening in his Government. He is a part of the Government and also of Parliament. The Prime Minister cannot draw a curtain of secrecy between himself and the President. The latter has a right to know how his Government is working. Naturally the Prime Minister is a conduit of all such information. It is his constitutional duty to furnish the fullest information asked for by the President.

Rajiv Gandhi denied that he had a hand in the tirade against me by the Congress MP K.K. Tewary in Parliament in April 1985. He said that the Government had stated in the House that Tewary's insinuation about extremists having links with the *Rashtrapati Bhavan* had been denied by the President's Secretariat. I told the Prime Minister to have a second look at the record of the proceedings of Lok Sabha.

I asked Rajiv Gandhi, who was responsible to give official files to Arun Shourie, the exuberant Editor of the *Indian Express,* to write two articles about my conduct as Home Minister in the matter of handling the Indian Postal (Amendment) Bill, in which it was alleged that I had mooted the idea of making the censorship of postal articles more stringent. In his write-up, Shourie had quoted from minutes and notings in the secret files of the Government with page Nos. and dates. I reminded PM that all Ministers at the time of swearing in took the oath of secrecy. Who was responsible then to place the secret files of the Government at the disposal of journalists to write articles? As the Prime Minister could not deny this, he said he would look into matter and bring the guilty to the book. I wondered if the Prime Minister was ignorant of the identity of those who had shown the secret files to Shourie. His assurances of investigating the matter and taking action against the 'Minister or Ministers, who had violated the oath of secrecy carried little weight and were also of little avail.

I reminded Rajiv Gandhi about the plight of some two hundred Nepali families, who had been ousted from Meghalaya. In Sikkim also there were a large number of Nepalese, who had sent away their families to Nepal and had stayed behind themselves in Darjeeling to create trouble.

I reminded PM that leaders of foreign countries had to call on me, and if I was not kept fully posted with the latest developments in our relations with other nations, it would mean a handicap. If the Government were not interested in keeping the President well-informed for his meetings with foreign dignitaries, then it would be more appropriate to see that they did not call on the President at all.

I mentioned about a write-up in the *Sunday* Magazine by a journalist, Vir Sanghvi, who had commented on the remarks allegedly made by me to the President of Yugoslavia that he should make efforts to bring India and China closer to each other. He also wrote about my alleged suggestion to the President of Bangladesh that he should appoint the Opposition leader, Sheikh Hasina Wajid, the daughter of the slain Sheikh Mujibur Rehman, as Prime Minister of that country

I told PM that I was aware that he had asked Vir Sanghvi to publish this article and to quote a friend of PM as source of this information.

I further reminded Rajiv Gandhi that there was a time when I was functioning as the Vice-President of the Punjab State Congress; twice I was a Minister in that State, for well over five year I had served as the Chief Minister and for more then five years, I was the President of the State Congress Party. There was nothing about Punjab that I was not fully conversant with. I personally knew each *Jathedar* of the District Units of the Akali Dal. I had no desire or intention of meddling in the affairs of that State.

Chapter 43

NO DESIRE FOR A SECOND TERM

Without responding to any of the points made by me, the Prime Minister asked me of my plans to settle down at the end of my tenure as President, because he knew that I had no intention of seeking a second term in office. I reiterated that I had no desire to get a second term as President, and I had let it be known to PM five months earlier. If I chose to fight re-election, the outcome would be difficult to predict, but, in effect, I was not interested at all to get another term.

I told the Prime Minister that I had heard that Congress(I) were preparing grounds afresh for my impeachment. He denied and described it as totally baseless. Such a move, he said, would be highly detrimental to the interests of the country.

To round up the discussions, I said that it was incumbent on the Government to provide full information to the President in the future and on adherence to this principle would depend the relations between the President and the Prime Minister. I would be keenly watching the attitude of the Government and would decide upon my equation with PM accordingly. He then said that he was hearing of the visits of several leading journalists to *Rashtrapati Bhavan,* when the President was giving them material and information. I said it was rather strange, because a list of all visitors to Rashtrapati Bhavan was published daily. People holding diverse views and belonging to different political parties visited the Head of

State. Visitors to *Rashtrapati Bhavan* included both the supporters and opponents of PM and the ruling group.

During this talk with Rajiv Gandhi the mood on either side became nostalgic. When he was inducted into politics by Mrs. Gandhi, our relations used to be more than cordial. He never missed an opportunity to discuss things with me then. His calm and consistent cordiality and warm exuberance used to be a fascinating feature of our mutual relations.

I reminded Rajiv Gandhi that I was not consulted by the Government before the Operation Bluestar was launched at the Golden Temple, Amritsar. After the Army action, I was prevailed upon by Mrs. Gandhi to visit the *Golden Temple* and *Akal Takht.* A few persons had expressed the opinion that reticence on my part would have been better. There was no need for me to address the Nation at that stage after the Operation Bluestar, because that implicitly gave an impression that I was endorsing the Government's action. Paradoxically the impression had gone round that Mrs. Indira Gandhi had tried to dissuade me from visiting the *Golden Temple,* and I had disregarded her advice and insisted on making a trip to Amritsar. My broadcast to the Nation on the Radio and Television network on 17 June 1984, had been appreciated and praised by Mrs. Indira Gandhi and many other people. It had been suggested by Rajiv Gandhi that I should speak extempore and not use a prepared script. Had the Government taken me into confidence about the Operation Bluestar, I told Rajiv, perhaps, things would have taken a different course and the national purpose could have been achieved without that tragic action and its aftermath. Tact and pragmatism would have been of greater value. Such large scale bloodshed could easily have been avoided. To me the unity and integrity of the nation were more important than anything else. My life would be of little use, if all my energies could not be harnessed to the protection of the unity and integrity of the Nation.

As a corollary to the open indifference shown by the Prime Minister to me, some disgruntled politicians started entertaining a vague hope that as a reaction to the Prime Minister's conduct, perhaps, I would use my constitutional powers to replace him with somebody more reasonable and rational. Among such persons were sitting and former Members of Parliament, public men and some journalists. They all had different reasons. Some were avaracious, some wanted to settle scores with Rajiv Gandhi and others wanted to be a part of some imaginary excitement.

Throughout my term as President, and even before, I had been meeting people freely. Having remained in politics from my early youth, it had been a way of life with me to meet as many people as possible. By habit I was accessible. There were often suggestions from my staff to be restrictive in giving appointments. But I could hardly turn down a request from anyone to see me. People came from far and wide to meet me and I had hardly any heart to turn them away.

I was surprised to discover during those days that some persons ostensibly close to Rajiv Gandhi had unfavourable designs about him. Some tried to level charges of corruption. Some thought that his so-called charisma was wearing out. Some others expressed the view that he was becoming a liability to the Congress. Some politicians held the conviction that they had overwhelming evidence to expose Rajiv to discredit him in the public eye.

I was astounded when a senior politician of considerable standing started hobnobbing with one of my officers, the stories about which were circulated in the press. I came to know later that they had known each other for quite some time. I took serious notice of the goings on and upbraided the officer. Being over-enthusiastic he had the habit of talking out of turn. I seriously thought of taking disciplinary action against him, but ultimately let him off with a reprimand.

With the Haryana elections going against the Congress and in favour of the Opposition in the State, some persons were emboldened. They wanted this as a rallying point to ask the Prime Minister to resign, as he had lost the confidence of the people. Some persons mentioned the names of V.P. Singh, P.V. Narasimha Rao, R. Venkataraman, V.C. Shukla and one or two more. But I was clear in my mind that an elected Prime Minister enjoying the mandate and confidence of the House could not be removed. In the heart of my hearts I had no desire to take such a drastic step. I could not think of doing anything which would go against the spirit of the Constitution. Though I let the persons talk and vent their feelings, I held my own counsel. That is why I directed my Secretariat and Deputy Press Secretary, Tarlochan Singh, to issue the following press release on 3 May 1987:

> The President has noted with distress the reports and comments which have appeared in the press persistently speculating that the President intends to dismiss Rajiv Gandhi from the office of Prime Minister. The President has so far refrained from commenting on these reports as also on the conjectures concerning what transpired in his recent meetings with the Prime Minister. The President feels that reports and comments concerning so grave a matter as the dismissal of the Prime Minister cannot be allowed to remain uncontradicted any longer.
>
> The President therefore wishes it to be known in the clearest terms that the said reports and comments are utterly devoid of any basis.

It goes to the credit of the veteran Congress leader and former Prime Minister of the country, Morarji Desai, that a day earlier, i.e. on 2 May 1987, when I was at Bombay to attend the Golden Jubilee celebrations of the Jain Acharya Tulsi's acharyaship, at which I gave away an Ahimsa award of Rs. one lakh to Desai, the intrepid fighter for the truth and the *karmayogi* told me in so many words that it was wrong on the part of the Prime Minister not to fulfil his constitutional obligations towards the President. But I had told him then that though the PM might have been unfair to me, I would never be unfair to him.

As regards my so much trumpeted desire for a second term in office, I had made it clear to the Prime Minister many months earlier that I had no such ambition.

Chapter 44

CONSCIENTIOUS OBJECTORS

Stoicism is one of the natural traits of people in this country. They have a tendency to take a fatalist view of events in their personal, social or even political life. Whatever has to happen will inevitably happen, they are convinced, and nobody can prevent the pre-ordained. Most people seem to be of the opinion that since they cannot change the course of events, it is futile to make any effort to do so. Some reason with themselves that in this vast country the voice of an individual or a few individuals would be ineffective, or even if someone took up the cudgels on behalf of the aggrieved, against the wrong actions of the authority, it would be of no use. Sometimes the efforts would boomerang on the complainants or petitioners. People, in effect, understood the meaning of the axiom "Silence is Golden." But there are some individuals, who can be described as Conscientious Objectors. I noticed this particularly when some leaders and intellectuals took unusual steps to approach me for permission to prosecute the Prime Minister, Rajiv Gandhi, for what they perceived as his wrongful actions.

On 13 June 1987, I received a letter from George Fernandes of the Janata Party outlining the information said to have been gathered by him abroad on the Submarine deal and the Bofors Gun deal. He suggested that the Prime Minister should be asked to step down from the office to facilitate proper investigation by any agency of Government or a Committee of Parliament. I forwarded a copy of this letter to Rajiv Gandhi the same day.

On 21 June 1987, Fernandes sent me another letter giving a list of specific questions on which he wanted clarifications to be sought from the Prime Minister. He requested me either to give permission for prosecuting the Prime Minister on charges of corruption or ask him to resign from office. And if he failed to resign, then to dismiss him in the national interest. I forwarded this letter to the Prime Minister on 24 June 1987, drawing his attention to the charges and the inferences drawn therein.

In his letter of 17 July 1987, Fernandes pleaded for sanction for prosecution of the Prime Minister particularly in the light of the Report in the *Indian Express* of 15 July 1987.

On 10 June 1987, I received a letter from Chandra Shekhar, President of the Janata Party, on the Bofors deal. After dealing with the various aspects of the deal, Chandra Shekhar pleaded that the Government should be asked to terminate the contract and to start prosecution against those responsible for payment of commission. He also suggested in the letter that if the Prime Minister did not respond reasonably, then a duty was cast on the President to take a view on the issue and take the people into confidence.

On 14 June 1987, Rajinder Puri, President, Ekta Party, and a renowned journalist, wrote to me seeking permission under the Prevention of Corruption Act to prosecute the Prime Minister on charges relating to the Bofors deal. He enclosed to his letter a note on the Bofors deal, prepared by Ram Jethmalani, a Senior Advocate of the Supreme Court, and a copy of the allegations submitted by George Fernandes. On 26 June 1987, Puri wrote to me again urging me to take action to protect the Constitution of India.

On 8 July 1987, a letter was received from Ram Jethmalani in which he had listed the various aspects of the Bofors deal, which, according to him, constituted the chain of circumstantial evidence of corruption against the Prime Minister. He suggested that I should remove the Prime Minister and instal a new Prime Minister to head a National Government.

In view of the repeated requests for sanctioning prosecution against the Prime Minister, I pondered over the matter in great depth. I was fully satisfied that the President has the power to sanction the prosecution of the Prime Minister and this power can be exercised without the aid and advice of the Council of Ministers. But taking into consideration that a Presidential sanction for prosecution of a Prime Minister commanding absolute majority in Parliament would have far-reaching consequences, I made a careful assessment of the material placed before me and came to the conclusion that even though the allegations were serious and required to be effectively refuted by the Government to allay the misgivings of the nation, the material before me was not sufficient to establish a prima facie case for according sanction for the prosecution of the Prime Minister.

Since the matter had attracted considerable attention of the media and the public, I thought of seeking legal advice before taking any action. I invited luminaries like Y.V. Chandrachud, retired Chief Justice of India, Ashok Sen, former Union Law Minister and R.S. Narula, retired Chief Justice of the Punjab and Haryana High Court to advise about the propriety of permitting the prosecution of the Prime Minister.

All of them were of the view that it was a borderline case. The Prime Minister could get the benefit of doubt in a court of law. In such a case, acquittal was not difficult. They, therefore, would leave the decision to me. Since there was no precedent to this since Independence, the prospects were uncertain. In fact, my decision had already been made against the grant of permission. This was in spite of Ram Jethmalani and Rajinder Puri's personal pleas that they should be allowed to proceed against Rajiv Gandhi. Jethmalani had gone to the extent that if permission were given, I would go down in history as upholder of probity in public life; otherwise history would not forget this omission.

Ashok Sen went a little further. He said that if I thought that the Prime Minister was not following the conventions and was not performing his duties in accordance with the provisions of the Constitution, he could be removed from office. In such an eventuality anyone could be appointed Prime Minister. And if nobody more suitable was available, then he was prepared to take up the job. For a moment I was puzzled at Ashok Sen's offer, because I had not even mentioned any intention about the removal of the Prime Minister. 1 politely told him that the matter under discussion related only to the petitions of certain. people for permission to prosecute the Prime Minister on corruption charges.

There were many others who had taken strong positions on this subject. An important Congress leader with notable family connections had taken it upon himself to repeatedly emphasize that it was a good case for prosecution and permission should be granted.

Another previously close confidant of the Gandhi family insisted that the country should be saved from the present government. Anyone else, he said, would be better than the present leader. According to him, differences were simmering in the minds of Congress (I) MPs. If some one gave them a lead, they would come out in the open.

Rajiv Gandhi deputed two of his Ministers to keep on meeting me in an effort to influence me for not giving permission for prosecution. Both Buta Singh and Rajesh Pilot faithfully carried out their assigned task and 1 did not mind their coming to me and talking to me about the undesirability of conceding the petitioners' request. 1 told them each time they talked that 1 had no personal illwill for Rajiv Gandhi and would never do anything prejudicial to fair and just practices. As far as this particular matter was concerned, 1 was convinced that there was no direct evidence against the Prime Minister and, therefore, permission for prosecution was not called for. I directed my Secretary, S. Varadan accordingly and asked him to send the replies to all concerned.

Chapter 45

THE INDIAN POST OFFICE (AMENDMENT) BILL 1986

On 22 December 1986, I received a Bill to amend the Indian Postal Act of 1898, passed by both Houses of Parliament for my assent. According to the amended Section 26, the Central Government or the State Government or any officer specially authorised in this behalf by the Central or State Government, if satisfied that it is necessary or expedient so to do in the interests of public safety or tranquillity, the sovereignty or integrity of India, the security of the State, friendly relations with foreign States or public order or for preventing incitement to the commission of any offence, or on the occurrence of any public emergency, by order in writing direct that any postal article or class or description of postal articles in the course of transmission by post, shall be intercepted or detained or shall be disposed of in such a manner as the authority issuing the order, may direct.

After going through the Bill, I realised that the amended bill was too sweeping in nature and wondered why the Government was keen on assuming the power to intercept any pry into postal communications indiscriminately. The Bill, I thought, undermined the fundamental freedom granted under the Constitution and was not in conformity with the Law Commission's 38th Report. It also went against the thrust of some Supreme Court judgements, which had interpreted Article 19 liberally.

I also noted that the Bill did not specify the categorisation of articles for censorship. This could mean that books, journals and periodicals could be subjectively censored and money orders could be withheld.

I asked the Law Ministry to be more specific. I wanted to know what category of officers would be entitled to censor the mail and other articles, as the amending Bill did not specify the rank of the official, who may be authorised to censor postal articles. I thought that a judicial magistrate shall be the authorised person to enforce censorship. It was reported that such a proposal had been made during the debate in Parliament, but the suggestion had been turned down by the Government on the plea that judicial scrutiny would be time consuming. Since the matter infringed on Fundamental Rights, hasty action was in no way justified.

The Indian Post Office Act of 1898, had not been challenged in any Court. The law, as already existed, was harsh enough. The new measure would impose fresh curbs on the fundamental rights of the people. In its report in 1968, the Law Commission had made several suggestions to bring the law on the subject in conformity with Article 19(2) of the Constitution, which deals with reasonable restrictions on the right to freedom of speech and expression. The Commission had said that Article 26 Sub-Section(i) need not be disturbed, but had recommended addition of a new Sub-section to the effect that the power of interception etc., shall in respect of letters, books, post-cards and newspapers be exercised only in the interest of the security of the State, public order, friendly relations with foreign states or preventing incitement to the commission of any offence. Thus the Commission had specified certain categories of postal articles which should not be intercepted in situations not falling under Article 19(2) of the Constitution, Giving reasons for this recommendation:, the Law Commission had said inter-alia that other postal articles would not ordinarily raise questions of freedom of expression, when they are intercepted in post, whereas these specified postal articles would. Therefore, Article 19(2) of the Constitution should apply to them.

According to the Law Commission, the expression 'public emergency' is capable of being given a rather wide meaning and may not be enough to make the power of interception of postal articles valid with reference to the freedom of expression, as it may embrace situations not falling under Article 19(2) of the Constitution. In the Amendment, as passed by both the Houses, this recommendation is not reflected. On the other hand, the situations listed under Article 19(2) of the Constitution have been added to the existing provision to cover any postal article, class or description of postal articles. I could not acquiesce in curtailing the rights of the citizens. If at all, the grounds had to be specific and there had to be safeguards against the misuse of the measure in the future.

The reply received from the Government did not satisfy me. They did not deal squarely with the points raised by me that the Bill amending the Indian Postal Act of 1898, was not in conformity with the 1968 recommendations of the Law Commission. Instead of showing an inclination to undo the wrong proposed to be done by the amending Bill, they stated that the Constitution also provided for special powers for the Executive during the state of emergency. They made a tentative promise to specify the rank of the officer ordering the interception, in the rules or the administrative instructions that could be issued after the bill came into force.

I once again wrote to the Government urging them to take a view consistent with the right to freedom of speech and expression guaranteed under the Constitution and the principles of natural justice. I was not in favour of postponing this exercise to a future review instead of using the present opportunity to comprehensively amend the Act, which was nearly 100 years old.

There were two options before me - either to give assent to the Bill as sent to me or to return it with a message to Parliament. I did not exercise either of these. In case I returned the Bill, Parliament was bound to reconsider it and, if it was passed by both Houses again, I could not withhold assent. Till then no Bill had ever been returned by the President under Article 111 of the Constitution. I could have set a new precedent. But my intention was not merely to carry out an exercise. I wanted to give a chance to the Government to peep into their hearts and consider if it was necessary at all to curtail the liberties of the people in the proposed fashion.

Some persons expressed strong reservations about the provisions of the Bill and described them draconian. Members of the Opposition had come to me in a delegation and asked me not to give assent. I wanted to know from the Government if the person, whose mail was to be intercepted would be asked to be present, when it was opened. The Home Minister, Buta Singh, came and tried to persuade me to give assent, but he could not advance any convincing argument about the severe nature of its provisions.

The' Rashtriya Samajwadi Congress President, Pranab Mukherjee, addressed a Press Conference and said that his Party welcomed the observations made by the President on the Bill. He urged an objective and non-partisan view to be taken on the President's observations and recommendations, in case the Bill was returned to Parliament for reconsideration.

Unfortunately, some people construed my reservations on the Bill as confrontation between the President and the Parliament or between the President and the Prime Minister. Nothing was farther from the truth. There were no personal feelings. I only thought that the Government was trying to arm itself with arbitrary powers to intercept the postal communications indiscriminately. There was a possibility of its gross misuse by the officials, inspite of the assurances to the contrary by the Government. The Congress Party was always opposed to such measures when enforced by the foreign rulers. But now they were trying to impose these curbs themselves on the people in a free and democratic India. I found myself unable to back the intentions of the Government and did not give my assent. I did anticipate that my successor in office would likewise be reluctant to endorse such a measure, as it militated against the basic freedoms guaranteed to the citizens.

Chapter 46

POLITICISATION OF SIKH FAITH

Some extremist elements amongst the Sikhs have been raising slogans, all the implications of which are not very clear even to them. At first an attempt was made to claim a separate nationhood for the Sikhs, a description which was based neither upon the teachings of the Sikh Gurus nor upon any contemporary political logic. The forum of the Sikh Educational Conference which held a few meetings at Chandigarh was grossly misused by an American citizen to extend support to this claim. Even though the resolution passed at the Conference declaring Sikhs as a separate nation was countermanded by the Chief Khalsa Dewan, the sponsors of Sikh Educational Conference, the mischief already done did create some misgivings not only about Sikh politics but also about Sikh religion as such. To add to the confusion the Shiromani Gurudwara Prabhandhak Committee, a purely religious body dominated by Shiromani Akali Dal, a political party, deemed it expedient to pass for the first time in its existence an uncalled for resolution declaring Sikhs a separate nation.

The lead given by S.G.P.C. was followed by Akali Dal after some time. The issue was further complicated by some foreign based elements by putting forth the demand for Khalistan as also for associate membership for Sikhs in the U.N.O. It is not very difficult to see some connection between these different extremist demands and some powers which are inimically disposed towards India and are keen to destabilise the Indian political and social structure. What is most heartening, however, is the fact that by and large the Sikh masses refused to be swayed by such empty though catchy slogans.

It needs no special pleading to say that the Akali doctrine that religion and politics are inseparable for Sikhs has meant, as shown by the historical experience, only subordination of the faith of the Sikh Gurus to the vagaries of power-politics and not the manner in which Akalis are trying to interpret it. In fact they are debasing the Sikh religious heritage and misleading the Sikh masses. It is a sad day that a statutory body like S.G.P.C. deriving its legitimacy from a Legislative Act to provide for proper management of Sikh Gurdwaras should have thought of passing a resolution that the Sikhs as a political entity are a distinct nation, because for them religion and politics are inseparable. The passage of the resolution by the S.G.P.C. was a glaring act of overstepping its specified sphere of activity and thus committing a constitutional impropriety. It also exposed the *Khalsa Panth* to ridicule. Firstly, it was none of the business of a body charged with the specific task of providing good administration of the Gurudwaras, which according to Sikh ideology and Sikh tradition are the places of worship, service and religious congregation to dabble into politics. Secondly their pronouncement has far reaching consequences which should not have been made without a sound basis and also without looking into their wider implications.

It is quite ironical that a religious body, which has failed so far even to evolve a self-regulating system for its own election and management, arrogated to itself the authority of reducing a universal faith, the Sikh Panth, into a narrow political grouping. Whatever the protestations of some of the Akali leaders, the resolution declaring the Sikhs, a nation, is at best a political monstrosity and at worst a thinly veiled move for disturbing the integrity of our country by promoting Sikh separatism. If religious identity alone is accepted as a determinant of nation-hood, the Sikh nation would imply a super-national status because Sikhs are residents not only in Punjab and citizens not alone of India, but of many countries in the world. What shall be the constitutional status, of a Sikh citizen of America if not an American? Any other suggestion will be received with ridicule. On the other hand the separatist implications of the move are quite apparent because in political theory a nation is a category which has either attained Statehood or is struggling for that. No religion has contained the boundaries of its faith to a State or a Nation State.

Sikhism, a faith and a way of life, is based upon teachings of Guru Nanak and his successors which are universal in nature. His spiritual quest took him not only to all the four corners of Indian subcontinent but even beyond its frontiers. The only reference of political import apart from the trenchant criticism of the kings of his times and their minions in his sacred hymns is to the invasion of India by Babar, the conqueror of India and founder of Mughal Empire of India. In this reference his vision of the unity of Hindustan is quite boldly expressed directly *(Khurasan Khasmana Kiya Hindustan Drayaya)*

To claim that only a portion of India is sacred to the Sikhs is to commit a blasphemy. The sacred Sikh geography extends far beyond the territorial boundary of Punjab or any imaginary "Khalistan". Leaving alone the places of Sikh pilgrimage in Pakistan and Bangladesh, I would like to point out that the Sikh Gurus extended the Sikh sacred geography to cover the whole of India. Right from Guru Nanak onwards, the Sikh Gurus maintained and continued strengthening integral links with the Sikh sangats all over India and abroad without any reference to any regional territoriality or racial grouping. Guru Amar Dass spread the Sikh prelacies all over Indian Sub-continent. Similarly, Guru Hargobind and Guru Tegh Bahadur made extensive tours all over Northern and North Eastern India restoring faith of and giving hope to a long suffering humanity. Some of the sangats established in different parts of India by the Gurus have survived up to our times. Two of the five centres of Sikh faith known as Takhats are situated outside Punjab. Similarly there are more than 100 Sikh shrines spread over the length and breadth of India. Any scheme of things or move that seeks to promote Sikh separation will ultimately lead to vivisection of the integrity and solidarity of the organic unity of the Sikhs.

Not in the matter of extension of the sacred geography of Sikhism alone but in the constitution of the Khalsa Panth as well, Guru Gobind Singh's view of Indian unity found expression in a pan-Indian base for the new order. The first five beloved ones *(Panj Pyare)* who formed the bedrock of the panth and the way of life, that Guru Gobind Singh revealed and laid out for the humanity, were drawn not from the narrow confines of the Punjab but from all over India. Bhai Daya Singh hailed from Lahore (Punjab), Bhai Dharam Singh from Hastinapur (U.P.), Bhai Mukham Singh from Dwarka (Gujarat), Bhai Sahib Singh from Bidar (Karnataka) and Bhai Himmat Singh from Jagannath Puri (Orissa). Castewise also they represented the whole spectrum of what were then believed to be outside the pale of civilized Hindu society, the weavers, the barbers, the water-drawers and the farmers. Only one of them belonged to one of the so-called high castes. Thus both by way of territorial and caste origin, Guru Gobind Singh aimed at an integrative and unified universal identity and not a separatist, disunited and parochial one within which some ill-advised protagonists of the Sikh cause are trying to quarantine Sikhism by declaring Sikhs as a nation. All religions are universal in their self-identity and not restrictive. Sikhism is all thc more open because it describes the Guru's faith as a door open to all and closed to none. How can a 'nation', a political grouping afford such openness?

Those who never tire of saying that for the Sikhs their faith is inseparable from their politics, conveniently forget that a distinction in this sphere was made even during the lifetime of the Gurus themselves. The holy precincts of the Hari Mandir (Golden Temple) were never used for political 'gatherings or other non-religious purposes. This distinction was very clear to Guru Hargobind who raised Akal Takhat outside the holy precincts of the Hari Mandir. It is being increasingly felt that instead of providing good administration of the Sikh Gurdwaras and propagating the universal teachings of the Sikh Gurus, the S.G.P.C. only politicised the management of the holy shrines and thus the conduct of all Sikh religious affairs. A reason for the present day decline of Sikh faith may as well be found in such politicisation of Sikh faith.

So far as the political aspect of the problem is concerned, it will be necessary to go back to pre-Independence days when Muslim League had raised the bogey of two nations based on religion. The Sikh political leadership was unreservedly opposed to the protagonists of the two-nation theory and never subscribed to the pernicious two-nation theory by deliberate choice. The Sikh leadership called upon the Sikh people to emigrate enmasse from the theocratic state of Pakistan to the democratic and republican State of India, which was creation of a secular faith in the theory of one nation and which cherished the value of equal respect of all faiths and equality of all men before God as cherished and nurtured by the Sikh Gurus. The wounds of the partition may have healed, but the memories of the holocaust in the wake of the communal frenzy have not yet faded. It will be crucial for the so-called protagonists of the theory of Sikhs being a separate nation or of Khalistan to ponder over the fact as to why the Sikh masses and the Sikh leadership chose to cast their lot with protagonists of India being one nation and not with those committed to the two-nation theory which was the real basis for creation of Pakistan. Any other course would have meant repudiation of the unique contribution of the Sikh patriots to the national struggle for India's Independence. It is in this background of the basic commitment of the Sikhs to the cause of Indian nation that one can appreciate the fact that the Sikh population migrated from the new state of Pakistan to India leaving behind their hearths and homes and even their holy shrines. Above all this migration was symbolic of their identification of the faith of the Sikh Gurus with the secular, democratic and socialist structure of the Indian polity.

The Sikhs were in the forefront of the national struggle of Independence throughout. Starting with the Namdhari movement which had begun in 1857 barely 8 years after the annexation of Punjab to the British Indian empire, the Sikhs made tremendous contribution to the national cause till the dawn of Independence. In large number of those who mounted the gallows in British India on charges of sedition against the British Government were Sikhs. The Ghadar Movement which blazed a new trail of patriotic fervour in the latter half of the second decade of this century was composed predominantly of the Sikh immigrants to North America. The victories of the Sikh Gurudwara Movement were hailed by Mahatma Gandhi as the first decisive victory in the war against the British imperialism. The Akali and the Babbar Akali Movements, the Bharat Naujawan Sabha and the Shiromani Akali Dal, Riayasti Akali Dal and Parja Mandal spearheaded the struggle for Independence in British provinces of Punjab and the princely Sikh states of Punjab. Never during their supreme involvement with the Sikh cause did the Sikh masses falter from their commitment to the cause of national freedom. For this cause they rose to great heights of self sacrifice, of suffering detention and long term internment in British jails and numerous other trials and tribulations. Surpassing it all was the havoc through which the Sikhs had to pass in the wake of communal riots preceding and consequent upon the partition of Punjab. During all these trials the Sikhs upheld their categorical stand against separatism and parochial sectarianism. The misguided or the misdirected elements which are today trying to create confusion and cast doubts in Sikh minds as also in the minds of others about the intentions of the Sikhs are trying to blot out this glorious and sacred heritage of the Sikhs in the modern history of India. The Independent India under the awakened and able guidance of the national leaders extended warm welcome to the Sikhs uprooted from Pakistan and provided them with all the opportunities to strike their roots and flourish anywhere in India as their motherland and homeland. The entire India is today the homeland of the Sikhs. Any wilful action in promoting Sikh chauvinism in Punjab is fraught with consequences which are against the interest of Sikhs themselves.

Here, I am reminded of "An appeal to the conscience of Commonwealth countries" addressed by Sant Harchand Singh Longowal, Presiderrt, Shiromani Akali Dal, to the Queen of Britain and other Heads of Commonwealth countries on the eve of Commonwealth Conference held at New Delhi in November 1983.

In his letter, Sant Harchand Singh Longowal had made the following points:

That the Sikhs had made tremendous sacrifices to save the integrity of the British Empire and the Commonwealth of nations. In the words of Sant Longowal, "during the two world wars when the very fate of this Body (British Commonwealth) and its members hung in balance, about 4,00,000 Sikhs fought on the side of the allied armies to save their integrity and independence".

Whereas the Muslim community developed misgivings about the bonafides of Hindu leaders and the future prospects of Muslims in a political set up dominated by the Hindu majority and laid claim to a separate sovereign state in the shape of present Pakistan, the leaders of the Sikhs put their faith in the solemn commitments held out to them that in free India their special interests as a national minority would be fully protected in the Constitution. In the words of Sant Longowal, "the Congress leaders, once in the seat of power, went back on all the solemn assurances held out by them to Sikhs and bluntly refused to provide any safeguard and protect their interests as a national minority". Ever since 1947 a calculated and callous campaign has been in progress at all levels to destroy their spiritual, cultural, economic and political health with a view to effecting their very national entity.

In more recent past, this campaign of ruthless repression against Sikhs has assumed such a horrible form that one is reminded of Jews suffering at the hands of Hitler. Such is the fate of Sikhs in India, which claims to be the biggest democracy in the world, that they do not enjoy even the most elementary human right i.e. right to one's life.

While concluding, Sant Longowal made an earnest prayer to the Heads—of Commonwealth, "to save the people who once helped save many members of the Commonwealth".

The contentions of Sant Longowal were not only contrary to Sikh history and traditions but were based on complete distortion of facts and history. The very act of choosing to write to Heads of Commonwealth in this fashion was in itself repugnant to the honour and dignity of the nation.

Coming to the merits, it is apparent that all the three issues raised by Sant Longowal are not borne out by the history of India's freedom struggle and the status and position of Sikhs in independent India.

By referring to the services rendered by the Sikhs for the protection of British Empire, Sant Longowal did not do justice to the Sikh martyrs and freedom fighters, who made tremendous sacrifices and underwent untold sufferings for the country's freedom. Starting with Baba Ram Singh in 1872, the history of India's freedom struggle recounts vividly the sacrifices made by the Sikhs. The role of Ghaddar Party, the Jalianwala Bagh massacre, the martyrdom of Sardar Bhagat Singh, Guru Ka Bagh Morcha, Jaito Morcha and the sacrifices made by a large number of Sikhs along with other communities constitute a glorious chapter in Sikh history, in which every patriotic Sikh takes pride.

To say that assurances given to the minorities including Sikhs by leaders of the freedom struggle had been betrayed is contradicted by certain fundamental provisions made in our Constitution.

In free India, minorities have been equal partners in the process of national development. To say that a calculated campaign has been in progress since 1947 to efface the national entity of Sikhs presents a travesty of facts. In every field of human endeavour, Sikhs have been playing a prominent role. Sikhs have risen to the highest positions in different fields of public life and in different professions. In political life, Sikhs have occupied positions of responsibility including the highest office of the land. Economically, Sikhs are among the most progressive and prosperous sections of the Indian society. Their economic activities are not confined to the state of Punjab, but extended to the remotest parts of the country. Culturally, for the first time in the history of India, Punjabi language has been given the status of an official language.

In my view Sant Longowal did not do any positive service to the Sikh community and India's secular polity by comparing the Sikhs in free India with the Jews in Hitler's Germany. The whole of India is the homeland of the Sikhs. In the holy scripture, Guru Nanak, the founder of the Sikh faith never talked of any single province, but twice mentioned Hindustan, which was known as Bharat. The last and the tenth Guru, Guru Gobind Singh was born in Patna (Bihar), spent his youth and laid the foundation of the Khalsa at Anandpur Sahib (Punjab) and breathed his last at Nanded (Maharashtra). The Gurus recognised the whole of the country, as their own. The Sikhs fought for the country's independence not only from the soil of Punjab, but made the whole of India their battlefield. They waged the sacred battles for freedom from Canada, USA, Malaysia. Singapore, Thailand, Burma, Japan and various other places. They belong to Indra and India belongs to them.

Chapter 47

SANT JARNAIL SINGH BHINDRANWALE

Sant Jarnail Singh Bhindranwale was a young preacher of the Sikh gospel in Punjab, who leapt into prominence in an aura of militancy in the early eighties. He became a menace to the law-keeping authorities, whereas he was considered a messiah by the fundamentalist elements. Though he lost his life during the Operation Bluestar, his spectre has been looming large. It has been variously alleged that I had a hand in creating him or propping him up from obscurity or bringing him into limelight from the sidelines for the sole purpose of using him as a pawn on the chessboard of politics or transforming him into a countervailing influence against the Akalis, who had adopted a confrontationist attitude towards the Congress Party and the government.

Sant Bhindranwala had started his life in an unpretentious manner in the Damdami Taksal (mint), whose main objective was to turn out devout and dedicated Sikhs with a spartan outlook, but with purity of mind and character. Meditation was their medium of attaining saintliness and service was their vehicle for achieving moral merits. But in a deluge of frenzy over a few years they were carried towards the fast currents of militancy thereby becoming a challenge to the traditional and even tenor of life.

It is further alleged that Sanjay Gandhi was looking for a religious personality, who could steal the thunder out of the Akali leadership and his choice fell on this particular personage of Chowk Mehta, Amritsar. In a book entitled *Amritsar* by

Mark Tully and Satish Jacob of BBC in 1985, it was insinuated that I had a hand in bringing the Sant on the centrestage. Their main source of information in matters relating to Punjab was none other than Darbara Singh, the then Chief Minister of the state.

The allegation that I had created the Dal Khalsa, whose avowed aim was to demand a sovereign Sikh state was also given currency. It was a most baffling and unrealistic statement. A man the very foundation of whose life was laid on the bedrock of patriotism and the unity of the country could not have thought of aiding the formation of an anti-national body. The purpose of spreading such a canard was to sow the seeds of confusion in public mind. As it was a common practice for voluntary organisations and social and cultural institutions to approach public bodies or established institutions for financial assistance for holding a public function or arranging a meeting, it is quite possible that a small amount of a few hundred rupees might have been provided by a philanthropist organisation in good faith. Obviously such a gesture could not be linked to any sinister motive of creating a frankenstein.

When in April 1980, the Nirankari Baba Gurbachen Singh was murdered in Delhi, the crime was linked to Sant Jarnail Singh Bhindranwale, as the incident was considered a revenge for the mowing down of eight Akalis by the members of the Nirankari sect. In reply to a question in Parliament, I as the Home Minister told the House that Bhindranwale was not involved in it. There was no concrete evidence to show his complicity, but my detractors seized upon this opportunity to criticise me.

In September 1981, a warrant for the arrest of Sant Bhindranwale was issued by the Punjab government. At that time the Sant was in Haryana. Before the Punjab police could reach ·Chandu Kalan, where the Sant was sojourning on some religious mission, he had left the place. An utterly false impression was tried to be created that I had a hand in it! When Sant Bhindranwale was ultimately arrested, he was released by the Punjab government. This again was attributed to me, which was a total travesty of facts. After some time Sant

Bhindranwale carne to Delhi and drove around the capital with his armed supporters. He did not break any laws and the arms borne by his followers were licenced ones.

Sant Bhindranwale undertook a trip to Bombay and engaged himself in some religious ceremonies without let on hindrance by the Maharashtra government. On his return to Punjab, he was not arrested by the Government headed by Darbara Singh. He made himself comfortable in Guru Nanak Niwas and my advice to Mrs. Indira Gandhi to arrest him was not heeded. Later he was invited by the Akali leaders, Jathedar Gurcharan Singh Tohra and Sant Harchand Singh Longowal to shift to the sanctuary of the Akal Takht. It was perhaps the first time in the Sikh history that somebody was permitted to turn the holy Takht into living quarters, but inscrutable were the ways of the Akali leadership.

I never had any occasion of meeting Sant Bhindranwale.

The nearest I got to him was at the Bhog (final prayers) ceremony of Jathedar Santokh Singh, the President of the Delhi Sikh Gurdwara Management Committee, who was shot dead by a friend- turned-rival, in December 1981. The Sant was sitting cross-legged as everybody does in a Sikh congregation and I had no communication with him whatsoever. There were a number of dignitaries present at the ceremony including partymen and Ministers. A fantastic lie was spread that I had touched the feet of the Sant. The perpetrators of this lie were not conversant with or pretended to be ignorant of the Sikh tradition that no one bows to a person in the presence of the Holy scripture, which is worshipped as a living Guru. The Sant was a short distance away from where I was sitting and it does not indicate that I had any proximity with him. I had no contacts with him whatsoever. Our ways were different. Our philosophies of life' were different. We had nothing in common. I always abhorred separatism from the national mainstream. He had his own ways. Mark Tully and Satish Jacob missed these points. Though they remained tenacious to their statement, they erred on facts. They were wilfully misled by someone who did not see eye to eye with me.

I cannot say if it was a mere coincidence that on the very day I took the oath of the office of President on 25 July 1982, Sant Bhindranwale had announced that he would continue , the agitation launched by him in protest against the atrocities committed on the Sikhs by the Centre and the Punjab government "I am ready to sacrifice my head", he had added,

It was really the responsibility of the State government of Punjab to apprehend anyone posing a threat to law and order or creating discord between the various communities, My advice to Mrs. Indira Gandhi to take a suitably hard line in time was not accepted, which, unfortunately, led to the tragic events of 1984.

—

Chapter 48

SOME MEMORABLE MEETINGS

General Zia-ul-Haq, President of Pakistan relished to come to India on unofficial visits, and whenever he came, he made courtesy calls on the President. Each time he came, he extended invitation to the Indian President to pay a visit to his country. When he asked me to visit Pakistan, I told him that this could be settled between our two governments and dates could be fixed as per mutual decision. I conveyed General Zia-ul-Haq's wish to the then Prime Minister, Mrs. Indira Gandhi.

Though the Pakistani President was an army General and was supposed to be a tough ruler, he was mild in speech and affable in manner. He impressed by his sincerity in what he said, and exuded a certain air of warmth and a good amount of cordiality.

General Zia was born in Jalandhar, the heartland of Indian Punjab and, as he said, he had a lot of goodwill and affinity for India. But since he was the leader of Pakistan, which had separated from India in 1947, he could take only such decisions as would provide satisfaction to the people of his country.

He said that my visit to Pakistan would be widely welcomed, and it might pave a way for establishing mutual friendly relations on a lasting basis.

After conversing with me for sometime in the Urdu language, General Zia burst into Punjabi, which was the mother tongue of both of us. The atmosphere became more informal. I told him that official talks on some important issues could be held between him and the Indian Prime Minister, but it would give me immense satisfaction, if he would like to open his mind on certain issues, which we could discuss without any reservation. I told him that India had chosen the path of democracy, and though Pakistan had opted for a different course, he was in command of his nation and his word prevailed there. Though we are very close neighbours and ought to have much larger cooperation with each other, there have been some basic differences, and if we could reach an understanding, we, as nations, could be much happier. I told General Zia that with the influence he wielded over his people, he could help remove the cobwebs of misunderstanding between our countries, so that the poor masses could devote greater attention to their own prosperity. It did not matter much how long one remained in power. But what really mattered was the contribution one made for the betterment of one's people. If we, the persons at the helm of our nations, could lead the masses on the road to development and reconstruction, we could contribute a great deal to the future of our societies. Unless the people of India and Pakistan started living in a friendly environment, they would not be able to move towards progress. A policy of conflict and confrontation impels our nations to seek support and sympathy from other countries, which in quite a few cases generates distortions. Pakistan and India have gone to war three times, but except material and human loss, hardly have any positive results been achieved. If we could resolve our differences amicably, we could utilise our limited resources for peaceful purposes. First of all, we have to make up our minds that our nations should abide in perpetual peace and solve our issues in a spirit of compromise and understanding. General Zia-ul-Haq then asked, "Sahib-e-Sadar, kindly advise me, what I should do. You need not tell me, what your country should do in the prevailing circumstances, But it would be helpful, if you could suggest the course I should adopt."

I reminded General Zia-ul-Haq that Pakistan was in illegal occupation of a part of Jammu and Kashmir, which is contrary to all legal and moral precepts. We could make a beginning from that point.

General Zia said that he agreed that Jammu and Kashmir was the main stumbling block in Indo-Pak relations, but, even before we could reach a settlement on this issue, we could improve our relations in the fields of free travel to ·each other's country, trade and cultural exchanges. Strengthening of ties in these spheres would be conducive to bringing an overall improvement. He then invoked God and suggested that we should be guided by the Divine will. If we looked towards the Almighty, He might show us the right way. Let us think deeply and sincerely, and then proceed in the right direction. Until we reached positive conclusions, we need not make our plans public.

At this stage, the Pakistani President suggested that we should exchange our thoughts exclusively. I agreed to the suggestion. The General was accompanied by his aides and one of my officials was also present. They were asked to withdraw. The General then remarked that he hoped there was no bugging in the room. I laughed and assured the Pakistani President that there was no question of any bugging here. He then used a Punjabi proverb, which means that even walls have ears and suggested that we better talked in the open, out of the fourwalls of a room. I then led the guest to the Mughal garden for a stroll, while our conversation continued. General Zia requested for a tangible suggestion for solving the Kashmir tangle, to which my reply was that Shimla Agreement signed by Z.A. Bhutto and Mrs. Indira Gandhi provided for a suitable framework for discussing the matter bilaterally and there could not be a better method than having a dialogue between the representatives of our two countries to hammer out a solution. On a repeated suggestion by President Zia, for a concrete proposal, I told him that a definite proposal could come from a Minister or a senior official of the government, but I could only express my personal opinion that Jammu and Kashmir being an integral part of India, it would not be possible to negotiate on the status of this territory. However, looking at the position on the ground, it might not be feasible for us to recover the territory occupied by you. And Pakistan can never have the Indian part of Jammu and Kashmir. If both countries could accept the line of actual control as the International boundary, then there could be a possibility of ending the conflict giving rise to a new era of friendship and cooperation. The tension between our two countries had been resulting in the wastage of our limited resources on the defence of our long border. "You are looking for allies and friends for projecting your viewpoint about India. We in turn have also to muster support for our stand. We could as well reach an agreement and divert our scarce resources to more constructive purposes," I said.

General Zia reacted slowly and spoke in measured tones. He said that it was a very delicate matter and needed a lot of deliberation. It was very difficult for him to frame an immediate response. But he felt that if India made a formal proposal to this effect, then he would make a sincere endeavour to get it accepted by his country. After a few seconds, he said that it was his personal promise that he would do everything possible to agree to this proposal, if the initiative came from India. With an air of resignation, the General said that people remembered only the major successes of their leaders and generally overlooked their transient achievements. I agreed with the General.

I narrated the whole conversation to Mrs. Indira Gandhi. She expressed the view that some major powers would not let the matter be settled on these lines. Though General Zia showed inclination to accept such a solution, there was little possibility of its going through to a logical end. She suggested that this proposal be kept in cold storage. She also requested that this need not be mentioned to anyone else. General Zia being a Dictator, had very little real support in his country. One day he was likely to be overshadowed by his opponents, especially the Pakistan People's Party. In his heart of hearts General Zia wanted a good equation with India. Mrs. Gandhi said that she too desired smooth relations with Pakistan and she had no prejudice against that country. But she doubted, if all Pakistani elements shared this view. She told me that if I accepted the General's invitation to visit Pakistan, he would get a boost in his country, to which his political opponents would not take kindly. If we pursued the proposal about Kashmir, we would also have to seek a consensus with other political parties. Personally, she said, such a line would be acceptable to her, though she was not sure of the reaction of the opposition ·parties. She endorsed my reaction to the General's invitation to visit Pakistan that a decision would be taken as per mutual convenience.

Mrs. Gandhi further remarked that though Zia had suggested that such a proposal on Kashmir would be acceptable to him, if put forward by India, we should obtain a guarantee to this effect, otherwise the entire effort would become futile leading to embarrassment. Let this be frozen for the time being, without any hurry for its resurrection.

When George Bush, then Vice President of USA came calling on me, I was briefed by the Ministry of External Affairs that he was a man of considerable reckoning and it was likely that he would be elected the next President of his country. After exchange of greetings and settling down for an informal conversation, Bush informed that he had visited India before and was very happy to come once again. He had great admiration for the Indian democracy and its openness. He also felt happy that most people here were religious minded and had unshakable faith in God. He himself had deep faith in God and religion and also had tremendous respect for individual's dignity, the sentiments shared by the Indian people in ample measure. Responding to his views, I told Bush that we Indians have a basic philosophy of religious tolerance and respect for one another's faith. Our Constitution guarantees to every individual freedom to profess the creed of his choice and our minorities have the right to run their own educational institutions.

Bush was happy to say that USA and India had close mutual relations. We were attached to each other emotionally. Ever since its freedom, India had been contributing to world peace. He was happy at the Indian people's policy of peaceful co-existence. He said that the exchanges of views in economic, political and cultural matters had been going on in a very satisfactory manner.

Expressing my appreciation for his views, I told Bush that the government and people of our country welcomed his visit, which, indeed, would help strengthen our ties further. I told him that he was known as an influential leader in his country and for us his visit was of great importance. We would have been happier, if the President of the United States could also have visited us, but probably he had a busy schedule.

I told Bush that during President Reagan's visit to China, the Chinese media by and large had ignored his speeches. Inspite of that, Reagan being a large-hearted man, had gone on with his tour unruffled. Bush said that President Reagan had re-affirmed to the Chinese leaders that the Americans regarded individual dignity very highly. He also reiterated his faith in God, human rights and freedom of thought.

At one point Vice-President Bush told me that he agreed that India and USA had not been able to forge as close and strong ties, as they ought to have done. With a little humour he said that if we could be a little less ardent in our friendship with USSR and a little more .enthusiastic in upgrading our relations with USA, then perhaps the scenario could change. In the same lighter vein, I told him that real friendships are never conditional. Our relations with USSR were based on certain time-tested principles and we had received unstinted support from the Soviets in our difficult moments and in matters crucial to us.

The meeting ended on a very cordial note. The illustrious visitor radiated happiness.

The high profile visit of the Soviet President, Mikhail Gorbachev was a big event for us. It received much fanfare in our mass media. Ever since the signing of the Indo-Soviet Treaty of Friendship etc. our two countries had become much closer. On many an occasion we received unstinted support from the Soviets. India's stance of universal peace and fair outlook had a moderating influence in the cold war situation. No wonder, therefore, that the Indo-Soviet mutual relations had assumed a special significance. The ambience was full of goodwill and sincerity.

When Gorbachev called on me, our conversation centred on our two countries' friendship and cooperation. The guest was full of praise for our contributions to peace. He was aware of our problems with our neighbours in the north and the north-west and he believed that with our steadfastness we would be able to overcome them.

I complimented Gorbachev for his efforts in softening the rigours of the cold war and bringing about reforms in his own country. He dwelt on his favourable subjects of glossnost and perestroika. I agreed with him that free debate and openness helped in the liberation of the soul and contributed to the development of the individual and the society. Freedom of thought and fearlessness in expressing one's feelings within the parametres of collective welfare of a particular society or a nation would allow the citizens to flourish. He said that his main objective was to transform the human spirit in a peaceful manner. He was keen to change the course of political and economic thought of the Soviet people, which had fallen in a groove. He hoped that he would be successful in his endeavours.

He was changing the course of history not only of his own people, but the whole world, I remarked. He laughed and modestly indicated approval of this observation. He was trying to go into the nuances of his philosophy, but trying to keep to the schedule, we moved on to the Mughal Gardens, where tea was laid and a number of guests were waiting. The informal atmosphere was full of joy and gaiety. The visitor was really feeling comfortable and he enjoyed every moment of it. The conversation naturally was being conducted with the help of an interpreter. Gorbachev did not seem to be happy with his performance, because his Secretary came and told my staff that our interpreter was not upto the mark and his translation was full of distortions.

After tea, Gorbachev held my hand and asked if another meeting would be possible between us the next day. No other meeting was listed in the visiting dignitary's programme. When my Secretary inquired of the Ministry of External Affairs, they did not react at all. I abandoned the idea of having another meeting with Gorbachev, but before leaving Rashtrapati Bhawan, he dropped in again alongwith his own interpreter. He confided that though he had launched upon a momentous programme of reforms, he could not gauge the reactions of the common man about the same. All the same he was determined to continue with his mission and to bring a new era of freedom, a liberal way of life and a spirit of enterprise among his people. He expected a wind of change to blow all over the place complimentary to human spirit. I expressed my best wishes for the welfare of the Soviet people and hoped that his efforts would usher in a new phase in their life and set them on a fresh course leading to greater happiness and prosperity. He also thanked me for my thoughts on his personal welfare.

Chapter 49

CENSORSHIP OF PRESIDENT'S BROADCASTS TO THE NATION

It had become a convention to send a copy of the text of the President's broadcast to the nation, to the Prime Minister before the President recorded it for Radio and Television. This was particularly relevant to the formal broadcasts by the President on the eve of Independence Day and Republic Day. Secretary to the President used to contact Secretaries in various Departments of the Government to send inputs for preparation of the script. Not all Departments complied. Those who did, usually provided notes lauding their achievements. While some of the notes received were balanced and objective, the others did not yield much useful material. During my tenure in Rashtrapati Bhavan, the draft script for each broadcast was prepared by my officers under my directions. The quality of my broadcast scripts and public speeches improved considerably, when a highly competent official, Manohar Singh Batra, a retired Deputy Director General of All India Radio joined as my Officer on Special Duty in early 1986.

When the text of my speech for broadcast on the national hook-up of All India Radio and Doordarshan on 14 August 1986, was sent to the Prime Minister's Secretariat, they did not furnish any comment or suggestion for over seven days. AIR and Doordarshan, both Government media started making frantic contacts with the President's Secretariat for the recording of the speech. All India Radio have set up a small studio in a room in the Rashtrapati Bhavan, where the recordings are made. *Doordarshan* bring their equipment each time the President is to be recorded, for which a bigger room close to the President's study is used. I went through both the exercises, but hours after the recording was made, a word was received from the Prime Minister's office that I should be requested to omit the following sentences from my recorded speech:

> "A Government gets the support of the people by its handling the issues with a liberal but firm approach. Consideration for the sentiments of the people earns their affection and goodwill. It is most essential for the Government to protect the life, property and honour of every citizen. Any government that is unable to discharge these obligations, will lose its credibility."

Buta Singh, Minister for Home Affairs came personally to me with the request that I should re-record the speech both for All India Radio and Doordarshan by omitting the above lines. It gave me utter surprise at this suggestion, as the script had been lying in the office of the Prime Minister for so many days, and now when it had been recorded, I was being asked to record it again. I was also amused at the fact that the Prime Minister had sent the Home Minister to me instead of the Minister incharge of the Information and Broadcasting Ministry. I told Buta Singh that the speech had to be recorded a couple of days before the date of broadcast, as All India Radio were very keen to have the text in their hands for transmission to their stations in the various State capitals for translation into regional languages, which are broadcast by them after the Hindi and English versions relayed from Delhi. I declined to re-record the message, as I did not find anything wrong in the four sentences, which I was being asked to omit.

Then came P.V. Narasimha Rao, another senior Cabinet Minister, along with Buta Singh and repeated the request. I asked them to specify the ground on which the Government found these innocuous sentences so offensive. Their reply was astounding. They argued that these lines would give an impression to millions of listeners and viewers that the Government had failed to protect the life, property and honour of citizens and it would bring discredit to it. I pointed out to the two senior Ministers that law and order and protection of citizens was primarily the responsibility of the State governments and the words used by me in the speech were 'a government' and 'any government'. I asked them if they were happy with the performance of several State governments in this matter, to which they did not have any definite answer. They insisted, however, that I should consider excluding these sentences from my recorded speech for broadcast to the Nation.

I pointed out to the Ministers that the External Publicity Division of the Government had already transmitted the text including these "objectionable" sentences to our embassies abroad, where Ambassadors were to read out the text to the gatherings at the Independence-Day Celebrations. Would they advise the Embassies separately to omit these sentences? Would they like to announce all over the world that the President's speech had been censored after it had been recorded?

I had strong reservations in the matter, I told them. But since the electronic media were under the direct control of the government, they could, if they wanted, tell the media to erase the "offending" sentences from the recorded speech. And this is exactly what they did. The broadcast and telecast speech on the eve of Independence Day was tampered with and the sentences were left out.

The next broadcast to the Nation by the President was to take place on 25 January 1987, the eve of the Republic Day. As usual, the script was sent to the Prime Minister's Secretariat. And again the Home Minister, Buta Singh approached me with certain suggestions, which largely were meant to boost the image of the Government. After noting that the economy of the country had grown at five per cent or higher, I had said in a forthright manner that our food production had crossed the 150 million tonne mark. But the Government added: "Despite persistent drought, our agriculture has demonstrated a remarkable resilience and the food-grain production has crossed the 150 million tonnes mark." Similarly, where I had said that the rate of industrial growth had been showing a rising trend, the Prime Minister's office wanted me to add that it was due to the dynamism of the new industries.

They deleted the sentence: "It is of utmost importance to simultaneously keep a check on price rise and inflation." As regards my suggestion that sustained efforts had to be made to wipe out the deficit in trade balance, which had risen from Rupees 5318 crores during the previous year to Rupees 8616 crores in 1985-86, the Government recast the sentence like this: "We should take heart from the impressive acceleration in exports and make sustained efforts to wipe out the deficit."

To crown it all, the Government wanted me to delete the following paragraph from my broadcast altogether:

To conclude, I would like to say, my brothers and sisters, that the Constitution has enjoined upon me, as President, the duty to preserve, protect and defend the Constitution and the law.

I have at all times done my best to discharge this duty resolutely with sincerity and devotion. I have endeavoured my utmost to maintain and strengthen the unity of India.

I was to leave *Rashtrapati Bhavan* for the airport at 1240 hours on 21 January 1987, for a visit to West Bengal, when Buta Singh came at 1205 hours to press for acceptance of these changes in the script. I asked him how it affected the Government, if I told the Nation that I had served them to the best of my ability. Surprisingly, his version was that if I said so in the broadcast on the Radio and Television, the people would get the impression that the President was indicting the Government indirectly that they had been found wanting in some way or the other. I told Buta Singh that as I was about to go to Calcutta, we would discuss this further on my return two days later. On 23 January 1987, the Home Minister came late in the evening and I told him that I had no mind dropping this paragraph from my speech.

Then came my address to a joint session of both Houses of Parliament in the Central Hall on the opening of the Budget session. The preparation of this address is a prerogative of the Government and the President has no say in it, except that he can informally suggest changes. While going through the text, I found that in the portion dealing with foreign policy, there was no mention about China. This was conveyed to the Cabinet Secretary by my Secretary, and promptly a word was received that they were going to make up for the omission. The second important point noticed in the script was the high encomiums showered on the then Akali Chief Minister of Punjab, Surjit Singh Barnala. I had nothing against the Government praising the Chief Minister, but I felt that the hyperbolic expression used in the Address reflected the Government's over-enthusiasm. My observation on this point was not accepted by the Government. Barnala was specially invited by them to take a seat in the President's gallery in the Central Hall to personally hear the Government's approbation from the mouth of the President. And it was only this portion in the Address that evoked the applause from the Parliamentarians, who expressed appreciation by thumping their tables. All eyes were rivetted on Barnala, while his face was beaming with pride and pleasure. But it was the same Barnala, who after three months, was abruptly removed from the office by the Central Government for incompetence and inefficiency in handling the situation in the State. Punjab was placed under the President's rule.

I was to demit office on 25 July 1987, when the President-elect R. Venkataraman was to be sworn in. I decided to bid farewell to the Nation on Radio and Television in the evening of 24 July. With the assistance of my OSD, Mr. Batra, I prepared the text both in Hindi and English and kept it with me. There were numerous inquiries from the Cabinet Secretary and Secretary to the Prime Minister about the contents of my speech. In fact, my Secretary, Varadan was hard put to it to oblige, as there were persistent requests for a copy of the script from these officials as well as the Directors General of All India Radio and Doordarshan, who were, perhaps, cautioned by the Ministry of Information and Broadcasting to ensure that nothing "objectionable" in the President's farewell speech should be recorded. My Secretary repeatedly assured them all that the President's script contained nothing "sensational" and they should have no cause for anxiety. The 'efforts to obtain a copy of the text in advance continued till the last moment, and they heaved a sigh of relief when the message was recorded, which was a simple acknowledgement of my gratitude for the Nation's trust and confidence in me and the love and affection showered on me during my tenure as President as well as the expression of my feelings for the unity and integrity of the country, This was the least I· could do at the time of my departure as the first citizen and servant of the Nation. This was my personal message, in which I did not need the aid and advice of my Council of Ministers.

Chapter 50

MY SUCCESSOR AND I

My five year term as President came to an end on 25 July 1987. R. Venkataraman, who like me was elected on the Congress ticket, took oath of office in the Central Hall of Parliament. On our return to Rashtrapati Bhavan after the ceremony, it was time for me to say goodbye. I was given an affectionate send off. I was touched by the gesture of the new President and his wife, Janaki Venkataraman to accompany me to 4 Circular Road in Chanakyapuri, the residence allotted to me by the government. I consistently had very cordial relations with Venkataraman, when he was the Vice President and was quite impressed by his pleasant countenance, poise and calm dignity. Most of the time his visage was wreathed in a self-confident smile and whenever we exchanged a few words in conversation, I found him affable and courteous. I had confidence in his fairness and objectivity.

But something happened in early 1988. That was the time when I seriously started working on my memoirs with the help of my friend and aide, Manohar Singh Batra. During my tenure in *Rashtrapati Bhavan,* I had not maintained a personal diary and was hard put to it while narrating my reactions and sentiments. That is one of the factors of my having dealt in these pages with only such events as I have considered of some importance to me and my countrymen.

During the entire period of five years in office I used to get press clippings made daily, which my Press Secretary, Suryanarayanan, used to place before me for my perusal, These cuttings related to my significant engagements including meetings with Indian and foreign dignitaries, functions attended and addressed in the capital and other parts of the country, State events and important articles written by eminent journalists and public men. A few days before the end of my term, Suryanarayanan showed me some volumes of those press clippings, which he had got bound, as per my desire, for my reference. But he failed to hand them over to my personal staff and retained all the volumes with himself.

On 17 February 1988, I addressed a personal letter to the President, R. Venkataraman, requesting him to lend me some of the volumes of the press clippings for my perusal. He sent me a reply on 29 February 1988, stating that he would be happy to provide facility for perusal and also for taking copies of a *limited* number of the press clippings to me or an authorised member of my staff, in *Rashtrapati Bhavan.* I would appreciate, he added, that since they now formed part of the official records, it would not be possible for these to be taken out of the Secretariat.

I was taken by surprise at this unexpected response, and though I was keen on taking it up urgently again with the President, I fell ill and was kept in the Cardiological ward of the Ram Manohar Lohia Hospital for a number of days. After I recovered somewhat, I sent another letter to Venkataraman on 7 May 1988. I thanked him for his offer of letting me read through the press clippings in the *Rashtrapati Bhavan* Secretariat, but pleaded my inability to do so. I drew his attention to the fact that the press clippings were made during the period I had held the office of the President, under my directions. Moreover, the process of going through these press clippings being time-consuming, it would not be practical for me to visit *Rashtrapati Bhavan* over a number of days. I suggested that the files containing the clippings could be loaned to me in small instalments like books from the library to be returned before another batch could be issued.

The President, however, replied to me on 14 May 1988, appreciating my difficulty, but reiterating that it would not be possible to send *official files, whatever the contents, outside the office.*

My next letter to Venkataraman on the subject was dated 10 June 1988. While expressing my surprise and dismay, I repeated my contention that these files contained no State papers. These were just cuttings from the newspapers and newspapers could not be treated as secret. I was constrained to point out that his fixed approach to an innocuous request made by his predecessor was really baffling. I added that in such a mundane matter, he had chosen to exercise his discretion in a very unhelpful manner. I told Venkataraman in my letter that the stand taken by him would remain an enigma to me. I wondered what constraints had come his way. I offered to make a cash deposit as security with his office for safely returning the press clippings, if this could help him change his mind.

The President's reply of 14 June 1988, was prompt. It said that he respected my feelings, and it was not a question of loss or damage but that of a principle that *official records* were not taken out.

I felt quite sad at this unrelenting attitude. I would not call it obduracy or petulance or even sheer lack of human kindness. It was, perhaps, irresilience of a pre-set mind. One view was that on receipt of my initial request, the President had sought the advice of the then government and he was told to offer me the facility of perusing the press clippings only in the President's Secretariat, which would also give them an indication of the nature of the clippings I was interested in, in case I wanted photocopies. Thereafter, the President was compelled to do the stonewalling. Whatever it might be, I sent yet another letter to Venkataraman on 29 June 1988, this time by Registered Post, informing him that I needed no photocopies of any press clippings. I only wanted to have a look at the clippings personally. I told him that his refusal to lend me the press clippings was not only beyond my comprehension, but it was also most distressing. I asked him to ponder over the matter quietly. I did not expect such an attitude from him. I told him that, perhaps, it was for posterity to judge how a man in this great country, who always took pride in norms of courtesy and decent behaviour, was being treated after he ceased to be a President!

There was no reply to this letter. In the meantime, I narrated my memoirs relying in major part on my memory and copies of whatever limited number of papers available with me. After I read through the first draft, I made some minor changes, again digging into the reserves of my memory. Though the changes made in the manuscript were to my entire satisfaction, I touched upon certain points once again.

In view of my indifferent health and various other factors, I did not feel inclined to publish this volume with a sense of urgency. I was approached by various Indian and foreign publishers to let them have the manuscript for early publication, but I procrastinated.

After the passage of time and on completion of the tenure of R. Venkataraman and the taking over of the Presidency by Dr. Shanker Dayal Sharma, I mentioned to him about the press clippings. Perhaps, I did so just for testing the waters. Without the slightest hesitation and with surprising promptitude, Dr. Sharma made available to me the first few volumes of the clippings and issued directions to his staff that whatever assistance or facility I needed, I should be provided without any hitch. But since the memoirs, however sketchy or incomplete were already prepared and since a sense of *ennui* had overtaken me, I decided not to reopen the manuscript and left it to my children, Joginder Singh, Joginderpal Kaur, Gurdip Kaur and Manjit Kaur and also my aide, Manohar Singh Batra to publish it, when I am no more.

INDEX

Abul Kalam Azad, Maulana, 57
Abdul Ghaffar Khan, 57
Abdul Ghani, 93, 95
Accords
-Assam, 236
-Mizoram, 236
-Punjab, 220, 236, 252
Adi Granth,129
Agricultural Price Commission, 120
Ahmed Din, (Munshi), 20
Ahmed, Fakhrudd in Ali, 113
Aiyar, Alladi Krishnaswamy, 261
Ajit Singh, 77
Akali Dal, 31-32, 47, 111, 280
Akali-januta Covt., 135, 137, 139
Akali Legislature Party, 109
Akali Party, 104-105, 113
Akali Party, (Longowal), 172
Akalis, B, 25, 106, 108, 110, 112- 114, 116, 131, 164, 166-168, 171-172, 187
Akal Takht, 179, 181, 183, 187, 191, 194-196, 283
Alexander, r.c.. 225
All India Gurdwara Act, 140
All Assam Gana Sangram
Parishad (AAGSP), 153, 156
All Assam Students Union (ASSU), 152-153, 156
All India Congress Committee, 34, 92, 113, 195
All India Congress Committee Session (1975), 137
All India State People's Conference,
Sixth Session, 26
Amarinder Singh, 167
Anandpur Sahib, 113, 125
Anandpur Sahib Resolution, 164, 166
Apprenticeship Act (1961), 123
Appropriation Bill, 111
Article 19, 278-279
Article 60, 260
Article 78, 255-257, 260, 262, 264- 265
Arun Singh, 180-183, 217
Arya Samaj Movement, 13
Assassination
-Indira Gandhi, 253
-Mahatma Gandhi, 60
Atma Singh, 190
Attack on Sikhs, 207
Baha Deep Singh, 129

Baba Gurbachan Singh, 290
Baba Ishar Singh, 13-14
Baba Kharak Singh, 48, 1$7
Baba Santa Singh, 187, 193
Bachan Singh (Master), 20
Badal, Prakash Singh, 112, 114, 135, 137
Balwant Singh, 111
Bansi Lal, 115, 133

Barooah, D.K., 83, 135
Barnala, Surjit Singh, 305
Batra, Manohar Singh, 301, 305, 307, 310
Beant Singh, 140
Bhagat Singh, 14, 17, 129
Bhai Mani Singh, 129
Bhai Santokh Singh, 11
Bhajan Lal, 151, 221
Bhajan Singh, 127
Bhargava, Gopi Chand (Dr), 20
Bhattal, Hira Singh, 50
Bhave, Acharya Vinoba, 133
Bhindrawala, Sant Jarnail Singh, 171, 179, 289-92
Bhola Singh, 58
Bhoodan, 88
Bhullar, Darbara Singh, 140-141
Blitz, 250, 253
Bofors, 258, 262-264, 272
Brar, Prithi Singh, 30
Brar, Zora Singh, 138
Brish Bhan, 72-73, 75, 76, 78, 80, 82, 87, 90
Buta Singh, 175, 232-233, 275, 279, 303

Censorship, 277
-Press, 132
-Postal Articles, 266
Chakma minorities, 230
Chakravarty, Inder Singh, 60
Chanan Singh, 11
Chanda Singh, 14
Chandi Ram (Lala), 20
Chandra, Prabodh, 95
Chandrachud, Y.V., 274
Chandrashekhar, 273
Charan Singh, Chaudhary, 142, 147
Chavan, Y.B., 105, 109, 135
Chidambram, P., 255
Chritos Sartzetalkis, 241
Citizen's Commission, 213-214, 216
Civil Liberties, 26
Commission of Inquiry (Amendment) Bill (1988), 232
Communal Riots, 148, 285
Communist Party, 108,]53
Congress Legislature Party, 114
Congress Parliamentary Board, 111-112
Congress Working Committee, 68, 85, 105, 136
CPI, 114, 139
CPI(M), 139

Damdama Sahib, 125, 127, 129
Damdami Taksal, 289
Dansinghwala, Jathedar Nahar Singh,2 1
Darbara Singh, 96, 118, 135, 163, 165-166, 252
Darbar Sahib, 179
Darshani Deodhi, 193-194
Das Commission, 100
Daya Kaur, 9
Dayal, Rajeshwar, 213
Desai, Morarji, 102, 133, 141-142, 245, 271
Desh Dardi (Patriot), 19
Dev Raj Urs, 136
Dhawan, RK., 144-145, 181-182, 204
Dhillon, Gurdial Singh, 135, 142
Dhingra, Madan Lal, 130
Dinesh Singh, 107
Dispute
-River Water, 34
Dod, Sant Singh, 30
Dowry Prohibition (Amendment) Act, (1976), 123

Elections
-General (1957), 91

-General (1962), 97
-General (1967), 107
-Midterm (1969), 111
-State Assembly (1972), 117
Electrification of Villages, 117
Emergency, 132-133
Emergency Excesses Enquiry Authority, 137, 139
Espionage Scandal, 224
Extremists *(see Militants)*

Fairfax, 258
Faridkot, Raja of, 70-71, 77,82-83
Fateh Singh, Sant, 110
Fazal Ali, Syed, 89
Ferozpur, District Congress Committee of, 20
Freedom Fighters, 16, 18-20
Freedom Movement, 17
Freedom of the Press, 120, 257

Gandhi, Indira, 93, 105-106, 108-110, 113-115, 118, 127, 130-131, 133-136, 141, 144, 147, 155, 158, 160, 163-164, 166, 168, 171, 174, 177, 181, 191-192, 202, 205-206, 210, 213-214
Gandhi, Rajiv, 159-160, 163-164, 175, 180, 195, 204, 206-208, 217-218, 227, 230-231, 234, 243, 247, 258, 26] -262
Gandhi, Sanjay, 133-135, 139, 144, 289
Gandhi Smarak Nidhi, 88
Garewal, Balbir Singh, 71
General Zia *(see Zia-ul-Haq)*
George Bush, 297
Ghaddar Movement, 18
Giani Kartar Singh, 106
Giani Mehar Singh, 31
Giani, Sahib Singh, 182-183
Gill, Lachman Singh, 109-110
Giri, V.V., 113
Golden Temple, 128, 171, 178, 180-183, 187, 192, 194-198, 269
Gorbachev, Soviet Leader, 241
Gujral, I.K., 107
Gupta Commission, 139
Gurdev Singh (Justice), 137
Gurdwara Keshgarh Sahib, 147
Gurdwara Sach Khand Hazoor Sahib, 126
Gumam Singh, 108-109, 111, 112, 114
Guru Gobind Singh, 11, 125-128
Guru Granth Sahib, 12
Guru Nanak Dev, 11, 129, 198
Guru Nanak Niwas, 291
Guru Ram Das, 129
Guru Tegh Bahadur, 125, 130

Haqiqat Rai, 129
Harcharan Singh, 77
Hardev Singh, 50
Harikekalan, 20
Harish, George (Rev), 127
Harmandir Sahib, 187, 192, 283
HDW, 263
Holy Book
-Guru Granth Sahib, 9
Howitzers, 258, 263
Hukum Singh Committee, 105

Impeachment, 221, 223
-President, 268
Indian Express, 247, 266
Indian National Congress, 20
Indian Postal Act (1898),266, 276-278
Indi Kaur, 9

Indira-Mujeeb Agreement, 153
Inquiry Commission, 238
Intelligence Bureau, 149, 223-225, 249
Ishar Singh, 17-18, 20
Issue
-Assam, 152
-Mizoram, 228
Jagjivan Ram, 113, 134
Jaito, 50
[akhar, Balram, 144
Jana Singh, 108, 111-112, 114, 131-132
Janga Singh, 13-14, 17,35,42
Jaruzelski, General W., 242
Jaswant Singh, 14-15, 19
Jathedar Harnam Singh Kabbarwachha, 47
Jathedar, KirpaJ Singh, 195
Jathedar Nahar Singh, 70
Jathedar Ram Singh, 40-41, 72
Jathedar Shivdev Singh, 146
Jatti, B.D., 159
Jeji, Harchand Singh, 47
Jethmalani, Ram, 273
Jogi, Karam Singh, 13
Joginder Singh, 310
Joginderpal Kaur, 310
Jugal Kishore, 22

Kabul Singh (Master), 20
Kachru, Dwarka Nath, 51-52
Kairon, Pratap Singh, 80-81, 87, 90, 92-93, 97, 99-100, 102
Kapur, Yashpal. 115, 145
Karam Singh [ogi, 13
Kar Sewa, 187, 200,
Kaur, Gurdip (Dr.), 160
Kaur, Manjit (Dr.), 227
Kaur, Mohinder, 46
Kehar Singh (Dr.), 16, 18, 29, 44
Kewal Kishan, 118
Khalistan, 179, 252, 280, 282-283
Khalsa Dal, 290
Khushi Mohammed (Sufi), 22
Kichlew, Saifuddin (Dr.), 20
Kishan Singh, 9
Kotkapura, 9, 14, 59
Kulwant Singh, 138
Kunzru, H.N., Pandit, 89

Lahore Central Jail, 17, 25
Lala Achint Ram, 20
Lala Jagat Narain, 132, 171
Laldenga, 228-231, 236
Lalthanhawala, 228
Land-Tenure Committee, 80
Legislative Assembly (1970),119-120
Lekh Ram, 21
Longowal, Sant Harchand Singh, 167-168, 173, 197, 217, 220, 252, 285-286, 288, 291

Major Harinder Singh, 106-10"
Major Harpal Singh, 68
Makwana, Yogendra, 147
Malerkotla, Nawab of, 127
Mandi Coniana, 60
Manisinghwala, Sandhura Singh, 21
Master Tara Singh, 46-47, 25
Maulvi Sulaiman, 21, ~9-40
Mauritius, 202
Mehr Singh, 65
Menon, V.P., 72-73, 76, 77, 81
Mikhail Gorbachev, 298
Militants *(see Exiremists/Terrorisis)*, 177-180, 182-183, 186-187, 194-196, 198, 251-252
Misra, Justice Ranganath, 217
Moga, 23

Mohali,122
Mohan Singh (General), 101, 108
Muchaki, Ajaib Singh, 138
Mukherjee, Pranab, 205
Muktsar, 15-16, 47
Musafir, Giani Gurmukh Singh, 73, 76-77, 91, 96, 106-109
Muslim League, 59

Nagoke, Jathedar Mohan Singh, 46-47
Nagoke, Jathedar Udham Singh, 87
NAM, 234, 238
Namdhari Movement, 284
Nanda, Gulzari Lal, 101, 104, 107
Nand Singh, 26
Narain, [ai Prakash, 132-133
Narain, Lal [agat. 171
Narula, R.S., 274
National Movement, 16, 20, 25
Nehru, Arun, 204, 217
Nehru, B.K., 220
Nehru-Harinder Pact, 57, 59
Nehru, Jawahar Lal *(see Nehru, Pandit)*
Nehru-Liaqat Agreemnt, 153
Nehru, Pandit, 26, 52-53, 56, 63, 67-68, 70, 85-86, 93-95, 104, 129, 261-262
Nepal, 226
Nihal Singh, Takshak, 77, 83
Nijalingappa, S., 110-111, 113

Onkar Chand, 137
Operation Blue Star, 178, 183, 186·209, 269
Ozal T., Turkish P.M., 242

Panchayati Raj, 69, 117
Pande, B.D. 171
Pannikar, KM., 89
Pant, Govind Vallabh, Pandit, 91
Pant, KC. 221
Papandreau, Andress G., 242
Parja Vi Pukar (Cry of the People), 28
Parja Mandai Movement, 19,46-47, 51, 53-58, 62, 65, 69, 72, 76-77
Parmar, Y.5., 90
Patel, B.R., 75
Patel, Maniben, 63
Patel, Sardar Vallabh Bhai, 59-63, 67-69, 71, 74, 76, 80
Patiala, Maharaja of, 25, 46, 72-73, 75, 83, 87, 109
Pavate, D.C (Dr.), 115
People's Democratic Republic of Yemen, 202
People's Union for Civil Liberties (PUCL), 211, 212, 216
People's Union for Democratic Rights (PUDR), 211-212, 216
PEPSU, 76-79, 81-83, 86-90, 99, 102
Phula Singh, 127
Pilot, Rajesh, 275
Political Conference, 20, 114
Political Meetings, 19-20
Prabodh Chander, 93, 95, 96, 101
Prakash, Baldev (Dr.), 132
President's Rule, 103-110, 112,114, 151, 153, 171-172, 231, 305
Prevention of Corruption Act, 273
Pritam Singh, 37
Prosecution
-Prime Minister, 273-75
Punjab Affiliated Colleges Bill, 24
Punjabi Linguistic State, 104
Punjabi Suba, 91, 105
Punjab Land Reforms Bill (19), 119
Punjab Mata, 129
Punjab Problem, 163-164, 221-222

Punjab State Congress Committee, 50
Punjab State Cooperative Bank, 121
Punjab States People's Conference (1946), 48
Puran Singh, 27

Qazi Obedullah, 21, 57-58
Quami, Copal Singh, 20

Ragi, Sarwan Singh, 13
Ram Chander, 22
Ram Kishan (Comrade), 106
Ram Tirath, 128
Ranjit Singh, Sardar Bahadur, 77
Ranga, Professor, N.C., 219
Rao, Cundu, 159
Rao, Narasimha P.V., 159, 205, 216, 302
Rarewala, Cian Singh, 73, 75, 82, 104, 110-111
Rasgotra, M.K., 203
Rashtrapati Bhavan, 145, 158, 160, 163, 181, 204, 21~ 224, 23~ 235, 249, 251, 258, 268
Rastr iya Swayam Sevak Sangh, 208
Rattan Singh Vandarjatana, 21
Ravi-Beas Waters, 120
Rawail Singh, 190-192
Reagan, President, 241
Reddy, Brahmanand, 135-136
Reddy, Neelam Sanjiva, 97, 113, 140, 161
Registration of Societies Act, 56
Relation
-President-Prime Minister, 226, 245-247, 249, 253, 259-260, 268
Riots, 237
Riyasti Parja Mandai, 20

SAARC, 243
Sachar, Bhim Sen. 94
Salve, N.K.P., 160
Sandhu, Mehr Singh, 333
Sandhura Singh, 32, 35
Sandhwan,9
Sanghvi, Vir, 267
Sant Chanan Singh, 105, 110-111
Sardar Bhagat Singh *(See Bhagat Singh)*
Satyagraha, 49, 51, 60, 62, 67
Sethi, P.C. 86, 165
Seth Ram Nath, 49, 53, 60, 75-77, 98, 108
Sew a Singh Thikriwala, 19
S.G.P.C., 110, 190, 194-195, 197, 280-281, 283
Shah Commission, 105
Shah, J. C. (Justice), 137
Shah Nahar Deeder Project, 120
Sharma, A.P., 113
Sharma, Bhagwat Dyal. 106
Sharma, Shanker Dayal, 106, 310
Sharma, Yagya Dutt, 142
Shastri, Lal Bahadur, 101-102, 104-106
Shiromani Gurdwara Prabhandak
Committee *(see SGPC)*
Shourie, Arun, 267
Shukla, V.c., 270
Sikh Educational Conference, 280
Sikri, S.M., 213, 215
Sinan Hasani, 241
Singh, L.P., 153
Singh Sabha Organisation, 13
Singh, V.P., 259, 270
Sitaramayya, Pattabhi, 62-63, 67- 68, 81
Sobti, Tirath Singh, 138

Srinivasavardan, T.CA., 213
Statehood
-Arunachal Pradesh,229-230
-Goa, 229-230
-Mizoram, 229
States Reorganisation Commission, 89
Sukhadia, Mohan Lal, 111
Suraj Prakash (EPCE), 11
Suryanarayanan, 307-308
Swaran Singh, 101, 107, 118, 134-136, 138, 165-166
Swarna Mandir *(see Golden Temple)*
Swaroop Rani, 129

20-Point Socio-Economic Programme, 123
Takht Kesgarh Sahib, 126
Talib, Niranjan Singh, 104
Talwandi, Jagdev Singh, 132
Talwandi Sabo, 126
Tandon, Balram, 132
Tankhahua, 187-188, 190-191
Tarkunde, V.M., 212
Tegh, Amar Singh, 14, 17-18
Tenancy Laws, 117
Terrorists *(see Militants)*
Tewari, K.K., 251, 266
Thakkar Commission, 238
Tohra, Jathedar Gurcharan Singh, 171, 197
Tripathi, Kamlapathi, 113, 135
Tur, Mohan Singh, 132
Twelve-Point Programme, 116, 123
Tyabji, Badr-ud-Din, 213

Udham Singh, 130
United Front, 108, 111

Varadan S., 275
Venkatasubhiah, 147
Venkataraman, R., 159, 205, 270, 307, 309-310
Vidhata Singh (Tir), 19
Virdi, Surinder Singh, 138
Visits
-Greece, 24'1
-Poland, 241
-Yugoslavia, 241
Yadavendra Singh, 109
Yemen Arab Republic, 202

Zia-ul-Haq, 293-297
Zimbabwe, 233